Additional Praise

"This book is a comprehensive guide to Enterprise Process Orchestration, offering invaluable insights and actionable strategies to streamline workflows, align teams, and achieve operational excellence. With its focus on a holistic framework, it's a must-have resource for embedding orchestration into any organization's DNA."

—Daivish Shah
Enterprise Architect, Atlassian

"Bernd and Leon deliver invaluable insights for achieving a successful digital process transformation, supported by their strong technical expertise. I especially appreciate the chapter on people and its impact on the transformation journey."

—Joerg Meisterjahn-vom Bey
Head of Group 2nd Line Workflow Automation, Vodafone

"I highly recommend this book to anyone looking to establish effective process orchestration or seeking to improve organizational efficiency within their company. It's an honor to see some of our ideas thoughtfully incorporated into its pages."

—Niko Vogel
Responsible for BPM at Axa Germany

Enterprise Process Orchestration

Enterprise Process Orchestration

A Hands-on Guide to Strategy, People, and Technology That Will Transform Your Business

Bernd Ruecker · Leon Strauch

This edition first published 2025

© 2025 Bernd Ruecker and Leon Strauch.

All rights reserved. No part of this publication may be reproduced, stored in a retrieval system, or transmitted, in any form or by any means, electronic, mechanical, photocopying, recording or otherwise, except as permitted by law. Advice on how to obtain permission to reuse material from this title is available at http://www.wiley.com/go/permissions.

The right of Bernd Ruecker and Leon Strauch to be identified as the authors of this work has been asserted in accordance with law.

Registered Office(s)

John Wiley & Sons, Inc., 111 River Street, Hoboken, NJ 07030, USA

John Wiley & Sons Ltd, New Era House, 8 Oldlands Way, Bognor Regis, West Sussex, PO22 9NQ, UK

For details of our global editorial offices, customer services, and more information about Wiley products visit us at www.wiley.com.

The manufacturer's authorized representative according to the EU General Product Safety Regulation is Wiley-VCH GmbH, Boschstr. 12, 69469 Weinheim, Germany, e-mail: Product_Safety@wiley.com.

Wiley also publishes its books in a variety of electronic formats and by print-on-demand. Some content that appears in standard print versions of this book may not be available in other formats.

Trademarks: Wiley and the Wiley logo are trademarks or registered trademarks of John Wiley & Sons, Inc. and/or its affiliates in the United States and other countries and may not be used without written permission. All other trademarks are the property of their respective owners. John Wiley & Sons, Inc. is not associated with any product or vendor mentioned in this book.

Limit of Liability/Disclaimer of Warranty

While the publisher and authors have used their best efforts in preparing this work, they make no representations or warranties with respect to the accuracy or completeness of the contents of this work and specifically disclaim all warranties, including without limitation any implied warranties of merchantability or fitness for a particular purpose. No warranty may be created or extended by sales representatives, written sales materials or promotional statements for this work. This work is sold with the understanding that the publisher is not engaged in rendering professional services. The advice and strategies contained herein may not be suitable for your situation. You should consult with a specialist where appropriate. The fact that an organization, website, or product is referred to in this work as a citation and/or potential source of further information does not mean that the publisher and authors endorse the information or services the organization, website, or product may provide or recommendations it may make. Further, readers should be aware that websites listed in this work may have changed or disappeared between when this work was written and when it is read. Neither the publisher nor authors shall be liable for any loss of profit or any other commercial damages, including but not limited to special, incidental, consequential, or other damages.

Library of Congress Control Number: 2025903746

Hardback ISBN: 9781394309672
ePDF: 9781394309696
ePub: 9781394309689

Cover Image: Abstract Technology Background © aleksandarvelasevic/iStock/Getty Images
Cover design by Wiley

Set in 10pt and SourceSans Pro by Lumina Datamatics

SKY10099459_030625

Contents

Foreword   **xiii**

Preface   **xv**

Why Automation? xviii

Avoid the Value Trap of Local Automations xx

Focus on Processes xxi

The Methodology Behind This Book xxii

How to Read This Book xxvi

Who Should Read This Book xxvii

About the Authors   **xxix**

Introduction   **1**

Process Orchestration in the Context of Automation 1

Process Automation = Process Orchestration + Task Automation . . 2

Challenges Process Orchestration Solves 4

Taming Process Complexity 5

Process Orchestration Engines and Executable Process Models . . . 6

The Benefits of Process Orchestration 7

Better Customer Experience 8

Operational Efficiency 10

Risk Mitigation and Compliance 11

Faster Time to Value and Greater Business Agility 12

Enabling Artificial Intelligence 14

Avoiding Technical Debt and Accidental Complexity 15

Understanding Process Types That Can Be Orchestrated 16

Tailor-made Digital Processes 16

Diversity of Business Processes 18

A Useful Categorization of Use Cases 19

Tailoring Your Process Automation Approach 20

Avoiding the Danger Zone Around Vendor Rationalization and Tool Harmonization 22

Typical Business Processes to Be Orchestrated 23

Financial Services 23

Insurance 25

Telecommunications 26

Public Sector 26

Retail 27

Other Industries 28

Technical Use Cases of Process Orchestration 28

Takeaways 29

Chapter 1: Vision

31

Strategic Alignment: Bridging Vision, Strategy, and Stakeholders 32

Scoping Your Transformation Journey 33

Defining Your Vision 34

Aligning Your Stakeholders 35

Building a Business Architecture to Realize Digitalization and Automation Benefits 38

The Business Architecture in a Nutshell 38

Customer Journeys and Value Streams 41

Strategic End-to-End Processes 42

Business Capabilities 44

The Role of Executable Processes 48

Avoid Lengthy Discussions About Process Hierarchies 50

Advantages of This Business Architecture 52

Making Informed Decisions About Where to Invest 53

Strategically Improving Your End-to-End Processes 54

Defining Clear Ownership 55

Composing Processes Out of Business Capabilities 55

Enabling Organizational Redesign 56

Establishing a Process-First Mindset 58

Building Your Transformation Roadmap and Implementing Change 59

Adoption Governance (aka Who Owns the Business Architecture?) . 60

Understanding Process Orchestration Work Streams 62

Building and Prioritizing Business Cases 65

Amplifying Organic Bottom-Up Initiatives 69

viii

Enterprise Process Orchestration

Getting Started on Your Adoption Journey 72
    Following a Wave Pattern on Your Journey 72
    Enterprise Adoption Phases 73
Questions to Assess Your Maturity 75
Takeaways 77

Chapter 2: People   79

How Software Is Being Built Today 80
    Focused Components That Implement Capabilities 80
    Agile and DevOps 81
    Product Thinking 82
    Process Ownership 83
    Team Topologies 84
    Diversity of Roles 84
    A Healthy Level of Centralization 86
Centralized Teams to Facilitate Process Orchestration 88
    The Business Process Optimization Group (POG) 89
    The Adoption Acceleration Team (AAT) 90
    The Relationship Between the POG and AAT 92
Delivery Models 92
    Federated Solution Delivery with the AAT as an Enabler 93
    Fully Decentralized Delivery 95
    Fully Centralized Delivery 96
Roles 99
    AAT Leader 99
    Enterprise Architect 100
    Rainmaker 101
    Business Analyst 102
    Solution or IT Architect 102
    Software Developer 103
    Low-Code Developer 104
    Operations Engineer 105
    Product Owner 105
Zooming in on the Adoption Acceleration Team 106
    The Scope of Your AAT 106
    What About Communities of Practice (CoPs)? 107
    What Should Your AAT Look Like? 108
    The Business Case for the AAT 110

Building Your AAT 113

AAT Tasks 114

Governance 121

AAT Anti-Patterns 123

Real-Life Examples 125

Defining Your Target Operating Model 126

Key Dimensions to Define Your Operating Model 127

Sketching Your Journey 130

Questions to Assess Your Maturity 134

Takeaways 135

Chapter 3: Technology — 137

Implementing Your Business Architecture 137

Implementing Business Capabilities 138

Technical Capabilities, Platforms, and Enabling Technologies 140

Business Orchestration and Automation Technology 142

Composable vs. Monolithic Platforms 144

Components Required for Process Orchestration 145

Operationalizing AI for Autonomous Orchestration with Guardrails . . . 157

Providing a Process Orchestration Capability to Your Organization 160

Enterprise vs. Solution Scope 160

Platform Thinking 162

Modern Process Orchestration Platforms Don't Become a Bottleneck — 165

Why Does This Work Now if SOA Failed a Decade Ago? 165

Chargeback Models 168

Operating a Process Orchestration Platform 169

Running the Platform 169

Isolation Needs and Multitenancy 170

Staging Environments 172

Sizing and Scaling 173

Resilience and High Availability 173

Selecting the Right Process Orchestration Technology 174

Types of Processes: Standard vs. Tailor-Made 174

Scope: Task Automation and Simple Integrations vs. Processes . . . 176

Process Complexity: Simple vs. Complex 177

Scale: Small vs. Big 179

Project Setup: Ad Hoc vs. Strategic 179

Contrasting Process Orchestration with Adjacent Technologies 180
    Robotic Process Automation (RPA) 180
    Data Flow Engines and Data Streaming 181
    Event-Driven Architecture (EDA) and Event Streaming 182
    BPM Suites and Low-Code Application Platforms 182
    Microservice Orchestrators 183
Tips on Evaluating Tools 183
Questions to Assess Your Maturity 186
Takeaways 187

Chapter 4: Delivery   189

Solution Creation Approach 189
    Discover 190
    Model 192
    Develop 193
    Run 194
    Monitor 194
    Being Agile Throughout the Solution Creation Lifecycle 195
Setting the Stage for Success: Your Early Projects 195
Derisking Your Start with Process Tracking 197
Typical Delivery Teams and Roles 199
Solution Design 201
    Greenfield Solution Architecture for Pro-Code Use Cases 202
    The Software Development Lifecycle and Model Roundtrips 203
    Simplified Solution Architecture for Low-Code Use Cases 205
    Typical Questions Around the Development Lifecycle 206
Accelerating Solution Building 209
Questions to Assess Your Maturity 211
Takeaways 212

Chapter 5: Measurement   215

Why Metrics Matter 216
Value Drivers of Enterprise Process Orchestration 218
Understanding Metrics 221
    Measurements, Metrics, Goals, KPIs, and SLAs 221
    What Makes a Good KPI? 223
    Example Metrics and KPIs 225

Operationalizing Your Metric-Driven Approach 228
   Metrics Are Not an Afterthought 228
   Mapping Metrics and KPIs to Value Drivers 229
   Mapping Value Flow Through Business Architecture Layers 231
   Modeling for Measurement 233
   Setting Up Continuous Measurements and Communication 235
   Can't We Just Delegate This to Our Existing Data Warehouse Folks? . 239
Questions to Assess Your Maturity 240
Takeaways 241

Closing Thoughts   243

List of Abbreviations   247

References   249

Index   259

Foreword

Organizations face an automation imperative, and for many it will be crucial to their survival. Automation at scale is no longer about driving efficiency or cutting costs; it's focused on building a foundation for business agility and innovation. As an industry analyst, I've spent the last decade tracking the market's interest in core automation topics like BPMN. I watched as interest in these topics waned until roughly eight years ago. Then, trends shifted dramatically. What happened?

Organizations began to get serious about the need for broadscale automation. We saw an increasing number of strategies coalesce around a very critical concept: orchestration. And one vendor became central to the trend – Camunda. So, when Bernd approached me to write a foreword for their book *Enterprise Process Orchestration*, my first thought was "Ooh, early access!"

I cracked open the book, and by the next day I had read it cover to cover. Our firm, Analysis.tech, was founded to address the reality that most automation initiatives currently fall short of driving true transformation. *Enterprise Process Orchestration* tackles this challenge head-on. I often use the analogy that huge automation projects are like turning an aircraft carrier, as they require massive budgets and resources. Make no mistake, most of these initiatives have been worth it; however, transforming your organization so it has a true process and automation mindset is like turning 5,000 speedboats in unison.

The central theme of this book is orchestration. From a business perspective, a focus on orchestration provides a context for breaking through silos created by legacy systems and organizational boundaries and driving true transformation at scale. This is where tomorrow's innovation and disruption will come from – but it's hard to get there.

What I truly appreciate about Bernd and Leon's approach to this crucial topic is the pragmatic advice backed by real-world examples and strong technical underpinnings. It requires careful thought and planning to drive organizational change. It also requires a well-thought-out technical architecture. In *Enterprise Process*

Orchestration, Bernd and Leon offer a detailed approach to technology selection, maturity models, and governance, and a guide to help your organization build a process-first mindset. I was particularly excited about the section that defined the different models for a center of excellence, a critical part of a successful process automation strategy.

If you're serious about the challenges of driving deep and meaningful change through automation in your organization, *Enterprise Process Orchestration* is a must-read. Bernd and Leon tackle the issues head-on with a pragmatic approach to drive success. It's a big job, but your organization's survival might be at stake.

—Rob Koplowitz
Former Principal Analyst at Forrester and Co-founder of Analysis.tech

Preface

At CamundaCon 2024 in New York, Sanjam Sarpal, a solution architect from Atlassian, joined us on stage[1]. You might know Atlassian from tools like Confluence, Jira, or Trello, which are ubiquitous in the business and software world. Sanjam explained how Atlassian had recently successfully completed a transition from one enterprise resource planning (ERP) system to another in just nine months. ERP transformations are complex, time-consuming projects that many organizations fail with, and they have likely cost many CIOs their role – yet, Atlassian managed it with a breeze. He further shared that when Atlassian acquired the company Loom, they were able to integrate Loom's billing workflows into Atlassian's systems in three or four months, whereas in the past such a procedure would have taken nine months to a year. What was the reason for these success stories, in which transformation projects not only were executed seamlessly but were completed in a fraction of the usual time?

You might have guessed it already: Atlassian had introduced process orchestration. This approach allowed them to understand, manage, and transform the billing and ERP processes with ease, swapping out systems where needed, incorporating new product variations, and adjusting data transformations and endpoint integrations along the way.

And they didn't stop with the ERP transformation or the billing workflow. Atlassian made process orchestration a strategic technology on the enterprise level and developed an operating model that allows the organization to successfully reap its benefits: a central team (often known as a "center of excellence") helps autonomous delivery teams (like the ones Sanjam led) apply the right technologies, patterns, and best practices easily and swiftly. This accelerated building of not only the billing workflow but many others, leveraging economies of scale, driving efficiencies, and improving the customer experience – for instance, by reducing ticket turnaround times within support requests by 93%[2].

Earlier the same year, the research firm Forrester reported that TK[3], a big German health insurance company, had reduced the happy path for its denture reimbursement process from about 1.5 weeks to 2.7 seconds (read: seconds!) through process automation and digital data exchange with dentists. This is another great example of hitting two targets with one arrow: Not only did they lower operational costs through process automation, but they also hugely improved the customer experience. What's more, the newly orchestrated processes can be infused with innovative technologies (like AI) to drive further improvements.

Those successes are part of a broader pattern that is currently unfolding in the market. Recognition is growing that process orchestration can enhance business agility, increase employee productivity, improve customer experiences, and reduce business risks. As you will see in "The Benefits of Process Orchestration" starting on page 7, the benefits to organizations have been proven, with a 2024 Forrester report estimating a return on investment of over 400%. And according to Camunda's State of Process Orchestration 2024 report[4], 91% of companies surveyed have seen increased business growth due to process automation within the last year. In addition, 95% say automation has helped them achieve operational efficiency, and 93% say automation has helped improve customer experiences.

Process automation has become table stakes for organizations to remain competitive. And applying process orchestration strategically on the enterprise level allows you future-proof your enterprise architecture. That is, it not only gives you strong advantages right now, but ensures you will be able to make any needed changes to your business processes in the future – and if we know only one thing for sure, it's that business processes need to adjust often and quickly. Adaptability is crucial for your organization to survive. As one of our marketing colleagues says, "Orchestrate or die!"

Consider Artificial Intelligence (AI), which has been taking the world by storm since the launch of ChatGPT. While ChatGPT and other generative AI tools have created tremendous hype about the possibilities of AI, to the point where no CEO can afford not to think about it, enterprise adoption is still lagging (as, for instance, technology analyst Benedict Evans points out in his article "The AI Summer"[5]). There may be multiple factors at play here, such as data readiness or compliance concerns, but one of them stands out: Most organizations are just not able to strategically integrate AI into their value streams, because their operations are – frankly speaking – too chaotic. Business processes are buried in a mess of wildly integrated legacy systems, with limited visibility and minimal understanding of how the full end-to-end process works. In such a scenario, you cannot magically transform your business by just throwing in AI. You need to build the foundation first; otherwise, you are betting your organization's survival on fairy dust.

Don't get us wrong: we are fully convinced of the transformative potential of AI (and are investing heavily in it ourselves). But it's not a surprise to us that, on the whole, it hasn't yet delivered the value organizations expect. A report from BCG[6], for example, showed that 74% of companies struggle to generate and scale value with AI, and only 4% of companies are creating substantial value. As the report notes, "A common misconception is that AI's value lies mainly in streamlining operations and reducing costs in support functions. In fact, its greatest value lies in core business processes, where leaders are generating 62% of the value."

To tie this back to Atlassian's story, with their process orchestration layer in place, it is clear how they could integrate AI into their billing workflow: for example, by leveraging a large language model for fraud detection. Once you have the foundation, AI simply becomes an endpoint in your process that can be orchestrated.

At the same time, according to the State of Process Orchestration report, on average just 50% of organizational processes have been automated so far, many of those in a scrappy fashion. So, there is a huge opportunity on the table.

How can you set up your company to drive the right process architecture across your business, to realize value today and be ready for tomorrow? With this book, we aim to provide a recipe for achieving this. It's about adopting process orchestration to automate more while being faster at it at the same time, and transforming your organization's enterprise architecture to a future-proof model centered around business processes and business capabilities. The focus of this book is less on the nitty-gritty details of technology stacks and more on how to scale usage across the organization to benefit the company. This includes shaping your business architecture, staffing teams, getting the wider organization and management on board, anchoring the technology in the organization, and a lot of other sociotechnical elements. That said, it's also critical to create a technically sound foundation to build great solutions, and we'll show you how.

The book you hold in your hands is based on our experiences over the last decade helping numerous customers drive enterprise process orchestration adoption to an impressive scale to transform their business. We hope you'll join them.

Preface   xvii

Why Automation?

If you're not yet fully convinced of the transformative potential of process automation and the pivotal role of process orchestration, let's take a closer look at how they deliver impact step by step.

A while ago, one of our customers, a Top 10 insurance company in Germany, was startled by the results of its latest customer survey. The company found that customer satisfaction with the speed of claim processing had declined dramatically over the last three years (Figure P.1). However, digging deeper into their performance, they found that the process time had remained stable over that period. So, why had customer satisfaction gone down? The most likely explanation: Customer expectations have shifted massively. We've all gotten used to the lightning speed of the digital economy on our smartphones. Have groceries delivered to your home in a few minutes? No problem. Instantly open a bank account online? Done. Get a new eSIM in a matter of seconds? Easy. Wait 10 days for your insurance claim to be processed? No thank you!

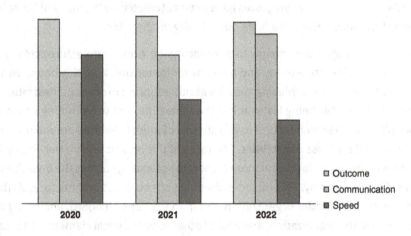

Figure P.1 Customer satisfaction with outcomes, communication, and speed.

This story of increased customer expectations is the reality in almost any business domain, and digitally minded organizations are beginning to eat up incumbent market share by providing a superior customer experience with high operational efficiency.

For example, a recent study around the Know Your Customer (KYC) checks[7] that banks need to do when onboarding new corporate clients found that 48% of banks lost clients because of slow and inefficient onboarding, and four out of five of those banks attribute that loss to delayed processing. To give you an idea of what "delayed" means, banks took on average 95 days to complete a KYC review in 2023. That's more than three months! And this finding needs to be viewed against the background that customers have more choices by the day, be it via FinTechs or BigTechs like Amazon Finance for Business. Those new players are disrupting with speed and agility. This has led to more and more traditional banks partnering with these players (for example, using Plaid for eKYC). But is your company ready to make such fundamental process changes?

At the same time, we are at the end of a decade-long period of virtually free money through near-zero interest rates. We're currently seeing a profound, global macroeconomic shift, with interest rates unlikely to return to pre-COVID levels. Accordingly, organizations will have to hone in on efficiency and achieve more with less.

The same goes for the looming threat of demographic change. As the US Bureau of Labor Statistics[8] points out, the size of the workforce in the United States will continue to decline over the next decade – and this amidst an already existing shortage of skilled workers. The situation is the same in the European Union and especially in Germany, where *The Economist*[9] reported in 2022 that almost 50% of companies said that they were unable to secure enough skilled workers (with the public sector being especially battered by this trend).

And it's not only market pressure that organizations are facing today. The ever-growing regulatory pressure is another hurdle, especially in the finance industry. In May 2024, the US security settlements cycle will be reduced to what is known as "T+1," which essentially means that a trade needs to be settled within 24 hours. Before that change, the cycle was two days. This is a huge challenge for banks. According to BNP Paribas[10], "The execution through settlement phases will need to be automated and modernized to enhance straight-through processing and minimize exceptions. While that will take investment, it will strip out manual workflows and bring operating efficiencies, cost savings and risk reduction." But at the time of writing, most banks are struggling to achieve T+1 through process automation. Until they do, they will need to do what is known as "throwing people at the problem," meaning they'll need to rely on an increasing number of people working on trade settlements under extreme time pressure. This is expensive and harms the employee experience; it is thus not sustainable and ultimately risky. Such regulatory pressure is not only evident in the finance industry, but among other verticals too; just think of healthcare, pharmaceuticals, telecommunications, utilities, and other areas where stringent regulations shape operations and compliance is paramount.

Preface   xix

Increasing customer expectations, cost pressure, demographic change, a growing regulatory regime, and more – how are organizations supposed to react to this? The intuitive answer is by leveraging technology to drive innovation, automate more, and optimize processes. But isn't this what most organizations have already been doing for a while now? Well, yes and no.

Avoid the Value Trap of Local Automations

When it comes to process automation, we have seen plenty of organizations driving improvements locally. For example, you might have used robotic process automation (RPA) to automate data entry in one of your core systems, or implemented a chatbot to automatically answer simple customer questions, or installed a new AI-fueled system for fraud detection.

Many of those initiatives doubtless generated initial business value and yielded local improvements. The challenge is that those are isolated projects and point solutions. Accordingly, they do not create an ecosystem within which an organization can improve its end-to-end customer journey. In fact, the data suggests exactly the opposite: As more and more tasks get automated locally, the overall end-to-end process becomes more difficult to maintain due to the increasing complexity of the IT landscape (so say 68% of IT decision-makers in our State of Process Orchestration 2024 report[11]). Point solutions tend to be brittle and hard to maintain, and due to their local nature they are often not embedded in a global corporate strategy.

This leads to a value trap for process automation. By automating locally, your organization accumulates technical and organizational debt that undermines the initially achieved value. Managing all those point solutions effectively makes it harder to control the core business processes, leading to reduced flexibility, longer time to market, and a lack of business visibility.

So, ironically, adding the local automations can make things worse in the long run, even if everything looks successful in the first place. The loss of process control hampers the ability to adapt or innovate, and you end up getting bogged down with maintaining your spaghetti integrations and legacy systems. This unfortunate situation nurtures the cliché of IT as a bottleneck for innovation instead of a business enabler, and widens the gap between business and IT. This can further diminish IT's influence in the decision-making process.

Notably, the current hype with AI fuels exactly the same pattern, as organizations try to take shortcuts and apply local AI solutions. These may yield some local

ROI, but by failing to consider the bigger picture, they end up falling into the same trap.

Focus on Processes

So, what to do? One of our customers recently described it very well: "We have our IT systems running, and somehow everything works, but it's very hard to change anything. What we need to do is think more in terms of processes."

This is where enterprise process orchestration comes into play. We have seen an increasing number of organizations successfully escape that value trap by orchestrating customer journeys end to end, which means that you do not need to rip your IT landscape apart but seamlessly integrate all the existing systems along the process chain, using graphical models that can be directly executed by process orchestration platforms. This is visualized in Figure P.2.

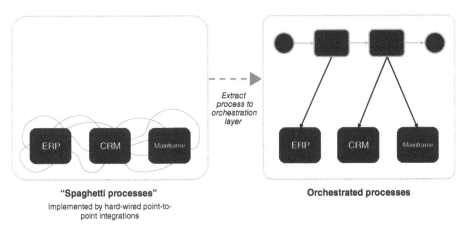

Figure P.2 Extracting the process into an orchestration layer makes it possible to manage the process end-to-end while easily integrating with existing systems.

The central component to achieve this is a process orchestration capability (Figure P.3). Without it, you simply can't achieve broad-scale automation. This is increasingly being recognized by analysts such as Gartner[12], who have declared that "The Future Is BOAT" (stands for "business orchestration and automation technologies").

As you will see in this book, building a successful process orchestration capability requires more than just a technical platform that allows you to integrate various

Preface

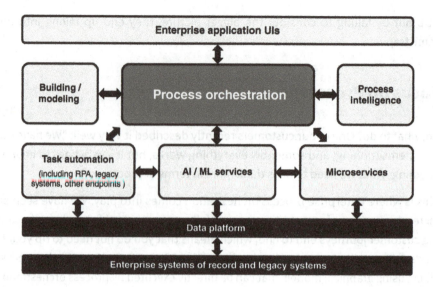

Figure P.3 Process orchestration is the central component of any large-scale automation effort.

systems and endpoints – you also need to define a vision, consider your people and their skills, define a delivery model, and identify and measure performance indicators. You will find information about all five of those pillars in this book.

Establishing a process orchestration practice allows you to tame the complexity of your existing systems and focus on generating business value today, while increasing your business agility for future requirements. Process orchestration brings together stakeholders across business and IT, with process models providing a common view and thus transparency on value streams. This enables you both to automate more processes to a higher standard of quality and to adapt to changes faster, all while bringing down technical debt.

The Methodology Behind This Book

Sounds good so far? Yes, indeed. Let's explore how to get there.

In contrast to siloed integrations, enterprise process orchestration is, as the name suggests, applied globally across an organization. This means that you need to involve a lot of people throughout the whole enterprise to drive the change you want to make, from top management to subject matter experts to software developers.

To help our customers with that, we have developed the *process orchestration adoption framework*. This framework can help you to transform your business by aiming for a strategic, scaled adoption of process orchestration. It provides guidance on all the steps of an iterative and agile journey that you can follow to generate value incrementally and learn fast.

The framework defines various maturity stages your company can be in, and it calls out the five drivers that are most important to look at when you want to define your current maturity and derive a roadmap from this. The five drivers, as visualized in Figure P.4, are:

- **Vision:** Are people aware of what process orchestration is and why it is valuable to the organization? Is there awareness of typical use cases? Why does enterprise process orchestration matter to the organization? What goals is the organization trying to achieve through its process orchestration practice?

- **People:** What people and skills do you need? How can you set up the right team structures? Who will define the standards and policies for how process orchestration should be used? Who is responsible for driving the change? What does the operating model look like? Are the right people empowered and enabled to do the right things?

- **Technology:** What technology philosophies, platforms, and solutions power the organization's process orchestration efforts? How does this fit into your overall enterprise architecture?

- **Delivery:** How are concrete process automation solutions being developed and deployed?

- **Measurement:** How does the organization define process orchestration success, and how well can the organization track that success?

You can rate your own organization's maturity for each of these drivers individually on a scale from 0 (undeveloped) to 4 (excellent). Doing so not only helps you understand your strengths better, but also your gaps. This allows you to develop an enterprise strategy and roadmap to build the required capabilities to succeed with enterprise process orchestration.

Table P.1 lists the different levels of maturity for each of these drivers as we have experienced them through our customer engagements.

Figure P.5 shows an example of what your maturity assessment might look like when you have started to apply process orchestration in a handful of first projects driven

Preface xxiii

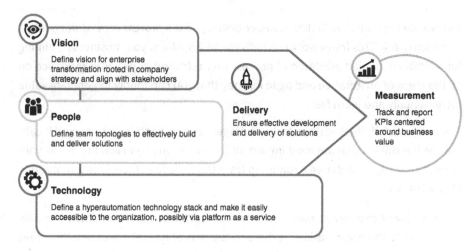

Figure P.4 The five key drivers of process orchestration maturity.

by IT (a situation we often see with our customers). You have some strength around process orchestration technology and solution delivery, but you need to evolve your vision, establish scalable structures in your teams, and improve at measuring success.

The process orchestration adoption framework, and hence this book, provides concrete hands-on guidance on how to increase maturity in all of those drivers.

In addition to the individual drivers discussed earlier, we also rate the overall degree of process orchestration adoption in the enterprise along five levels, which again will help you get an idea of where you stand and communicate the status quo alongside the target state internally:

- **Level 0 – No process orchestration:** No process orchestration solutions.
- **Level 1 – Single project:** Adoption in a single project or team, maybe as a proof of concept (PoC).
- **Level 2 – Broader initiative:** Multiple initiatives in one domain (e.g. the health insurance department in an insurance company may be orchestrating multiple processes).
- **Level 3 – Distributed adoption:** Multiple domains, with multiple initiatives (e.g. the health insurance and also life and composite insurance departments are strategically using process orchestration).

	Level 0: Undeveloped	Level 1: Basic	Level 2: Competent	Level 3: Advanced	Level 4: Excellent
Vision	Processes are not working efficiently or effectively. Some process tasks may have automated components, but those tasks are too dispersed for the effects of automation to be measured.	Focused on single, mission-critical process orchestration projects, or projects that center around a "broken" process.	Broader, scaled-up initiatives are focused on better business outcomes; measuring success remains a challenge.	Evolving toward a practice where process orchestration supports organization-wide digital transformation goals. This allows harnessing process orchestration to drive strategic business outcomes, at scale and at a rapid pace, for the entire organization.	There's a clearly defined strategy around technology, methodology, and people for enterprise process orchestration, matched by the ability to execute that vision. A demonstrated track record of delivering strategic value to the organization through process orchestration motivates teams to deliver business transformation at scale.
People	No teams established for process orchestration.	Disparate process orchestration projects are implemented in a fully decentralized manner (the "sprouting mushrooms" approach).	Centralization is initialized to share knowledge or enable teams, e.g. through a community of practice.	A center of excellence (CoE) focused on repeatability, enablement, and scale has been established.	A global CoE acts as a SaaS platform within the organization, providing enablement, training, and reusable components to accelerate delivery teams. Bottlenecks are avoided through strong focus on federation.
Technology	Teams may have implemented disparate automation technologies and local automations.	Teams are beginning to introduce process orchestration to integrate task automation and overcome the complexity of legacy systems and monolithic solutions.	Building a single process orchestration and automation technology stack that covers the entire process lifecycle.	Investing in elements that increase solution acceleration, with a focus on enabling multiple teams to build process orchestration solutions at scale.	Recognizing that there is no "one-size-fits-all" approach to hyperautomated tech stacks, the organization has instead built its own stack that fits its exact needs.
Delivery	Large gaps between business and IT create silos, leading to slow iterations and limited ability to deliver impactful process solutions.	IT increasingly acts as an enabler for the business, but lack of mature IT methodologies prevents agile delivery in small increments.	As business and IT alignment improves and the organization shifts to more agile development, teams begin to deliver continuous improvements in short sprints.	Multiple BizDevOps teams are involved in delivery and establishing best practices that speed up time to value; improved process monitoring allows organizations to track impact on business outcomes.	Business teams can self-serve on an increasing number of use cases with minimal IT involvement, enabled by the CoE; processes are purpose-built to drive business value and adjusted through continuous monitoring and improvement to maximize value.
Measurement	Processes are not well enough defined to measure anything.	Teams are focused solely on completing projects; success is defined as "project is in production." Process metrics are gathered manually or solely technical metrics from an engine are used.	Meaningful KPIs are defined and used for individual projects and/or processes. KPIs are mostly operational and not linked to strategic business value.	Clear success metrics and KPIs have been established for most processes, with a clear narrative to link those to business goals.	The contribution of process orchestration to business outcomes can be clearly shown using continuously measured strategic and operational KPIs. Those KPIs are also driving investment decisions.

Table P.1 The five maturity levels, across each key driver.

- **Level 4 – Strategic, scaled adoption:** Multiple end-to-end customer journeys across domains, automated intentionally through a holistic enterprise strategy.

We discuss the drivers and adoption levels further in "Introducing the Process Orchestration Maturity Model"[13] on the Camunda website.

Preface

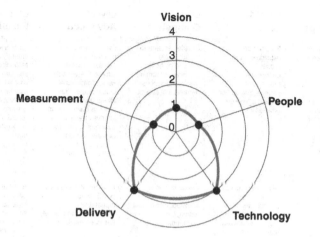

Figure P.5 An example maturity assessment for a company getting started on its process orchestration journey.

The process orchestration adoption framework serves as a holistic methodology that organizations can use to drive their process orchestration maturity. We derived this framework by speaking to hundreds of our global customers about their successes and failures, best practices, and lessons learned – and we've distilled that knowledge into this book.

How to Read This Book

The drivers described in the previous section form the five main pillars (or chapters) of this book: vision, people, technology, delivery, and measurement. We have planned the book so that you can read it cover to cover, but you can also start with the section that is most important to you at the moment.

In the "Introduction", we will explain the basics of process orchestration and the business value you can achieve by adopting it. Understanding this is crucial to building a vision to get both IT and business stakeholders onboard for your initiative. Building that vision is the focus of "Chapter 1: Vision". In that chapter, we will also discuss how you can align your stakeholders, set up a proper business architecture as well as governance to implement the changes associated with process orchestration, and develop an adoption roadmap.

"Chapter 2: People" is all about people and team structures. We will look at how software is being built today, and how this will affect your process orchestration initiative.

We'll also explore the delivery models organizations can choose to realize these initiatives, and which roles need to be involved. Then we will discuss a concept that's key to successful adoption: how to set up the right operating model for your adoption acceleration team (AAT), a center of excellence to support your goals and company culture.

Getting the technology right is, of course, equally important. In "Chapter 3: Technology", we will focus on the process orchestration tech stack and (enterprise) architecture. We will look at the components you will need, the accelerators you can build, and how to operate and run an internal platform.

In "Chapter 4: Delivery", we will explore best practices for successfully delivering solutions across all the project stages, from modeling a process to implementing typical solution architectures.

Once you have your solutions in place, you will need to continuously measure and monitor the value you are achieving with those solutions. In "Chapter 5: Measurement", we will look at ways you can do that successfully, to sustain your gains and get further buy-in.

Who Should Read This Book

We wrote this book as a practical guide for every person involved in your process orchestration initiative – all the way from the C-suite to the operational level.

Those who are driving initiatives holistically – especially IT leaders, CoE leaders, and business, enterprise or IT architects – will benefit from reading the book cover to cover. If you are one of those leaders, ideally you will then pass it around, pointing others to specific parts that are relevant to their roles. This can help you get stakeholders on board with process orchestration across your organization. For example, business leaders that you want to get interested in process orchestration should at least read through the "Introduction".

Many roles can benefit from the information in this book. Here are a few pointers:

- **C-suite executives** (especially CIOs) that want to transform their business with process orchestration should read the "Introduction" and "Chapter 1: Vision", as they are most often responsible for kicking off the necessary changes and getting relevant stakeholders on board (the CEO, CFO, IT leaders, and different business domains). CIOs should also read about team structures, mapped out

Preface   xxvii in "Chapter 2: People", as well as the technological underpinnings discussed at the beginning of "Chapter 3: Technology".

- **CoE leaders** can read this book from start to finish to learn how to drive enterprise adoption of process orchestration.

- **IT leaders** that are enabling process orchestration initiatives should mostly focus on the "Introduction", "Chapter 2: People", "Chapter 3: Technology", and "Chapter 4: Delivery". But typically, it makes sense to also look at "Chapter 1: Vision".

- **Business leaders** should read the "Introduction" to identify use cases for their lines of business.

- **Business and enterprise architects** who are playing a key role in the process orchestration initiative should read the book in full, as they are instrumental in unifying all parts of the business around a shared process orchestration vision.

- **Developers** will benefit from reading "Chapter 3: Technology" and "Chapter 4: Delivery" to understand the technology behind process orchestration and how solutions are built. They should also at least skim through the "Introduction" and "Chapter 1: Vision".

- **Business analysts** will benefit from the overview of the project lifecycle in "Chapter 4: Delivery". This will help them understand their contributions in context. "Chapter 5: Measurement" is also important to understand how to measure performance and business impact, and we recommend reading the "Introduction" as well.

Of course, there are even more people that can benefit from this book. If we didn't mention your specific role, please don't put it down just yet. Skim through, read the parts that are of interest to you, and let us know if you think we should call out your role explicitly in the previous list.

We wish you happy reading, and great success with your transformation initiatives!

About the Authors

Bernd Ruecker is co-founder of Camunda, the leading process orchestration platform, and has over 15 years of experience innovating process automation deployed in highly scalable and agile environments of industry leaders like Atlassian, ING, and Vodafone. Over the years, he has witnessed the evolution of process orchestration from small-scale implementations to transformative, enterprise-wide initiatives in some of the world's largest organizations, giving him unique insights into what drives success at scale. With a strong technical background, Bernd has contributed to multiple open-source workflow engines and authored the books Practical Process Automation and Real-Life BPMN. A sought-after speaker and technology writer, he draws on his extensive real-world experience to share both the opportunities and challenges of process automation and orchestration in this book.

LinkedIn profile: https://de.linkedin.com/in/bernd-ruecker-21661122
Author title(s) and affiliation(s): Co-founder and Chief Technologist at Camunda
Author pronouns: he/him
Email: bernd.ruecker@camunda.com

Leon Strauch is a Process Orchestration Strategist at Camunda, dedicated to helping organizations achieve their digital transformation goals. With experience across diverse roles in the software industry, Leon has guided a wide range of enterprises in navigating the complexities of process automation and adopting new technologies. With an interdisciplinary background spanning B2B management, communication studies, SaaS, and enterprise software, he develops and applies strategic methodologies to effectively scale process orchestration in large organizations.

LinkedIn profile: https://www.linkedin.com/in/leon-strauch/
Author title(s) and affiliation(s): Process Orchestration Strategist at Camunda
Author pronouns: he/him
Email: leon.strauch@camunda.com

Introduction

First things first: In this chapter, we'll dive into what process orchestration is, explore how it differs from process automation, and make a compelling business case for using it. As you'll see, there are very different types of processes that you can automate, and this influences how you build solutions in a big way. While this is not surprising at all, it is surprisingly often ignored in real life.

Process Orchestration in the Context of Automation

Automation is a big field. This book concentrates specifically on the automation of processes, and even more specifically on the (automated) orchestration of tasks (rather than on the automation of the tasks themselves). Figure I.1 visualizes this relationship. As the distinction can be a little confusing, we'll emphasize it once more – while process automation and task automation are closely related to process orchestration, they are not the same:

- **Task automation** is the use of technology to automatically perform certain tasks without human intervention.

- **Process orchestration** is the coordination of the different tasks of a process, both automated and manual.

- **Process automation** is a mix of process orchestration and task automation to automate a process, where the degree of automation can vary.

Process orchestration is often compared to the role of a conductor in an orchestra who makes sure everyone performs at the right time – they tell the musicians when each instrument needs to play to ensure that the song sounds as it should. The process orchestrator is the "conductor" of a process, coordinating and managing the interactions and dependencies of all the tasks in the process, be they human or automated. You can orchestrate a process comprising only human tasks very well.

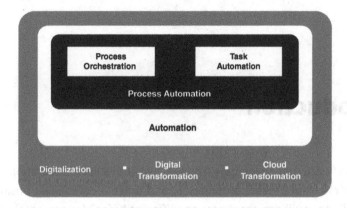

Figure I.1 Process orchestration in the context of automation.

Process Automation = Process Orchestration + Task Automation

Let's dive a little more deeply into this. Successful automation of (end-to-end) processes includes two distinct ingredients:

- **Task automation**, which focuses on automating individual tasks. This is often also referred to as *local automation*. For example, in a bank account opening process, the credit scoring of the applicant might be done by an Robotic Process Automation (RPA) bot instead of manually by a clerk. Or, even better, an Application Programming Interface (API) might be used to do the scoring automatically.

- **Process orchestration**, which coordinates the tasks of an end-to-end process throughout the process flow, maintaining a constant awareness of the status of each instance and what happens next. This includes automated tasks (e.g. via APIs) and manual tasks (e.g. handled by clerks) in a central task list. Using process orchestration allows the gradual automation of human tasks, using RPA or fully API-driven automations. It also provides the basis to inject AI into processes.

The two concepts are orthogonal to each other, as illustrated in Figure I.2.

Depending on where you start, different automation journeys are possible. Let's look at a few scenarios, knowing that the reality might be anywhere in between:

1. **You start with process orchestration and automate tasks later.** You could capture a completely manual process in a process model, orchestrating only human tasks. The automated process controlled by an orchestrator will replace sending emails, for example, with a task list, thereby standardizing the business process and improving time to resolution and the quality of

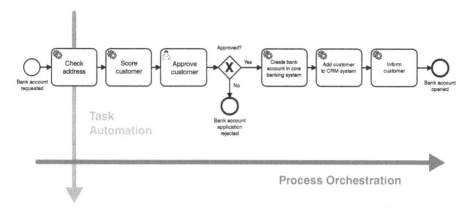

Figure I.2 An example of a bank account opening process.

results. This allows you to make sure that processes are finished as intended and service level agreements (SLAs) are hit. It also allows you to analyze cycle times and uncover bottlenecks in your processes.

This is a good starting point to incrementally automate discrete tasks within a process, step by step, with the priority driven by the value of task automation. For example, in our hypothetical bank account opening process, you might want to automate the address check first, as this is both simple to do and a monotonous and error-prone task when performed by humans.

This journey involves a lot of change management to get your people on board.

2. **You started with task automation, and now you need to add process orchestration.** Many organizations run local automation projects, for example to automate an address check or grab an order from a Comma-Separated Values (CSV) file in some email inbox. Sometimes, RPA is used for those projects. While the automations have a local return on investment (ROI), they don't necessarily improve the overall end-to-end process, as process instances might still go south between those local automations. So, you introduce process orchestration to coordinate the existing local automations.

This requires removing any direct integrations between the local task automations, so that the orchestrator can take over. An interesting technique to derisk this transition is to use process tracking, as described in Chapter 4 under "Derisking Your Start with Process Tracking".

In summary, you might be starting with process orchestration of human tasks and looking to automate tasks later on a step-by-step basis, or you might already have discrete or locally automated tasks that you need to roll up into seamlessly automated end-to-end processes. Regardless, *for successful process automation, you need both process orchestration and task automation*.

Note that we will speak of "endpoints" when we refer to what process orchestration orchestrates. Those endpoints can be systems and APIs, devices or bots, or, of course, humans.

Challenges Process Orchestration Solves

Process orchestration coordinates many different process endpoints and can tie multiple processes together, for example, to orchestrate end-to-end customer journeys.

Without process orchestration, you have a disconnected set of local tasks and (potentially) automations, which leads to challenges such as:

- **Lack of understanding:** The end-to-end process is not fully visible, and key metrics are hard to track.
- **Lack of flexibility:** Changing the end-to-end process is difficult since it will likely lead to changes in many different systems.
- **Lack of standardization:** Silos in business and IT, as well as point-to-point integrations, prevent standardization and thus hamper business and IT collaboration.
- **Broken end-to-end automation:** Since local automations are not integrated with one another, the end-to-end process is not fully automated.

A process orchestration solution needs to:

- **Bring business and IT together:** To automate business processes, you need to involve many stakeholders from all parts of your organization. You will need a common language to talk about processes.
- **Promote innovation:** Process orchestration promotes innovation by connecting business and technology silos faster, more smoothly, and at a lower total cost.
- **Operate at scale:** Of course, the chosen technical solution needs to run at the scale you require for your business. Fortunately, most modern process

orchestration platforms can run at any scale, so, for example, at Camunda we have large banks running payment flows via the orchestration platform without issues.

Taming Process Complexity

Real-world processes tend to be complex to integrate, orchestrate, and automate. There are two main reasons for this:

- **Endpoint diversity:** Processes commonly span a number of endpoints, potentially of very different types. The software must be able to easily orchestrate all of those, accommodating a diverse set of technical protocols as well as humans (via graphical user interfaces or chat-like communication).

- **Process complexity:** End-to-end processes are typically more than just simple sequences of steps, so to orchestrate them your software needs to be able to execute complex flow logic, such as exceptions, parallel processing, and loops. A powerful modeling language like Business Process Model and Notation (BPMN) is key to achieving this.

Additional drivers of complexity might include process variants (like selling online or in brick-and-mortar stores), new regulatory constraints, and of course the dynamic nature of market demands.

How can you tame those complexities with process orchestration? To deal with endpoint diversity, you need technology that can integrate with various systems, preferably via existing connectors. The ability to use software development for specific requirements is also very important, to make sure you don't hit a boundary where you can't progress any further. And you need to be able to pull people into the loop, which requires providing proper task lists and user interfaces or integrating with existing front-end applications like Microsoft Teams or Slack.

When it comes to dealing with process complexity, the modeling standard BPMN is a great tool. It was created to design and execute advanced workflows, and it implements advanced workflow patterns. Modeling tools that support BPMN enable effective collaboration between the different stakeholders of a process, such as business users and developers. In addition, execution tools that support BPMN ensure reliable, scalable orchestration of the end-to-end process, regardless of its complexity.

Introduction

Good examples of advanced workflow patterns are the dynamic parallel execution of many tasks at the same time (like provisioning a bulk shipment of SIM cards in parallel), message correlation (like passing a customer complaint directly to the right running process), or time-based escalation (like sending a reminder email if a customer's identity verification is not completed within a specific window of time).

Process Orchestration Engines and Executable Process Models

To get everybody on the same page, let's take a very quick look at how process orchestration with executable processes really works (without going into too much technical detail).

To orchestrate a process, you start by defining a blueprint of it, called the *process definition*. This is a model typically expressed in BPMN, the ISO standard for modeling processes graphically, that is then directly executable. Figure I.3 shows an example.

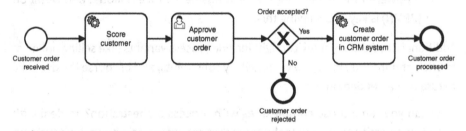

Figure I.3 An onboarding process described in BPMN.

The model defines where the process starts and ends, including all tasks along the way and the relationships between them. It can also have decision points where the flow goes one way or another. We won't explain BPMN in detail in this book, but it can execute the very advanced patterns required to automate the complexity of everyday processes very well. For more information, we recommend taking a look at *Real-Life BPMN*[1], by Jakob Freund and Bernd Ruecker.

Behind the graphical part, the process model contains various technical attributes that are needed to execute the process definition on an orchestration engine – for example, the exact logic to make the decision about whether or not to accept an order, the glue code or connector configuration for integrating the scoring system, or forms for the human interaction around approval.

The orchestration engine, often also referred to as a *workflow engine*, now automates the control of process instances. For example, it starts process instances upon receipt of new customer orders, and it keeps track of their state throughout their entire lifetime.

Here are a few key points to keep in mind:

- Process orchestration does not necessarily mean that the entire process is fully automated. What is automated is the *coordination* of the process.
- The central component is the orchestration engine, which executes an executable process model.
- The orchestration engine controls the process by informing humans of tasks that they need to do, and it handles the result of what those people did. This can be done, for example, through user interfaces like task lists or by leveraging chat infrastructure.
- The orchestration engine also communicates with internal and external IT systems.
- The orchestration engine decides which tasks or service calls take place and under what conditions, based on the results of previous tasks and service calls. Thus, the people involved can still influence the operational sequence of an automated process via data.
- Processes can be long-running in nature, meaning they can run for minutes or for hours, days, weeks, or even months.

We typically illustrate what an orchestration engine does with a screenshot of the graphical tooling that comes with it. As an example, Figure I.4 shows the overview page of Camunda's operations tool: You can see the number of technical incidents relating to customer scoring and a list of process instances waiting for approval.

The Benefits of Process Orchestration

In early 2024, Forrester conducted a Total Economic Impact™ (TEI) study for Camunda. As part of this study, Forrester interviewed customers that had been using the Camunda platform for a while to quantify the achieved ROI. Their key finding was that "Strategic, scaled investments in process automation with Camunda can: 1) improve customer experiences, 2) increase employee productivity,

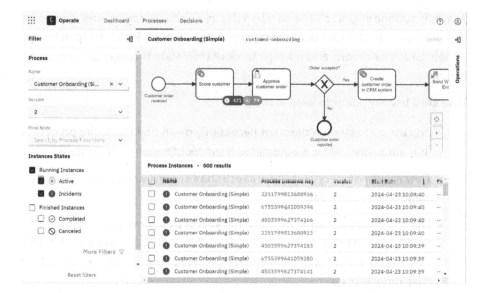

Figure I.4 Camunda Operate.

3) enhance business agility, and 4) reduce business risks. Leaders who center process orchestration within their businesses do more than increase efficiencies – they transform their organizations."

Forrester also put this finding in concrete numbers for a composite organization that it created based on the learnings: The organization achieved a total ROI of 410%, which translated to $116.11 million! You can find more information on this quite impressive number in the TEI study from Forrester[2].

So, there's definitely a huge opportunity here. Let's dive a bit deeper into the business value that process orchestration offers, so that you can understand how those numbers came about and, in turn, create more tangible business cases that are tied to your own corporate strategy. We believe it's crucial to lay this out in detail, as we have seen so many organizations struggling to qualify and quantify the potential business impact.

Better Customer Experience

As discussed in this book's Introduction ("Why Automation?"), today's customers expect:

- Immediate processing of their requests (e.g. purchasing a new mobile data plan).
- Self-service options (e.g. a public services portal for community citizens).
- Transparency on the current status of request processing (e.g. updates on insurance damage claim settlements).

To achieve all of that, organizations need to automate (customer-facing) value chains to orchestrate the customer journey in an optimal way. This is obviously not a trivial task. For example, most organizations need to satisfy omnichannel requirements, as different customers might expect them to be available via their preferred channel (e.g. website, chatbot, email, messenger, etc.). Technologies and customer expectations in this area are evolving rapidly, and organizations need to keep up to maintain their market share (or better, move fast to gain market share).

At the same time, most businesses – especially large incumbent organizations – have core business capabilities in existing legacy systems of record, like a core banking system, customer relationship management (CRM) system, or enterprise resource planning (ERP) system. Those systems are typically slow-moving and stable; they don't have a lot of changing requirements on a daily basis. They are also typically very difficult to replace, as they have many dependencies attached to them.

What do change frequently are the business processes stitching together the value chains and customer interactions with the core business capabilities, along with the company's product offering and business model.

Process orchestration is an important ingredient to balance the different paces of change in the customer interactions and business model vs. the core IT systems of record. It also allows organizations to easily pull in new capabilities, provided as separate tools or SaaS services (see Figure I.5).

An example may help to illustrate this. Suppose your car insurance company provides a new app for submitting claims. The app allows you to attach pictures of the damage along with documents like invoices. It guides you through everything you have to do to get your claim settled, giving you immediate feedback when you upload your photos and providing an estimate of the payout you will receive. In the best case, you get paid within minutes or hours.

This functionality is not part of the core insurance systems. Instead, the app on the front end is very likely a custom-developed component that uses some core business capabilities (e.g. to retrieve customer and contract data, create claims, trigger

---

Introduction 9

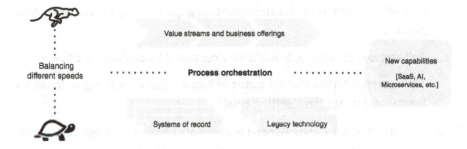

Figure I.5 Process orchestration stitches together new and existing business capabilities into end-to-end processes.

payouts, etc.). At the same time, the claim settlement process requires orchestration of not only these tasks, but others as well (e.g. determining responsibility, estimating damages, making payments). The orchestration layer permits you to add new tasks or adjust the process easily, even allowing you to experiment, for example, with new AI capabilities. Still, all the important data and the core business functionality is provided by the existing core systems.

Process orchestration thus allows organizations to innovate business models and improve their processes, without having to replace all of their legacy infrastructure at once. In turn, this allows customers to benefit from new service offerings, better transparency, and faster cycle times, all of which greatly improve the customer experience.

Operational Efficiency

In addition to being innovative, staying cost-efficient is a priority for many organizations – especially when they need to grow their business while keeping operating expenses under control. And while customers are always looking for a better experience across multiple channels, businesses can't always charge their customers for this. In fact, often they cannot. This creates further pressure on operating margins and forces organizations to drive efficiency in operations.

Process automation, in general, drives operational efficiency by, for example:

- Decreasing the amount of human involvement thanks to straight-through processing.
- Reducing the time spent manually routing requests.

- Reducing the amount of rework and reassignment (rerouting).

- Reducing manual and duplicate data entry into systems.

In addition, **process orchestration** in particular provides insights into what is going on, allowing both technical and business operation teams to:

- Identify areas of high human involvement as candidates for automation.

- Allocate available resources where the highest volume of business is observed.

- Identify technical incidents quickly and derive and apply appropriate fixes fast, removing stuck processes and clearing up customer inquiries.

- Identify gaps in business projections and real-life execution to adjust in an agile way.

Process orchestration technology gives you all of that right out of the box – a huge advantage when, as is so often the case, you simply don't have the time and resources to gain these insights through process mining or Big Data analytics solutions. Process orchestration opens the door for continuous delivery and improvement of processes.

Risk Mitigation and Compliance

Process orchestration plays a crucial role in risk mitigation and compliance. Orchestrated processes are structured, well-coordinated, and well-documented. This enables organizations not only to proactively identify and manage risks, but also to guarantee adherence to regulatory requirements.

Standardized processes ensure that best practices are consistently followed, reducing the likelihood of errors and discrepancies that can lead to operational and compliance risks. Regulatory requirements can be integrated directly into workflows, making sure that compliance steps are included in relevant processes. Periodic reviews can keep processes aligned with changing regulations. Compare this with the typical chaotic integration spaghetti many organizations have to automate processes, where it is very expensive to even understand where processes need to be adjusted to adhere to regulations, and you'll quickly see the benefits of orchestration.

Audit data from the process orchestration platform allows you to track process performance in real time, enabling prompt identification and mitigation of SLA violations before they escalate. This audit data is also an important input for proving process compliance to auditors, without the need for manual collection or costly audit projects. Furthermore, process orchestration helps with setting up robust internal controls, such as access restrictions and approval workflows, by preventing unauthorized actions and ensuring that critical tasks are performed by qualified personnel.

These capabilities don't just protect the organization from potential threats and legal issues but also contribute to a culture of accountability and continuous improvement, supporting long-term success and stability.

Faster Time to Value and Greater Business Agility

Business requirements change continually and rapidly, requiring companies to adjust fast and modernize their infrastructure to stay competitive. A rigid or chaotic implementation of processes and rules (hardcoded, or with complex choreography) can become a serious impediment for business agility and project cycle times. Technology leaders like CIOs therefore need to reduce the cycle time for automation projects and make sure they provide value to the organization as quickly as possible.

The agility that good process orchestration technology brings to the table is achieved through three things:

- A common language for processes.
- Developer-friendly tooling.
- Reusable technology components.

Let's look at these one by one. The first key element is a standardized graphical model to express business processes. In the earlier example we used BPMN, an internationally adopted ISO standard from the Object Management Group (OMG) for process models that are not just modeled graphically, but can also be executed by an orchestration engine. This is a real superpower. With BPMN, you can draw graphical process diagrams that can be understood by various stakeholders in your organization – and those diagrams are not dead documentation artifacts, but actually the directly executable source code of running software systems (as discussed in "Process Orchestration Engines and Executable Process Models"). You can see any runtime incidents and statistical data visualized on top of those process diagrams. And if you want to change a process, you know exactly how it is implemented today and have a great tool to demonstrate and discuss possible modifications.

BPMN is a very powerful language. It implements many advanced workflow patterns[3], which means that you can directly express situations that occur with real-life processes elegantly in BPMN without the need for clumsy workarounds that make process models hard to understand. (You can find some examples in "Why process orchestration needs advanced workflow patterns,"[4] on the Camunda blog.)

In short, BPMN is a great choice for process modeling; we are not aware of any other language that provides this triad of easy understandability, broad industry adoption, and powerful execution semantics.

We concentrate on process orchestration in this book, but if process orchestration is Batman, it must have a Robin. Process orchestration's sidekick is *decision automation*. Decision automation requires creating business-readable decision models, typically expressed as decision tables in the OMG Decision Model and Notation (DMN) standard. As you might expect, the ideas behind DMN are pretty close to BPMN; what's more, BPMN process models can natively invoke DMN decisions, and some tools (such as Camunda) support both standards.

The advantage of a common language and understanding should not be underestimated. One project manager in a customer's context once told us that while they now put in 20% more effort in the early analysis phases, as the graphical process models trigger more discussions, they save roughly 10 times that effort in the implementation, because the requirements are pretty clear by then. This is in line with the findings of a well-known study by the Systems Sciences Institute at IBM[5]: Problems found during tests are **15 times more expensive** to fix than problems found during design.

Another good perspective to view this from has to do with the lifespan of software. Automated core processes will be in operation for at least a couple of years (different studies commonly report numbers between 4 and 12 years). Within that time frame, you will need to make adjustments to the processes, quite possibly at a point where your people have already forgotten how the software was developed in the first place. A graphical diagram helps everybody involved get up to speed quickly and find the right places to make changes.

The next key to agility is developer-friendly tooling. So, let's briefly get a bit more technical and consider the duo of developer friendliness and open architecture. This is one of the main differentiators of the Camunda platform, and it has proven to be incredibly powerful. A developer-friendly platform allows you to apply state-of-the-art software development paradigms while building on existing skills (e.g. Java

---

Introduction   13

or C#) and tools (like CI/CD and testing frameworks) instead of spending time learning proprietary languages, and an open architecture lets you easily integrate new and existing technologies (like your ERP or CRM system). A platform with both of these qualities makes it easy for an organization to keep its existing engineering practices in place and simply add process orchestration into the mix, greatly improving time to value. This is in sharp contrast to the technology available a decade ago – namely business process management (BPM) suites, which were effectively aliens in the IT landscape, leading to very proprietary approaches that hardly anyone understood and typically making everybody quite unproductive.

Productivity can be further increased by providing reusable technology components and building a business architecture that fosters reuse on a business capability level, which is something we will dive more deeply into in "Building a Business Architecture to Realize Digitalization and Automation Benefits".

To give you a concrete example of what faster time to value can mean, T-Mobile Austria has said that it can bring new products to market four times faster[6] thanks to the adoption of a modern process orchestration platform.

Enabling Artificial Intelligence

These days, there's a lot of hype around AI, machine learning (ML), and large language models (LLMs) – but organizations need to be smart about where they can apply these innovations to have an impact on their business. For sure, there will be some experimentation involved.

Process orchestration is a great enabler here, as it makes introducing new software endpoints easy – and AI solutions are always software endpoints. Having an orchestrated process allows you to pinpoint where such services can be introduced and makes it easy to implement those changes. Without process orchestration, the reality is that processes are kind of chaotic, either manually driven or spaghetti-integrated, which makes it hard for organizations to find the right places to introduce new functionalities (let alone run A/B tests to experiment with new technologies).

So, the process orchestrator is a catalyst for strategically adopting and integrating new technologies like AI. We gave an example earlier around automatically assessing accident pictures and estimating damages in claims processes for insurance companies, but you can probably think of many more (say, fraud detection in Know Your Customer (KYC) processes).

Without understanding your process and knowing where to integrate AI endpoints, you can't leverage AI properly, let alone use it to transform your business. Process orchestration is table stakes in the AI economy.

Avoiding Technical Debt and Accidental Complexity

In addition to the previous benefits, an orchestration engine simply solves some technical problems that would be hard to solve otherwise and would slow down your IT teams. This is largely about long-running processes, as they require certain technical capabilities. Chief among these are:

- **Durable state (persistence):** The orchestration engine keeps track of all running process instances, including their current state and historical audit data. While this sounds easy, durable state is still a challenge to handle, especially at scale. It also immediately triggers subsequent requirements around understanding the current state, which means you will need operations tooling. An orchestration engine needs to manage transactions too; for example, handling concurrent access to the same process instance.

- **Scheduling:** An orchestration engine needs to keep track of timing and possibly escalate if a process gets stuck for too long. Therefore, there must be a scheduling mechanism that allows the engine to become active whenever something needs to be done. This also allows tasks to be retried in the event of temporary errors.

- **Versioning:** Having long-running processes means that there is no point in time when there is no process instance running. In this context, "running" might actually mean waiting. Whenever you want to make a change to a process, such as adding another task, you need to think about all the currently running instances. Orchestration engines support multiple versions of a process definition in parallel. Good tools allow migrating instances to a new version of the process definition, in an automatable and testable manner.

Ignoring those requirements and working without an orchestration engine just means that you need to code a lot of those features in your own project, which leads to a lot of accidental complexity and your developers working on issues that do not deliver direct business value. This also increases technical debt, as the resulting code needs

Introduction 15

to be maintained over time. With an orchestration engine, you get all of this out of the box (Figure I.6).

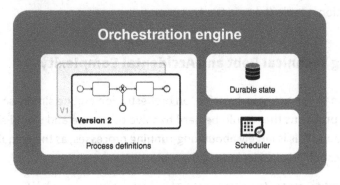

Figure I.6 An orchestration engine provides versioning, scheduling, and durable state out of the box.

Understanding Process Types That Can Be Orchestrated

The term *business process* is quite loaded, and of course there is a huge diversity of processes. In this section, we'll attempt to bring a bit of order to that chaos.

Tailor-made Digital Processes

Let's first sketch out the boundaries of what this book covers. When we talk about process automation in this book, we mean the following processes:

- **Business/digital processes:** These are the typical business processes that are common to most companies (like customer onboarding and order fulfillment), spanning multiple systems end to end. Some people prefer to refer to these as "digital processes," considering the term "business process" somewhat old-school.
- **Integration processes:** These are processes that focus on the point-to-point integration of systems or services, for example, to orchestrate microservices. There is not always a clear boundary between business processes and integration processes, as almost any automated business process will also integrate endpoints.

Other types of processes are explicitly out of scope. These include:

- Processes between untrusted participants (such as separate companies). This is a potential setting for blockchain.

- Infrastructure provisioning or IT automation processes (e.g. Ansible, Terraform). This is a domain on its own with specialized tools.

- Continuous integration/continuous delivery processes (e.g. Jenkins, GitHub Workflows). CI/CD build pipelines are standard processes in software engineering that are automated by standard software.

- Internet of Things (IoT) processes (e.g. Node Red). IoT use cases are often tackled with dedicated tooling that we would categorize as task automation software.

Of course, those processes might still be included in bigger business processes as tasks; for example, an internal employee onboarding process might directly invoke infrastructure provisioning processes to perform single actions within the overall process.

It's also important to recognize that there are two very different types of digital or integration processes:

- **Standard processes:** Whenever your company doesn't want to differentiate via the process, you can buy commercial off-the-shelf (COTS) software, like ERP, CRM, or human resources (HR) systems. In this case, you typically adapt your working procedures to the software.

- **Tailor-made processes:** Some processes are unique to an organization and because of that need to be tailor-made to the organization's needs. While these processes might be the same across different organizations (e.g. customer onboarding, order management, claim settlement), the way the organization designs and implements them is unique and can help differentiate them in their market. This enables organizations to be more competitive, conduct their business more efficiently, reduce costs, increase revenue, and transform into a more digital business. Sometimes, the uniqueness simply stems from a zoo of bespoke legacy systems that need to be integrated.

There is some overlap between these two categories when you customize your standard software, but companies have become more and more cautious about doing this because of bad experiences in the past.

Introduction

The decision about the type of the process to use needs to be made separately for every process in the company. There's no right or wrong choice, as long as your decision reflects your business strategy.

To recap, Figure I.7 shows the types of processes you might encounter and zooms in on the ones we're focusing on here.

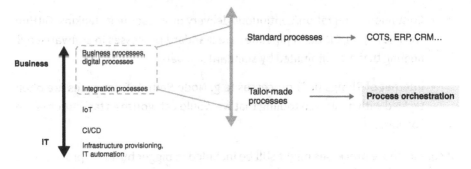

Figure I.7 The diversity of processes in an organization, and the ones this book focuses on automating.

Diversity of Business Processes

You can use process orchestration for a huge variety of use cases (see Figure I.8). The use cases with the biggest value are core end-to-end business processes, like customer onboarding, order fulfillment, claim settlement, payment processing, trading, and the like. But organizations also automate smaller processes. These processes are less complex, less critical, and typically less valuable, but they're still there, and automating them will have some ROI (or may simply be necessary to fulfill customer expectations). Good examples are master data changes (e.g. address or bank account data), bank transfer limits, annual mileage reports for insurance, delay compensation, and so on.

It's important to recognize that **nonfunctional requirements might differ** depending on the complexity of the use case. While critical, highly complex use cases are always implemented with the help of software engineering methods, to make sure the quality meets the expectations for this kind of solution and everything runs smoothly, the use cases on the lower end of the spectrum don't have to comply with the same requirements. For example, if a solution is not available for some time, it might not be the end of the world. If it gets

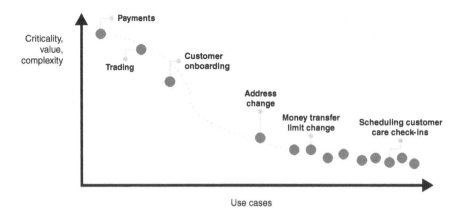

Figure I.8 Process ≠ process – there are typically some highly critical core processes to automate but also a long tail of simpler ones.

hacked, it might not be headline news. If there are weird bugs, it might just be annoying.

A Useful Categorization of Use Cases

The important thing is to make a conscious choice and not apply the wrong approach for the process at hand. An approach that we have seen work successfully is to categorize use cases and place them into three buckets, which we typically color red, yellow, and green.

Red processes are mission critical for the organization. They are also complex to automate and probably need to operate at scale. Performance and information security can be very relevant, and regulatory requirements might need to be fulfilled. Often we talk about core end-to-end business processes here, but sometimes other processes might be similarly critical. For these use cases, you need to do professional software engineering using industry best practices like version control, automated testing, continuous integration, and continuous delivery. The organization will want to apply some governance, for example, around which tools can be used and what best practices need to be applied.

Yellow processes are less critical, but the organization's operations will still be seriously affected if there are problems with these. So, you need to apply a healthy level of governance, but you also need to accept that solutions here may not be created to the same standard of quality as for red-use cases, mostly because you simply have a shortage of software developers.

Green processes are often local to one business unit or even an individual. The automations are often quick fixes stitched together to make one's life a bit easier, but the overall organization likely wouldn't realize it if they broke apart. The organization can afford to leave people a lot of freedom when it comes to these noncritical use cases, so typically there is no governance or quality assurance applied.

Figure I.9 provides a summary of the different categories.

Category	Description	Non-functional requirements	Value contribution	Governance
Red High complexity	Processes that are mission-critical for the organization (typically core end-to-end business processes, but sometimes other processes might be similarly critical)	• Complex to automate • Need to operate at scale • Performance and information security • Regulatory requirements	Very high; large influence on operational efficiency, customer experience, and business agility	Strong governance and quality controls need to be in place (e.g., standardized tooling, development stacks, version control, automated testing)
Yellow Medium complexity	Less critical processes, but ones where the organization's operations will still be seriously affected if there are problems	Depends	Not very high for individual cases, but together the long-tail processes deliver significant value	Require a healthy level of governance
Green Low complexity	Simple processes, often local to one business unit or even an individual	Low	Very low, on an individual case basis	No governance required

Figure I.9 A possible taxonomy of process categories within an organization.

Going back to our diverse set of processes, we can now map those to their respective categories, as visualized in Figure I.10.

Tailoring Your Process Automation Approach

When dealing with red use cases, organizations typically apply traditional software engineering methods, strict governance, and industry best practices, incorporating a process automation platform like Camunda into those efforts. Green use cases, on the other hand, are usually handled with Office-like tooling or low-code solutions like Airtable or Zapier. The yellow bucket is where the rubber hits the road: This is the long tail of processes that all need to be automated. This requires balancing nonfunctional requirements and effort, and establishing a fair level of governance,

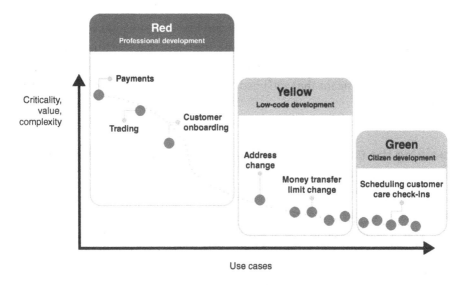

Figure I.10 Categorizing processes by their criticality and complexity.

quality assurance, and information security. We see our customers automating those processes with Camunda by making use of low-code accelerators like Connectors[7], rich forms, data handling, integrated tools like Tasklist[8], and browser-based tooling.

A good example of an organization using the same tool to automate both red and yellow use cases is Goldman Sachs. In addition to using the platform as a foundation for automating core banking use cases[9], they have built an extensive low-code platform[10] based on Camunda for the yellow use cases. As those case studies show, they've tackled the solutions quite differently, but based on the same technology foundation (as a sidenote, Goldman Sachs built the low-code platform themselves because they started on it several years ago, when there were no out-of-the-box solution accelerators available from Camunda).

In short, solution design, governance, and team structure are different for red and yellow use cases. We'll point this out throughout the book, so we'll refer back to these two categories of use cases often.

We want to add one important caveat: Processes in real life are often complex and heterogeneous. Some phases in a process might be complicated and require advanced technologies, whereas others might be simple. So, you may want to blend different approaches – such as pro code and low code – within one end-to-end process, perhaps in different phases. On the one hand, this is a strong argument to use platforms that are flexible enough to support a large variety of use cases. On the other hand, it also means that you need to add nuance in how you categorize your use cases.

Avoiding the Danger Zone Around Vendor Rationalization and Tool Harmonization

Reducing the number of vendors and tools in use across an organization is a common goal. This is understandable on many levels, but it can be very risky if the different nonfunctional requirements of green, yellow, and red processes are ignored. For example, procurement departments might not want to have multiple process automation tools in use, but they might not fully understand the difference between a platform like Camunda and a low-code platform. And while teams may be able to argue why they can't use a low-code tool for red use cases (as those tools simply don't fit into professional software development approaches), it gets more complicated for yellow use cases.

This can lead to a situation where low-code tools that are made for green use cases are applied to yellow ones. Whereas this might work for simple yellow processes, as Figure I.11 shows, it can become risky if the processes are more complex, or simply if organizational requirements around stability, resilience, ease of maintenance, scalability, or information security rise over time. On the other hand, Camunda's low-code acceleration features seamlessly extend its sphere of usability into yellow use cases: You don't have to involve software developers for everything, but you know that if additional nonfunctional requirements arise you'll be able to fulfill them, as the platform is built for red use cases. For example, if a solution starts to get shaky you can easily add automated tests, and you can easily scale operations if you face an unexpected spike in demand (Think of flight cancellations around the time of the COVID-19 pandemic; this was a yellow use case for airlines, but practically overnight it became highly important to be able to process them efficiently).

To summarize, it's far safer to target yellow use cases with a pro-code solution like Camunda, which has added low-code acceleration layers that you can (but don't have to) use. This allows you to use a single process orchestration stack for a large

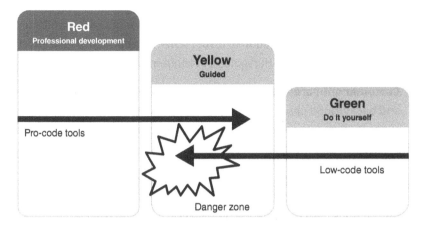

Figure I.11 Using low-code tools to automate yellow use cases can be risky, especially if nonfunctional requirements change over time.

variety of processes, while avoiding getting stuck with low-code solutions that cannot cope with changing nonfunctional requirements.

Typical Business Processes to Be Orchestrated

Now that you have an idea of what process orchestration can do for you, let's explore some concrete use case examples. We'll focus on a few specific industries here, and give some ideas of use cases that might be encountered in other industries as well. Of course, these lists are far from exhaustive.

To get more inspiration, you might also want to look at industry-specific reference models such as BIAN[11] for banking, ACORD[12] for insurance, eTOM[13] for telecommunications, or ITIL[14] for IT service management.

Financial Services

Possible use cases for process orchestration in the financial services industry include:

- **Loan and mortgage processing:** Orchestrating the journey from the initial application through document verification, credit checks, underwriting, and finally loan approval. This makes the entire process seamless, while decreasing the time from application to disbursement, reducing manual effort, and ensuring compliance with regulatory requirements.

- **Customer onboarding:** Orchestrating the verification of customer identities and background checks to comply with KYC regulatory standards, and the entry of customer data in all relevant systems to set up new accounts and services for customers.

- **Payment processing:** Ensuring seamless processing of payments, including cross-border transactions, while also automating the reconciliation of transactions between different financial systems and ledgers.

- **Trade settlement:** Orchestrating all the necessary steps to settle transactions. This not only increases efficiency but, importantly, ensures compliance with regulatory SLAs, like the T+1 regulation that requires trades to be settled within 24 hours.

- **Investment management:** Orchestrating the submission, approval, and payment of invoices in supply chain finance, and coordinating interactions and transactions with suppliers and vendors.

- **Know Your Customer or Anti-Money Laundering (AML) compliance checks:** While this is not a single process, KYC or AML checks affect many other processes. By orchestrating these, you can make sure the right checks are performed at the appropriate places in those processes, and also ensure the right data is written to the relevant systems. This approach lowers the risk of non-compliance, possible penalties, and damage to reputation, building trust with both customers and regulatory authorities.

When discussing use cases with financial services organizations, we typically use process overviews, as provided for example by the industry standard BIAN. Figure I.12 shows an example overview for consumer banking processes, highlighting investment priorities we discussed with an international bank. Processes marked in blue, for instance, have the potential for achieving an increase in efficiency or reduction in cost of over 20%, a net promoter score (NPS) improvement of more than 10 points, an increase in customer acquisition rate of more than 10%, 100% regulatory compliance, or an automation rate (STP = straight-through processing) of 70%.

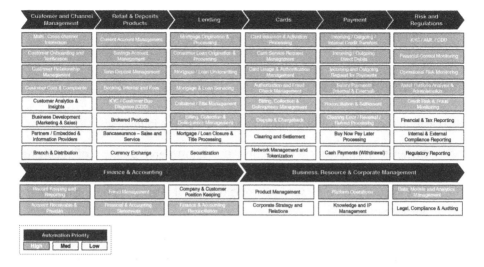

Figure I.12 Visualizing investment opportunities for process orchestration in consumer banking value chains.

Insurance

Process orchestration has many use cases in the field of insurance. Here are a few examples:

- **Claims processing:** Orchestrating the collection of claim information from customers through various channels, coordinating the assessment of claims (including fraud detection and validation of coverage), streamlining the approval process, and ensuring timely payouts to policyholders. Orchestration will lead to faster payouts and happier customers, and it can increase efficiency by automating a bigger percentage of claims.
- **Underwriting:** Orchestrating the collection and analysis of applicant data to assess risk and determine premium rates, as well as coordinating the issuance of policies, including document generation and customer notifications.
- **Customer onboarding:** Orchestrating the verification of customer identities and background checks to avoid fraud, and setting up accounts and services for customers in all relevant systems.
- **Policy administration:** Orchestrating the process of policy renewals, including notifications to customers and adjustments to policy terms, as well as

managing changes to policies, such as updates to coverage or beneficiary information (e.g. address changes).

Telecommunications

Use cases in the field of telecommunications include the following:

- **Order fulfillment:** Orchestrating the end-to-end process of receiving, validating, and fulfilling customer orders for new services or equipment. This includes not only service provisioning but also coordinating hardware delivery.

- **Service provisioning:** Orchestrating the activation of new services, such as mobile plans, internet connections, and TV packages. This might include setting up new customer accounts and configuring their services.

- **Network management:** Coordinating the deployment of new network infrastructure and upgrades (including the provisioning, monitoring, and management of IoT devices connected to the network), as well as detecting, diagnosing, and resolving network or hardware issues to minimize downtime and service disruptions. We have even seen processes to plan and build 5G cell towers or to manage reforestation required due to construction work.

- **Field service management:** Orchestrating technicians for network management.

- **Tariff changes:** Orchestrating the process to adjust tariffs for customers. Depending on the old and new tariffs, this might involve hardware return, new order fulfillment, and specific service provisioning steps.

- **Customer administration:** Orchestrating all things related to customer data, such as in the case of the customer moving to a new address. This can trigger further order fulfillment steps, for example, if landlines are involved.

Public Sector

In the public sector, use cases for process orchestration arise in areas such as the following:

- **Citizen services:** Orchestrating the submission, verification, and approval processes for various citizen applications (such as permits, licenses, and social services) and coordinating responses to citizen requests for services like waste collection, road repairs, and public safety issues.

- **Education administration:** Orchestrating the process of student registration, enrollment, and records management, and coordinating the allocation of educational resources, such as textbooks, classrooms, and technology.

- **Social services:** Orchestrating the assessment and distribution of social benefits, such as unemployment aid, food assistance, and housing support.

- **Public safety and law enforcement:** Orchestrating the management of criminal cases, including evidence tracking, court scheduling, and communications.

Retail

Possible retail use cases include the following:

- **Order management:** Orchestrating the process of order intake, processing, and fulfillment, ensuring accurate and timely delivery to customers with a high degree of transparency.

- **Inventory management:** Orchestrating the reorder process to maintain optimal inventory levels and avoid shortages or overstock situations, and streamlining warehouse operations such as receiving, storing, picking, and shipping products.

- **Customer service:** Integrating various customer service channels to provide consistent and efficient support, while also orchestrating the process of handling returns and exchanges to improve customer satisfaction and operational efficiency. Automating the refund process ensures timely and accurate reimbursements to customers.

- **Supply chain management:** Coordinating with suppliers to ensure timely delivery of products and materials and orchestrating logistics.

- **Customer relationship management:** Orchestrating the management of customer loyalty programs, including enrollment, points tracking, and rewards redemption.

Other Industries

While we have limited space in this book to go into detail, there are many other industries that will benefit from process orchestration. For example, in **manufacturing**, you can find use cases related to asset management or production scheduling. In **healthcare**, it can be beneficial to orchestrate processes relating to the patient experience like care coordination or automated claims processing. In the **automotive** industry, examples include processes for order management, after-sales services, and dealer management. Orchestrating **pharmaceutical** processes can be helpful for ensuring regulatory compliance or dealing with product recalls. **Energy** organizations might orchestrate processes centering around the distribution, management, or trade of electrical power or other resources. **Logistics and transportation** providers might automate processes for parcel management, routing, or rerouting. **Media and entertainment** companies might want to orchestrate the scheduling and distribution of content, possibly coordinating production or post-production processes. In the **hospitality** industry, room reservation, cancellation, and check-in and check-out processes are good candidates. **Legal service providers** might orchestrate processes for case tracking, document management, and communication.

Technical Use Cases of Process Orchestration

As we saw earlier, there are use cases for process orchestration in almost any industry, and it is the key ingredient for a successful digital transformation. But despite its critical role, process orchestration is rarely implemented as a standalone initiative. Instead, it is often embedded within broader strategic programs, serving as an enabler and accelerator. Here are some of the most common contexts in which process orchestration is introduced in an organization:

- **Value stream transformation:** Transforming value streams is key to driving customer-centric processes. Process orchestration helps align workflows, tools, and data sources to support this shift. It ensures that processes run smoothly across departmental boundaries, allowing organizations to better align with customer journeys, improve service delivery, and reduce friction.

- **Cloud migration:** Most cloud migration efforts include some application migration tasks, like transitioning to newer, cloud-first alternatives to legacy applications. Migrating workloads to the cloud requires understanding the current integration spaghetti, so that you can switch the integration logic from on-premise to cloud endpoints. All of this requires a deep understanding of end-to-end processes and the ability to adjust – and as companies like Atlassian have discovered (as reported in the Preface), these are among the key benefits of process orchestration.

- **Architecture modernization:** Process orchestration is essential to building more future-proof architectures. It enables microservices, APIs, and other architecture components to communicate and work together, creating a cohesive system that can adapt quickly to changing business needs.

- **Replacing legacy technology:** Modernizing legacy systems is a complex, multiphase endeavor in which process orchestration plays a pivotal role. Orchestration helps to bridge new and legacy systems, coordinating processes and workflows across both environments. This minimizes disruption and helps ensure continuity during transitions, allowing for a more manageable phased upgrade path.

- **Enabling AI:** Understanding end-to-end processes helps organizations decide where to apply AI and how best to do this. We explore this topic further in "Operationalizing AI for Autonomous Orchestration with Guardrails".

Of course, those initiatives are not mutually exclusive. For instance, a cloud migration can go hand in hand with architecture modernization, the replacement of legacy technology, and an architecture modernization, in order to transform an organization's value streams and enable the use of state-of-the-art technologies like AI.

Takeaways

Here are the key insights from this chapter:

- Process orchestration coordinates manual and automated tasks, ensuring seamless execution of end-to-end processes.

- Successful automation of (end-to-end) processes requires both task automation and process orchestration.

- Orchestration addresses challenges like disconnected workflows, lack of visibility, and limited adaptability by adding a separate process layer.

Introduction

- BPMN enables organizations to model and execute complex workflows, handling diverse endpoints and advanced process logic effectively.

- Categorizing processes as red (critical and complex), yellow (important, but simpler), or green (simple) helps prioritize governance and resource allocation appropriately.

- By blending seamlessly into your enterprise architecture, process orchestration facilitates gradual technical innovation, such as cloud migrations, AI integration, architectural modernization, and legacy system migrations.

- Process orchestration improves operational efficiency, enhances customer experiences, ensures regulatory compliance, and drives business agility across all industries.

Chapter 1: Vision

Now that we've explored process orchestration, the value it can bring, and typical use cases, let's turn our attention to using that knowledge to build a compelling vision for your process orchestration initiative.

We'll kick things off with a not-so-nice story, as often you can learn more from failures than from successes. A while ago we agreed on a strategic collaboration with a large infrastructure provider in Europe. They'd already had some initial success stories with Camunda, and the CIO wanted to set up a centralized process orchestration platform to increase process automation rates, harmonize tool stacks, and accelerate time to value for future initiatives. Efficiency was only one concern; the ultimate goal was to advance automation across the organization, to ensure business continuity with the looming threat of talent shortage because of the expected demographic change in the decade to come.

We had a few meetings with the CIO to better understand the company's strategic vision and the challenges they faced. We presented how a process orchestration strategy could help in meeting those challenges and how they could advance their initiative through Camunda's technology and services. Ultimately, we aligned on a shared vision, shook hands, and patted ourselves on the back for having done a great job.

Next, we spoke with the affected business domains with the goal of identifying potential use cases and kicking off concrete projects. But frustrations quickly arose. The first domain had already settled on a specific standard software, because they wanted to act independently from IT. Two other domains didn't consider process orchestration a strategic priority. Only the fourth domain committed to starting with a specific use case, but not with the urgency, we had hoped. All that made us lose the momentum we had built up initially. Consequently, our IT contacts became elusive; they deprioritized the topic because of limited bandwidth, and the initiative began to stall.

There is one core learning from this story: Even commitment from the CIO is not enough to ensure successful adoption of process orchestration. It requires buy-in from IT *and* the business. In this example, the roadmap and vision had been crafted within IT, without involving senior leadership from the business domains. This led to a lack of understanding of the potential of process orchestration and a lack of commitment, which resulted in a lack of urgency in the respective domains.

This chapter will guide you through how you can avoid these and other pitfalls and set up a successful process orchestration initiative that can truly transform your organization.

Luckily enough, in this particular case things still turned out well, as we still had a CIO that believed in process orchestration. We sat down with senior IT leaders, adjusted our approach, and initiated a close dialogue with senior business leaders to course-correct the collaboration and reignite the bold vision that had been set, getting us back on track.

Strategic Alignment: Bridging Vision, Strategy, and Stakeholders

As the story we just recounted illustrates, to set up your process orchestration journey for success you need to:

- Clearly define the **scope** of your initiative.
- Understand which **use cases** can benefit from process orchestration across the different domains.
- Link selected projects to your corporate **strategy.**
- Align the expectations of different **stakeholders** across the organization.
- Repeatedly **convey the value** and potential of process orchestration across the enterprise, not only to IT stakeholders, but also to the business domains.
- Create a **mutual vision and roadmap,** involving IT *and* business leadership, that is aligned on how process orchestration will transform your organization.

Let's dive into this in more detail.

Scoping Your Transformation Journey

Sometimes the path is the goal, but when you aim to transform your organization through process orchestration, you'd better have a clear target state in mind. Defining that target state begins with deciding on the scope of your initiative. In other words, which areas of the business do you want to focus your efforts on?

Process orchestration can be applied on different levels, as indicated in Figure 1.1:

- Enterprise-wide.
- Business domains (e.g. consumer vs. commercial banking).
- Specific processes within a business domain (e.g. a credit origination process).
- Local tasks within a process (e.g. a customer background check within a credit origination process).

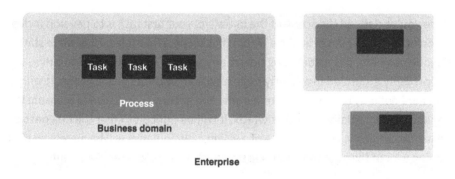

Figure 1.1 Potential scopes of process orchestration initiatives.

We recommend focusing your journey on using process orchestration at the enterprise level or, to get started, the business domain level. This is because when it comes to automation, it's important to think globally instead of locally. While a quick fix like using RPA to automate one task in a process might work in the short term, such point solutions will prevent organizations from effectively implementing end-to-end processes in the long run. By drawing a global scope, you will also make it easier to achieve the economies of scale needed to build sustainable competitive advantages through process orchestration, without getting bogged down in a myriad of minor initiatives with marginal impact.

This makes the strategic adoption of process orchestration a top management play. For an enterprise scope, the initiative should ideally be sponsored by the C-suite to ensure prioritizing investments and executing on the vision. For domain transformations, the initiative should be sponsored by the VPs or SVPs of the respective units. As we mentioned earlier, however, it's crucial that you have both IT and business leaders on board. IT typically makes the technical magic happen, but the business domains will leverage the technology to create business value, which means they need to understand why they need to use it.

Very often, we see process orchestration being tied to existing strategic initiatives (for example, around digitalization, cloud migration, or automation in general). That's normally a good thing, as it can have the advantage of being able to leverage existing funding and momentum.

Defining Your Vision

Once you've defined the scope of the initiative, your first task is to develop a clear vision of what you plan to achieve within that scope. While it feels like we're stating the obvious here, it is astonishing how many process orchestration initiatives are not properly grounded in a clearly defined vision. Without such a vision, it will be very hard not only to communicate the why and get buy-in, but also to measure the impact of your initiative. In other words, it will be difficult to "get the business on board." Accordingly, in the absence of a vision, your initiative will be merely tactical, leaving a lot of the potential of process orchestration on the table and putting first wins at risk of being stopped for other tactical reasons.

With a clear vision in mind, you'll be able to tie your initiative to your enterprise goals, identify appropriate success metrics, and track the ROI of your investments. Hence, it's crucial to invest time and thought here.

In their recent book *Rewired*[1], McKinsey executives Eric Lamarre, Kate Smaje, and Rodney Zemmel lay out what it takes to create a good vision: "Strong vision statements have some common ingredients: an aspiration, often anchored around the customer, as well as a time dimension and a quantification of significant value." The vision must be specific and tied to your business strategy, so that it can provide guidance on how your business will be transformed through technology – in our context, process orchestration.

To craft such a vision, close alignment with all relevant stakeholders is needed. As the McKinsey authors point out, through constant dialogue and dedicated workshops, the leadership teams need to build a shared understanding of the potential a technology (such as process orchestration) offers and how to integrate it into the organization. This relates to the business value and potential use cases for the technology, which capabilities are required, and how to develop a roadmap to build them.

Next up, we'll look at all the different stakeholders that are involved in a process orchestration transformation journey.

Aligning Your Stakeholders

Ultimately, such a complex transformation journey is a team effort across the whole organization. That's why it is crucial to align everyone's expectations. We think of the diversity of stakeholders in two dimensions, along a vertical and a horizontal axis, as shown in Figure 1.2.

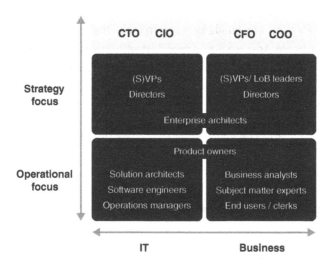

Figure 1.2 Alignment is required among diverse stakeholders across the enterprise.

On the vertical dimension, we group the personas according to their strategic and operational focus in the organization, with the C-suite acting as a governing entity across all domains. Strategy-focused stakeholders usually define the vision and provide the budget, while operational stakeholders execute it. In that sense, it's important to link the strategic goals of the organization to the initiative and think about how you can not only enable operational stakeholders to drive adoption across the organization, but also amplify their voices in order to generate a flow of fresh ideas and make sure their valuable experience is leveraged for further improvements.

Along the horizontal axis, we distinguish IT and business stakeholders as well as the multiple domains across the organization. For now, this distinction between "business" and "IT" is helpful to understand the different focus points, mindsets, and motivations. In some digitally mature organizations, the distinction between business and IT is eroding, as it should be, in order to deliver business value at scale (we will tackle this topic further in the next chapter). But in reality, for most organizations, business and IT are still operating as different entities that need to be aligned.

If you're targeting an enterprise transformation initiative, it's crucial to have a shared understanding in the C-suite about the potential of the technology and how to tie it to the business strategy. This helps to ensure you have the necessary funding and leadership buy-in to drive this change. Continuing to the (senior) vice presidents (SVPs), line of business (LoB) leaders, and directors, it is equally important to understand their goals and challenges and to make them aware of the value such a transformation holds. As you will typically start with a few use cases in a few domains (1–3), you'll want to focus on those leaders first so as not to overstretch your capacity. But of course, you should always be open to talking to anyone who approaches you about the value of process orchestration!

Let's look at how a vision for a process orchestration initiative could be crafted in an organization such as a large bank:

C-Suite/Senior Leadership:

- **Objective:** Define the global enterprise vision for process orchestration and automation.

- **Example:** "Our vision is to implement process orchestration across all global operations within the next four years, streamlining 80% of key customer-facing processes. This will drive a 30% improvement in response times, reduce manual interventions by 50%, and elevate personalized service by integrating real-time data insights. By orchestrating these processes, we aim to deliver a seamless end-to-end customer experience that positions us as a leader in operational excellence and customer satisfaction."

SVP/LoB Leader (e.g. of commercial and retail banking):

- **Objective:** Transform the domain/business unit according to the vision.

- **Example:** "Our objective is to leverage process orchestration in commercial and retail banking to automate 70% of routine operations by the end of next year, reducing manual errors by 40% and cutting transaction processing time by 50%. This will enable faster loan approvals, smoother payments, and seamless onboarding, leading to a 25% increase in client satisfaction and retention. By driving efficiency and accuracy through orchestration, we will strengthen relationships with our business clients and enhance loyalty across our retail banking segment, resulting in an increase in net promoter score."

Process/Product Owner (e.g. for the credit origination process in commercial and retail banking):

- **Objective:** Improve processes and products based on strategy.

- **Example:** "Our objective is to implement process automation in the credit origination process from end to end within the next 18 months, reducing approval times by 60%, cutting error rates by 35%, and improving process efficiency by 40%. This will ensure clients gain faster access to credit while maintaining compliance and reducing risk. By orchestrating critical steps, we will deliver a smoother, more reliable credit experience that significantly enhances customer satisfaction."

You should also directly define success **metrics** to be tracked. This will most likely happen on the process/product owner level, as you can define very specific metrics that are tied to the business value and should be reported back to the owner of the initiative and the strategic sponsors. For example:

- **Average approval time:** Measure the average time taken from the initiation of a credit application to its approval, aiming for a significant reduction post-automation implementation.

- **Error rate in credit applications:** Track the percentage of credit applications with errors or discrepancies pre- and post-automation, aiming for a decrease in error rates as automation reduces manual input and enhances accuracy.

- **Customer satisfaction (CSAT) score for credit origination:** Conduct regular surveys or use other feedback mechanisms to gauge customer satisfaction specifically related to the credit origination process, aiming for an improvement in CSAT scores post-automation as a reflection of smoother, faster, and error-free experiences.

Vision

To drive the transformation, organizations need to consider their business architecture and how it aligns with the transformation program. We'll explore that topic in the next section.

Building a Business Architecture to Realize Digitalization and Automation Benefits

To provide great products and services to customers, enterprises need to transcend organizational silos. Customer journeys and end-to-end processes, especially in large organizations, are simply too complex to be handled in just one team, or even in one department. This makes it crucial to define a business architecture for the whole organization that can support customer journeys that span those silos. Of course, it also needs to reflect modern requirements around business agility and efficiency.

But what might such a business architecture look like? That's what we plan to sketch in this section. Please keep in mind that such a reference architecture is always just an idealized target picture; in reality, you will see a lot of deviations from it. Still, it can serve as a North Star and will hopefully provide you with inspiration on how to gradually adjust your organization to allow for true digital transformation.

Before we dive in, let's start with a quick definition to get everybody onto the same page: a **business architecture** is, in essence, a methodology to connect your business strategy with your organizational setup and your technology.

The Business Architecture in a Nutshell

In his book *The Software Architect Elevator*[2], Gregor Hohpe uses the metaphor of a skyscraper to describe the business and enterprise architecture of a large corporation. The penthouse office at the top houses the executive suite, responsible for global business strategy. Riding the elevator down, you'll gradually enter more operational territory in the business domains, until ultimately you arrive at the engine room, where the foundational technologies are implemented. For a successful business transformation (and to be a good architect, as Gregor puts it), you'll need to ride the elevator both ways and be able to make stops at any point, talking to different roles in very different languages.

We've used this metaphor as the basis for our business architecture as well, as we believe it provides a great outline of what you need to be successful. To make things more hands-on in this section, we will use the example of a retail bank and a typical consumer loan application process.

Figure 1.3 shows an overview of the business architecture, which consists of five levels.

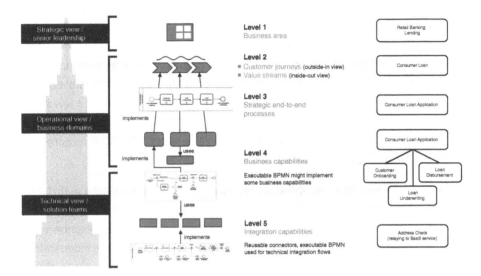

Figure 1.3 A business architecture that supports your digital future.

Let's break down what you'll find at each of these levels:

- **Level 1 – Business area:** Typical organizations are separated into manageable units that represent functional areas where the business competes for market share. The business area is at the top of the architecture. In our example, this is the lending area within a retail bank, which means the part of the bank working with consumers (B2C).

- **Level 2 – Customer journeys and value streams:** On this level, you look at the customer journey within the selected business area holistically. In our example, this means from the desire to borrow money, through receiving the money, until the loan is finally paid back and closed. In addition to the customer's perspective (the outside-in view), organizations can sketch their internal activity streams that show how those customer demands are met (the inside-out view). Those are called *value streams*; they're abstractions of processes or product lifecycles including the most important steps.

- **Level 3 – Strategic end-to-end processes:** Customer journeys and value streams typically focus on the whole lifecycle of a product or service, and as such are often too long to be fully discussed within automation projects. Instead, you focus on bursts of activity within the overall journey and distill those as end-to-end processes. For example, within the consumer loan journey, there is a phase from when the customer applies for a loan until it is disbursed, which is the loan application process. You'll want to describe this end-to-end process as a strategic process model, which is a general, results-oriented representation of a process, to create the quickest possible understanding for a wide audience. The process is sketched out in just a few steps: Errors or variations are not shown at all, and the model typically fits on a single sheet of paper. It links to the main business capabilities required for the process to be successfully implemented.

- **Level 4 – Business capabilities:** The business capabilities are the main building blocks the organization needs to complete the end-to-end processes (and therefore also whole value streams). Business capabilities describe what needs to be done, but not how it happens. Accordingly, they are independent of their technical implementation. This is handy when you want to gradually modernize your IT landscape, as it means, for instance, that you can migrate your billing capacity from a monolithic legacy ERP system to a flexible microservice without requiring a change in capabilities using billing.

- **Level 5 – Integration capabilities:** These are the technical details required to make certain capabilities available to the overall architecture. They often include integration flows, perhaps expressed as executable BPMN processes, that abstract the technical details required to integrate a specific system. They may also be reusable connector building blocks, easing the implementation of business capabilities.

Naturally, a business architecture such as this provides only a very high-level view of your organization. And truth be told, the specific set of business capabilities will often look very similar across organizations within the same industry. This is why industry-specific reference models like the ones mentioned earlier (BIAN[3] for banking, ACORD[4] for insurance, or eTOM[5] for telco) work well, and they are typically a good starting point. As we will see soon, competitive advantages are built through the implementation of the business capabilities and how they are brought together to transform the end-to-end processes and value streams.

Reading this section, savvy automation and process veterans might also think of process landscapes or maps. Those concepts typically describe initiatives to document all business processes within an organization, ranked in hierarchies. In that sense, they aim to provide a structure to core business functionality and as such are not so different to identifying value streams and business capabilities. However, those initiatives too often are not connected to IT implementation projects and simply document processes, without the ambition to transform the business or boost automation rates. So while they might provide some value around visibility and understanding of processes, their impact is, frankly speaking, often limited, and they are likely to be detached from reality. We have seen many organizations where these efforts caused the term "business process" to have a negative connotation.

This is why we prefer business architectures based on customer journeys, value streams, and business capabilities that are linked to executable processes. Yes, there is still a risk of those initiatives taking place in enterprise architecture ivory towers, but done right (keep riding the architect elevator!), those architectures can strongly influence organizational structures and connect business strategy to tangible IT initiatives – which makes them much more practical and valuable.

Customer Journeys and Value Streams

Level 1 of the business architecture should, hopefully, be self-explanatory, so let's zoom in on Level 2 and look more closely at customer journeys and value streams. Defining these starts at the top, with the customer. Every organization needs to understand which journeys and touchpoints the customer goes through to achieve the desired value. A simplified customer journey for a consumer loan is depicted in Figure 1.4.

While customer journeys provide the external view, value streams depict the high-level activities the organization needs to perform in order fulfill those customer needs. Accordingly, they provide a different perspective on the same process. Value streams can also point out the resources and costs associated with the required activities. Figure 1.5 shows the value stream for our consumer loan journey.

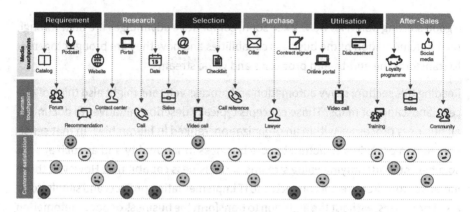

Figure 1.4 A sample customer journey, which is more basic than it should be in real life.

Figure 1.5 Value stream example for the consumer loan journey.

Value streams, by nature, are at a high level of abstraction. Their purpose is simply to provide an overview of the activities the organization needs to be able to perform. Typically, the value stream is stable even for deviations from the happy path and for variants of the journey (perhaps for different customer segments, regions, or input channels), and it runs through multiple teams and domains.

One big advantage of this level of abstraction is that you can avoid endless analysis in this phase, as the aim is just to identify and describe the essential activities. You may be surprised, though, how hard it can be to sketch out the value streams for core products – and how different sketches from different executives may look.

Strategic End-to-End Processes

At the next level, below customer journeys and value streams, are the end-to-end business processes. These are arguably the most important drivers of value in an organization. Bringing together the high-level nature of value streams with tangible business capabilities, they orchestrate all the activities required to deliver a particular product or service to the customer. For example, ordering a new fixed-line internet service starts with the customer's desire to have internet access, and that desire is only fulfilled once all the necessary hardware is installed and configured and the internet is working for the customer. Only if all of the required activities are executed properly and in full is the real value unlocked. Whenever the process stalls, there is frustration ("Why is my internet still not working?!") and additional operational costs are incurred (e.g. to support and appease the customer). This can sometimes also lead to regulatory consequences (for example, fines when lines are not provisioned according to regulators' SLAs) or customer churn.

The main difference between a customer journey/value stream and an end-to-end process is that the customer journey starts much earlier, at the moment when a customer discovers their desire, and ends later, when the journey is completed. It describes the full product (or service) lifecycle, which may extend over a very long time span. Consider, for example, a life insurance contract, or the mortgage on your house. From an operational perspective, it doesn't make sense to implement one end-to-end process for this complete time frame.

Accordingly, the duration of the process is the main differentiator. There are typically bursts of activity within that lifetime, interspersed with long periods of waiting. Those bursts of activity constitute end-to-end processes. Order-to-cash (O2C) is a textbook example: The end-to-end process comprises all the steps involved from the moment a customer places an order until the company has received and recorded the payment, but it does not contain information about the preliminary stages of the customer researching what to order and from whom, or any service requests during the subsequent use of the product.

For our loan example, the loan application process is such a burst of activity, starting when the customer applies for a loan and ending when the money is disbursed, as indicated in Figure 1.6.

Figure 1.6 End-to-end processes depict bursts of activity in value streams.

Afterward, there is a phase where the bank simply monitors the repayment, and finally there is another burst of activity when closing the loan, or perhaps negotiating a replacement loan. Along the way, there might be other activities or processes happening in the customer journey; for instance, a customer might move to a different address at any time, and this change will need to be processed. Such activities are entirely separate from the loan application process and are handled independently.

The goal at this level is to describe the end-to-end process strategically, as laid out in the book *Real-Life BPMN*[6] – that means we want to enable comprehension of the process, without including the nitty-gritty details. The resulting process model typically fits on one sheet of paper and is not executable, but it still should show the trigger, the results, and the main activities. It is a refinement of a part of the value chain.

For every end-to-end process, you should create a process profile describing the goals and key performance indicators (KPIs). Figure 1.7 shows an example of what this might look like for our loan application process.

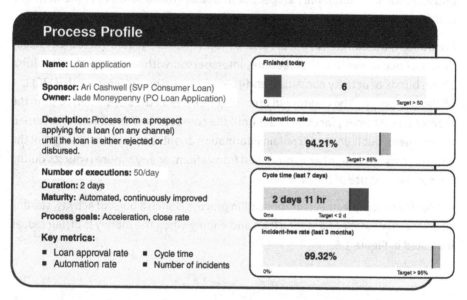

Figure 1.7 Process profile giving an overview of a process, including core KPIs.

Business Capabilities

To implement the end-to-end processes (and thereby also the value streams), you need to define the business capabilities that will perform the necessary activities. A business capability describes what needs to be done in business terms, independent of its implementation. Figure 1.8 shows the elements that should be included.

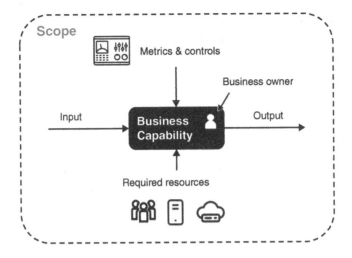

Figure 1.8 The elements of a business capability definition.

When defining a business capability, you need to consider all of the following:

- **Scope:** What is the exact scope of the business capability? Where do the boundaries of what the capability is and is not responsible for lie? For example, an underwriting capability is responsible for all loan decisions from a banking and risk perspective, but not for technical checks around address verification.
- **Input:** What is the trigger for this activity? What data needs to be provided to perform the business capability? How does the capability interface with the rest of the organization? There may be a manual trigger (e.g. a clerk gets an email with the loan request attached as a PDF and responds with the underwriting decision), but more often this refers to some technical means of communication, like APIs (e.g. one REST API triggers underwriting, another REST API polls for the results) or events (e.g. the fraud check might react to certain events and publish its own events).
- **Output:** What is the intended result (which should create value in some way)? Like with the input, you also need to define the type of the interface and the data that should be submitted.
- **Resources:** What resources are required (or available) to fulfill the capability? These may include people (roles, teams), IT systems and services, or other business capabilities.

- **Metrics and controls:** What are the KPIs that are measured for this business capability? What SLAs are provided?

- **Business owner:** Who owns the capability and is responsible for delivering the agreed-upon level of quality and continuously improving it? For example, the SVP of credit risk will sponsor the underwriting capability, while the corresponding process owner will be responsible and accountable for its successful operation.

Again, a business capability should be defined independently of its technical implementation. For example, the business capability for loan underwriting could be implemented manually by a risk officer using a pen and paper, or it might be automated, with only edge cases presented to a human to decide on via a web-based user interface. In the latter case, it would not matter if AI or traditional software tools were used.

As mentioned earlier, business capability maps are often quite similar across organizations in specific industries (in our case, banking). However, the implementation of those capabilities will vary widely, as each organization has its own structure and unique set of systems – and this implementation has a significant impact on the customer experience and operational efficiency. Accordingly, this is an important area where organizations can differentiate themselves: In short, **the exact implementation of your business capabilities is a decisive factor in your organization's success.**

For example, manually handled loan applications will not only take much longer to process, making customers unhappy, but also be very costly. An automatically orchestrated loan application process can be more efficiently operated and better scaled if demand increases, and it leads to a better customer experience and higher customer satisfaction. It also allows for further incremental technical innovation, such as plugging in AI to perform fraud checks for your loan decisions. You can then track the impact of these innovations by looking at the metrics of the business capabilities – for example, when implementing AI, has the number of manual checks for edge cases been reduced? (We'll talk more about measurement in "Chapter 5: Measurement".)

To define the business capabilities in our example, we need to identify the core functions and processes that enable delivering the consumer loan. The typical approach is to analyze the value stream in more detail, and list all the activities involved.

For example, in the Credit Evaluation and Underwriting phase, we might identity the following activities:

- Perform address check.
- Perform fraud check.
- Perform credit check using credit bureau services.
- Calculate internal credit score based on customer's financial history and current obligations.
- Decide whether to approve application based on evaluation results.
- Request additional information or require additional action from customer.
- Finalize terms of loan (e.g. interest rate, repayment schedule).
- Notify customer of loan approval.

Are all of those activities business capabilities? While you could define them as such, it's not advisable. This is because if you end up with thousands of unordered business capabilities, it will be hard to derive a meaningful business architecture. Instead, you should aim to group activities into meaningful business capabilities, taking into account your organizational layout and the responsibilities of the different teams (which we will dive into in "Enabling Organizational Redesign").

For example, we might define a "Loan Underwriting" business capability that can perform all the activities related to the financial evaluation of the loan and the risk assessment for the bank. This could be separate from the more technical evaluation of a customer, like address and fraud checks (which, notably, are not needed if the customer is already known). Those checks might better end up in a "Customer Onboarding" capability.

Figure 1.9 shows possible business capabilities and their main tasks identified for our loan example.

While business capabilities might require other capabilities to work, we intentionally do not add any hierarchy or layering within capabilities, as in our experience this can get confusing very quickly and lead to unnecessary discussions about how to structure the hierarchy. We like to think of business capabilities more as a long list of items, all at the same level. Of course, you can apply tags to individual capabilities to make that list manageable. We have found this more flexible way of categorizing capabilities more successful in real life.

Vision

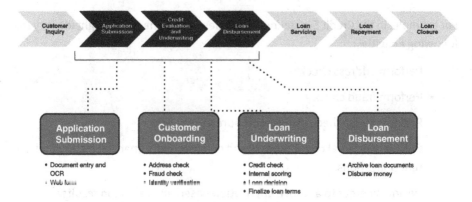

Figure 1.9 Deriving business capabilities from the end-to-end value stream – each capability can contain multiple tasks.

The Role of Executable Processes

At this point, you've defined your end-to-end processes and your business capabilities. But how are those connected to process orchestration? This is where the rubber hits the road.

Of course, business capabilities can be performed by humans. Or they can be implemented via point solutions or standard software, for simple, standardizable capabilities. But if you want to digitalize and automate your business strategically, most often business capabilities are implemented by process orchestration, using executable process models in BPMN. In the context of our business architecture, you would set up autonomous, stream-aligned teams, each developing and maintaining exactly one business capability. This is a very powerful approach, as it means every business capability has clear boundaries and a defined interaction with its environment. This in turn allows you to accelerate development.

Let's look at an example. Figure 1.10 shows the executable process model we might use to orchestrate all the tasks in the Customer Onboarding business capability described in the previous section.

As mentioned earlier, business capabilities can require other capabilities. For example, in the third step, the Customer Onboarding capability might require an Identity Verification capability. From the point of view of the Customer Onboarding capability, this is a black box; it has no idea about the other business capability's internals. This is why the identity verification task is not a call activity (aka subprocess), which is something you might be wondering about if you are familiar with BPMN already. But

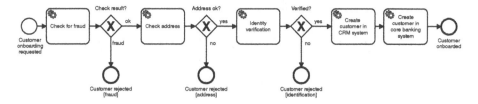

Figure 1.10 Executable process model implementing the Customer Onboarding business capability.

at this level we don't want to know that there might also be a process at play in the identity verification step, as this is an implementation detail of that step.

It's actually very likely, though, that the implementation of the Identity Verification business capability also uses an executable process model—for example, the one shown in Figure 1.11.

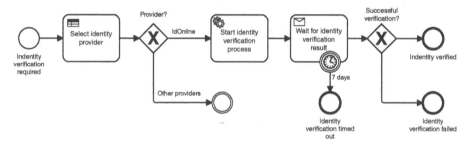

Figure 1.11 Executable process model implementing the Identity Verification business capability.

Using process orchestration, you can easily also bring humans into the loop of a business capability and mix manual and automated work. This is illustrated by Figure 1.12, where the process can be escalated to a human user to perform a manual identity check should a problem occur.

One special case that's interesting to look at is the end-to-end process itself. In our example, that's the loan application process. We looked at the strategic process model earlier, but of course it also makes a lot of sense to treat the end-to-end process as its own business capability and implement it via an executable process, as shown in Figure 1.13.

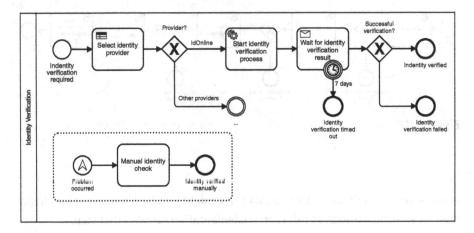

Figure 1.12 In BPMN, you can easily push tasks to humans, even if only for exceptional cases.

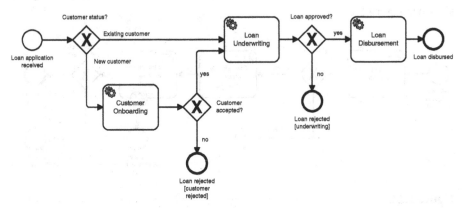

Figure 1.13 The end-to-end loan application process as an executable process model.

Even if this executable end-to-end process model is relatively simple, it is valuable to have so that you can benefit from visibility as well as collect audit data and metrics. It also enables you to discuss process improvements and redesigns on the end-to-end process level.

Avoid Lengthy Discussions About Process Hierarchies

We see one discussion come up so often that we want to address it up front in this book, in the hopes of saving you this discussion time. To understand the problem, let's look at the loan application example again and try to map the value stream to the end-to-end business process and the business capabilities (Figure 1.14).

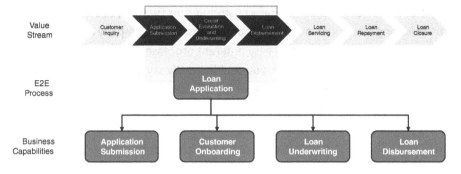

Figure 1.14 Mapping the value stream to an end-to-end process and to business capabilities.

As you can see, the end-to-end business process spans multiple steps of the value stream. At the same time, it is a business capability on its own, probably implemented by an executable process model that orchestrates other business capabilities.

While this all sounds great (and it actually is), this architecture has one implication: You cannot "zoom into" elements from the high-level value stream down to the executable processes in a consistent manner. Most prominently, the end-to-process cannot be referenced from the value stream, as it is not its own box there. This feels inconsistent to some, but we recommend simply ignoring this inconsistency – that might sound cavalier, but in such a high-level view it's really not a problem. The mapping from value streams to strategic end-to-end processes to business capabilities does not have to be an exact science.

If this still triggers too many discussions in your organization, you could adjust the value stream to include a Loan Application activity instead of the three more detailed activities (Application Submission, Credit Evaluation and Underwriting, and Loan Disbursement). Keep in mind, though, that while this will fix the hierarchy, you'll lose a bit of information in the value stream. This can be problematic if some people or roles look only at that and don't dig down to the end-to-end process or business capability levels.

Another topic of discussion that frequently comes up is whether it's possible to clearly differentiate between end-to-end processes and business capabilities, and if you should add layers to form a hierarchy. Again, we advise you not to go down this rabbit hole, as there is nothing to gain. It's often quite hard to differentiate them, as even elevated "end-to-end business capabilities" can still be used from within other capabilities. For example (as visualized in Figure 1.15), onboarding a new customer

Vision

might be a standalone process that a customer runs through, but it might also be part of issuing a new insurance policy, and an insurance company might offer very different types of insurance with very different processes for issuing the different kinds of policies. In such a context, you couldn't really say if customer onboarding is a top-level (end-to-end process) or lower-level (business capability) capability – and it actually doesn't matter.

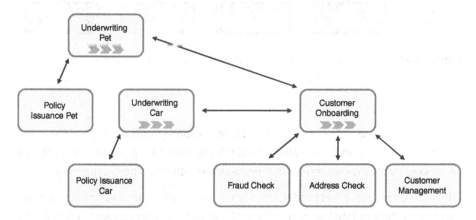

Figure 1.15 Processes implement business capabilities: they might also be invoked from other capabilities.

To summarize, in the proposed architecture, a strategic end-to-end process can be a business capability or not. This does not make a difference to the overall structure. Also, try not to create a hierarchy of business capabilities. It's much more valuable to simply attach tags to your business capabilities to make them more easily sortable or searchable. You might have a tag for "implements an end-to-end process," but that doesn't mean business capabilities with that tag are hierarchically above the others; it's just useful information. As with the other topics we've mentioned here, don't let conceptual discussions around hierarchies slow you down in your transformation journey!

Advantages of This Business Architecture

The proposed business architecture brings together business strategy with IT implementation. Its structure offers a powerful methodology to determine where to invest your scarce resources and provides strategies for incremental improvement of key end-to-end processes. It makes ownership clear and helps accelerate delivery through the reusability of business capabilities across teams. It also serves as a tool for promoting organizational redesigns to address the complexity of these processes, while enabling a process mindset.

That's quite a mouthful, so let's go over this in more detail.

Making Informed Decisions About Where to Invest

Understanding all the layers of the business architecture is essential to gain a comprehensive overview of your business. Otherwise, you might fly either too high, looking at business models without a good idea of how they are actually implemented in the organization, or too low, focusing on individual point solutions, teams, or pain points in isolation.

As an example, suppose you're considering investing in a new AI-based customer support system to handle customer calls more efficiently. This project would yield a sound ROI, and looking at it in isolation, it might seem like a no-brainer.

But if you were to look at the overall value stream holistically, you might find that investing the same amount of money into properly orchestrating the loan application process would lead to a dramatic drop in support requests in the first place. When you consider the big picture, the latter option (which might ensure that all required documents are requested up front and make the status at each stage of the process transparent to customers through a self-service web application) is the better investment choice – but this can only be seen when you take a high-level view of the value stream. This example also points to the effectiveness of a "shift-left" strategy, where you try to improve tasks as early as possible in the process, to avoid problems later.

In general, the business architecture, and of course the people overseeing it, give you a valuable framework to understand the status quo of your organization and discuss priorities for action. This helps you to avoid blindly following market trends or vendor marketing. It will help you drive improvements that are aligned with long-term transformation goals and further allow you to judge if local point solutions are legitimate in the bigger picture, or will need to be replaced in the future.

To summarize, the business architecture allows you to identify great automation candidates, either driven by risk or by opportunity. A collaborative discussion of the whole value stream is the best way to pinpoint the biggest automation or

Vision

orchestration opportunities. The business architecture provides the comprehensive overview you need to make investment decisions on the organizational level and can be a great enabler of a successful top-down transformation journey. (We will dive further into this topic in "Building and Prioritizing Business Cases".)

Try to be as data-driven as possible when planning improvements. Ideally, you will base your decisions not on opinions, but on data. By defining KPIs to measure right from the start, you can make sure any changes also yield the desired outcomes (this is further explained in "Chapter 5: Measurement"). The organizations we've seen have the most successful outcomes are really good at defining hypotheses, act accordingly, and measure the results.

Strategically Improving Your End-to-End Processes

Discussing process improvements at the end-to-end level avoids teams making local optimizations that could actually have negative effects on the overall business process. To give a real-world example, one lending organization we worked with saw the following improvements after making adjustments to their end-to-end process – results that they recognized they could never have achieved by making isolated changes to the individual tasks involved:

- **Processing time:** Reduced average time taken to disburse money from 3 to 5 business days down to 1 to 2 days by reducing waiting times for human work through the use of clearly orchestrated tasks. This time was distributed amongst the different business capabilities.

- **Contact rate:** Reduced the contact rate of inbound and outbound calls before loan offerings from 86 to 32% by enabling multichannel customer self-service.

- **Underwriting time:** Reduced average handling time for processing and underwriting a loan from more than 45 to 14 minutes through data prefill, enrichment, and decision support using AI/ML, which could be hooked into the orchestrated process.

Take another example. If you're introducing a new channel like a banking app for your customers, those changes can't be handled locally because they affect the entire end-to-end process. That means you have to do a holistic redesign of your value stream. The new app might allow customers to register and apply for a loan, but it will support a different customer experience than your existing customer journey; for example, the identity verification is done as an integral part of the registration flow, instead of being triggered via email later on as with traditional applications.

In this scenario, a new Customer Self-Registration business capability might own the customer flow through the app, which embeds the identity verification task and then kicks off the existing loan application process. You might also need to make some adjustments to the loan application process or the Customer Onboarding business capability, though. Distributing responsibilities correctly to the various business capabilities requires a high-level view of the various end-to-end processes that need to be supported.

Defining Clear Ownership

The business architecture allows you to define ownership of various artifacts. At Level 2 (customer journeys and value chains), the owners are usually C-level executives or SVPs. While the ownership here is typically very clear, establishing a transformation office and business process optimization group (discussed in "Adoption Governance (aka Who Owns the Business Architecture?)") will help ensure a regular meeting cadence is maintained, and they are kept up to date and incrementally improved.

You also need to define owners for every end-to-end process (Level 3) and business capability (Level 4). If an end-to-end process is also defined as a business capability, this can be a joint owner. In existing organizations, this type of ownership is often missing, leading to chaotic end-to-end processes and unclear responsibilities for every capability that crosses a team boundary. Doing this right provides a huge opportunity to drive improvements and optimizations holistically. We'll talk about this more in "Enabling Organizational Redesign".

Composing Processes Out of Business Capabilities

Reusability is a key feature of business capabilities. An often-used metaphor is LEGO building bricks: You can put together new business capabilities, processes, or even whole business models using existing bricks. The clearer the responsibilities and interfaces of your business capabilities are, the better this can work. Reusing functionality can require some flexibility on the part of your business and the way it works, though. Do customers in a branch office really need special handling? Strategically, is this worth the deviation on a business capability level? Or could the clerks simply fill out the same online form as customers would do themselves, and get a shortcut link afterward to do identity verification on the spot.

Composability also allows you to exchange the implementation of a capability more easily – say, when you want to switch your homegrown subscription billing service for an off-the-shelf SaaS offering. In this example, the end-to-end process can remain the same; only the implementation of the business capability changes.

Enabling Organizational Redesign

Traditional organizational structures, arranged in functional silos, are usually not aligned with the business architecture sketched out in this book. Hence, they might hinder your success with process orchestration and prevent your organization from staying competitive in the long run. In functionally designed structures, end-to-end processes need to span tasks in multiple silos and teams. None of those teams are responsible for the end-to-end success of a process, and as such nobody looks at the holistic value creation for the customer. This leads to inefficiencies and local optimizations that don't take into account the big picture. This problem is visualized in Figure 1.16.

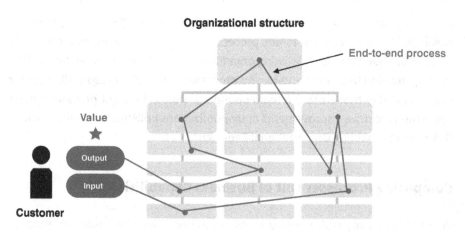

Figure 1.16 In traditional organizations that are structured in functional silos, an end-to-end process touches too many teams, with nobody overseeing value creation (taken from this CamundaCon 2024 presentation[7]).

Eliyahu Goldratt's *The Goal*[8] is a great book about this phenomenon. In one episode, the main character observes the inefficiency of a group of Boy Scouts on a hike:

because the fastest people are always out in front, they keep having to wait for the others, which then turns into a break for the whole group, making the hike last even longer. Only by looking at the group holistically and letting the slowest people set the pace could they optimize the end-to-end hike. A chain is only as strong as its weakest part, and processes are only as good as their bottlenecks.

To improve your operational model, you need to align your team structures with the value streams, end-to-end processes, and business capabilities mapped out in the business architecture. This observation also aligns with overarching trends in organizational development, such as microservices, domain-driven design, team topologies, SAFe, and other frameworks.

One typical pitfall is to not be radical enough here. Even if you see local successes, if the broader organization is still operating within the constraints of the existing structures, such an approach fails to address the underlying inefficiencies and silos that stand in the way of true improvements on the end-to-end level. You need to make the necessary bold and comprehensive changes to achieve effective process orchestration. A transformative mindset is required – one that is willing to challenge and overhaul entrenched systems, reconfigure team structures, and embrace a holistic, end-to-end perspective on business processes. Without such a fundamental and courageous shift, efforts at process improvement remain piecemeal, preventing the organization from realizing its full potential.

Of course, this cannot and does not have to happen overnight; you should follow an incremental approach that derisks your endeavor. But you should be clear on the goal. A typical journey we observe is to start by designating owners and dedicated teams for a few initial business capabilities, which the teams often view as "products," and identifying a selected end-to-end process where improvements need to happen. After a successful pilot, this structure is slowly rolled out to other business capabilities.

It is very important to clearly assign ownership as part of this exercise, as this enhances the accountability and empowerment of employees. Teams have a clear mandate and the autonomy to optimize their capabilities and processes, leading to improved performance and innovation. A good business architecture also ensures that business capabilities are tied back to the business model or customer journey, so that it is clear why those capabilities exist and what their goals are.

This organizational structure is particularly powerful for processes spanning multiple teams or departments, as you start to have one person being responsible for overseeing the entire end-to-end process, ensuring coherence, efficiency, and alignment with strategic goals. Such an owner has a holistic view of the process, bridging gaps between different teams and functions, and makes sure optimizations are done globally, not locally. This end-to-end oversight is essential for identifying and eliminating the bottlenecks, redundancies, and inefficiencies that often arise in siloed structures.

Of course, this is a big change, and it requires a significant cultural shift. Proper change management is a necessity, as is a good understanding of the **process-first mindset**.

Establishing a Process-First Mindset

The business architecture laid out here will help facilitate a process mindset. In this book, we often allude to the advantages of processes as first-class citizens. They are the key to aligning your strategy with your operations, increasing customer satisfaction, conquering new markets with new business models, and streamlining your operations to reduce waste, minimize errors, and generally reduce effort. Furthermore, standardized processes will improve consistency and quality across the organization. When processes are clear, employees are empowered to fulfill their roles more confidently and autonomously, having a clear understanding of their responsibilities and part in the process. Last but not least, a process-centric culture, using measurements as described in "Chapter 5: Measurement", leads to a more data-driven mentality, which in turn leads to better-informed decision-making that's connected to your business strategy.

So, there's a lot to gain – but to fully reap the benefits, you need to establish a process mindset throughout your organization, where processes are at the front of people's minds and everybody is aware of the potential of process orchestration. Communicating the importance of process orchestration to the organization is a top management task, so you need commitment and dedication from your C-level leaders, expressed through concrete actions and resource allocation.

A process mindset can be fostered by getting as many people as possible involved, for example, by providing easily accessible modeling tools and actively promoting them within the business domains, so that business analysts can take over process modeling in automation initiatives. A useful first step can also be to show all the process models developed within automation projects to all stakeholders, including business leaders (perhaps in the context of KPIs and dashboards, so they can better understand the value). This can help foster closer collaboration between business and IT, make new use case generation easier, and enable better time to value for projects.

As we will discuss in "Chapter 5: Measurement", part of a good process orchestration practice is expressing business value properly by defining concrete metrics and KPIs. Ideally, this starts a communication cycle between business and IT that will lead to the business being involved in the metrics definition process and goal setting. This will ultimately lead to a shared responsibility for metrics between business and IT, which is an important building block for better collaboration on automation solutions.

It's equally important to facilitate the developer experience by providing access to a process orchestration platform, enablement, and potentially further artifacts to reduce the cognitive load of building solutions. Often, you can even enable tech-savvy business users to develop simpler business processes (yellow processes, in our categorization from "A Useful Categorization of Use Cases") on their own.

Finally, a group that is sometimes forgotten but that is very important if you want to continuously improve your processes is frontline employees. They know how well (or badly) processes are working in practice, so they're a great source of ideas. With the shortage of skilled workers around the world, you want to retain your employees and not have them suffering because they're working with bad processes. Facilitating discussion and giving them all the context they need to understand what's in it for them with process orchestration will help secure their buy-in and give them the opportunity to fix those processes with you.

Establishing a process mindset that extends throughout the entire organization, from the C-suite to the process users themselves, is key. The business architecture sketched out earlier in this chapter and the transformation journey laid out next will help you achieve this. It will require strong leadership buy-in, but it has the potential to make a huge impact on your organization's bottom line.

Building Your Transformation Roadmap and Implementing Change

Enterprise process orchestration and the corresponding business architecture can touch hundreds or even thousands of processes across all domains of your organization. Managing this organizational change properly is crucial, but certainly not trivial.

Over time, we have identified some best practices that can help on that journey. First and foremost, it's important to understand who is involved in governing adoption, meaning which teams are responsible for implementing your vision and what their roles are. Identifying the relevant stakeholders and understanding their motivations is also critical. Then, you need to create a method to evaluate opportunities, a transformation roadmap, and a communication plan to bring it all together to empower your people to take a stake in the initiative.

Adoption Governance (aka Who Owns the Business Architecture?)

The question of who owns the business architecture and is responsible for governance correlates with the question of who drives your process orchestration program, as it brings together your process landscape with your organizational structure. In our experience working with hundreds of enterprise customers, we have frequently seen leading organizations adopt the kind of structure illustrated in Figure 1.17.

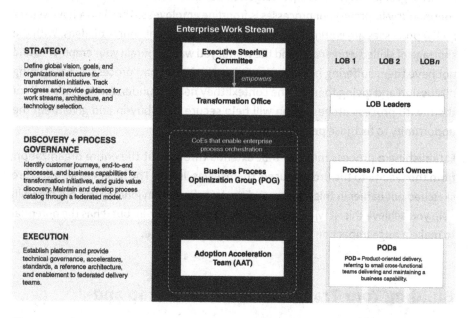

Figure 1.17 A successful governance structure for establishing a transformational business architecture.

The **steering committee** is in charge of defining the global vision and strategy for the transformation initiative. It should consist of high-level sponsors from the C-suite – typically the CIO, CFO, and/or COO – providing funding and setting the foundation for establishing the program structure together with the lines of business. They should track the progress of the program in a quarterly steering review, where success metrics are discussed and strategic direction is decided.

To drive the initiative and operationalize the program, the steering committee empowers a **transformation office**. It typically consists of members of the enterprise architecture team and manages the different work streams together with the lines of business, providing architecture guardrails and guidance on strategic technology decisions. The transformation office has mostly a mobilizing role, referring to the lines of business for their ideas on the transformation program.

The program management rubber hits the road in the **business process optimization group (POG)**. This group acts as a CoE that, together with the wider business, keeps an eye on the existing customer journeys, value streams, end-to-end processes, and business capabilities. It oversees the methodology and tooling used and can build process landscapes or business capability maps. The group is staffed with process excellence experts, leveraging best practices such as Six Sigma and Kaizen and technologies like process mining or process modeling tools to discover and map processes together with the respective process owners. This can also happen in a federated manner that is governed by a global process CoE. The business process optimization group typically reports to a COO-type role.

Based on the process catalog, a portfolio management team can be created to identify transformation opportunities at Level 2 of the business architecture (customer journeys and value streams), develop business cases based on strategic goals, capture existing bottom-up projects, and then prioritize the initiatives and set up a procedure to govern change. The book *Digital Transformation Success*[9] by Michael Schank, a former EY executive, gives a great example of how to set up such a practice by providing a global process inventory framework.

Meanwhile, the **Adoption Acceleration Team (AAT)** is a more technically focused CoE that provides the required technical platforms, standards, and enablement to build process orchestration solutions. The setup of such a team is described in "Zooming in on the Adoption Acceleration Team". It typically reports to a CIO or CTO, or a senior executive in their reporting line.

Note that there might be overlap between the two CoEs (the business process optimization group and adoption acceleration team), especially when you're starting out on your journey or in smaller organizations. Both activities can also be combined in one CoE. In general, when we talk about CoEs in this book, we are referring to both concepts (unless we specifically call out the AAT or POG). However they are

Vision 61

structured in your company, CoEs are crucial to implementing your enterprise strategy and driving change, so they should be led by someone who is capable of articulating the vision broadly across the organization, reporting the value to senior leadership, and helping to identify business use cases.

The solution building and delivery happens in federated, stable, cross-functional teams that have clear ownership of either end-to-end processes or business capabilities. Those teams are often called **PODs**, standing for **product-oriented delivery**. For example, there might be two pizza-sized Scrum teams, consisting of business and tech stakeholders, that can build and operate microservices implementing a specific business capability. This is detailed in "Chapter 2: People" and "Chapter 4: Delivery".

Understanding Process Orchestration Work Streams

It's important to differentiate between two separate types of work streams in an organization when adopting process orchestration. We call them the **enterprise work stream** and **delivery work streams**. Based on the adoption governance framework described in the previous section, organizations typically have one overarching enterprise work stream that enables the delivery work streams. Multiple delivery work streams can exist simultaneously, depending on the level of adoption.

A well-crafted enterprise work stream, consisting of the steering committee, transformation office, business process optimization group, and adoption acceleration team, will remove friction for the delivery teams. Figure 1.18 shows the responsibilities of each type of work stream.

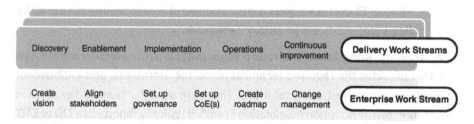

Figure 1.18 Process orchestration work streams.

A strategic adoption journey starts in the enterprise work stream. This is where you create your vision, align your stakeholders, and align with business leaders to identify processes and customer journeys to be orchestrated. In this work stream, you will also evaluate technology, often with the help of an architecture board – for example, deciding on a suitable process orchestration platform – and set up that technology to serve the wider organization. Later in your journey, you will also build governance structures like the CoEs in this work stream.

As with most initiatives, ideally you will follow the typical PDCA or Deming cycle[10] for your transformation journey to set up your work streams:

Plan:

- Define vision for process orchestration.
- Assess capabilities (which skills and technologies are needed, and which currently exist?), and prioritize business cases.
- Define adoption governance.

Do (communicate):

- Establish communication channels and events to communicate vision.
- Set up center of excellence and community of practice (See "Zooming in on the Adoption Acceleration Team").
- Build change champions across the organization.

Do (implement):

- Start executing on your vision.
- Implement program structure and business architecture.
- Deliver process orchestration solutions.

Check:

- Measure and monitor achieved value of process orchestration solutions.
- Communicate value across management levels (vertical) and business domains (horizontally).
- Continuously align on strategy between steering committee, transformation office, CoEs, and LoBs.
- Get feedback from users and community of practice.

Vision 63

Act:

- Celebrate milestones.
- Improve upon learnings.
- Understand challenges and iterate the plan accordingly.

As a quick side note, big international organizations with hundreds of thousands of employees might actually even distribute that one enterprise work stream by having a central global CoE and some federated local ones (Figure 1.19). This is driven by practical concerns, as one central unit could easily be overwhelmed by too many requests and would not be able to provide a localized experience to internal customers, either time zone–wise or culturally.

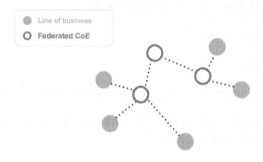

Figure 1.19 CoEs can also be federated to support scale; then, a central CoE enables federated local units.

Developing and deploying concrete solutions takes place within one or more **delivery work streams**. These may be driven by the enterprise work stream, especially when you're just getting started and want your CoE to be directly involved in the first use cases. Conversely, sometimes an enterprise work stream is only derived after a first successful lighthouse project, so you might implement one or two delivery work streams before amplifying the vision to the enterprise level. In that case, adoption follows a wave pattern (as we will further examine in "Following a Wave Pattern on Your Journey"): Organizations start by looking at a specific problem, elevate the solution approach to the strategic level, derive a strategic vision from this, and then get operational again to build additional hands-on projects while evolving a strategic enablement function over time.

Ideally, you'll have multiple cross-functional teams working in parallel on their delivery work streams to avoid bottlenecks. This means you can have multiple delivery work streams in progress, which all follow a similar pattern that the CoE can support:

- Discovery (is the technology a fit for my problem?), goal definition, and planning (what do we want to achieve, how do we want to track it, and how can we achieve this?).
- Enablement (building up required process modeling and development skills in the team).
- Modeling (creating the process model of your solution).
- Implementation (implementing the process orchestration solution).
- Operation (running the solution in production).
- Continuous improvement and value reporting (to capture whether the solution is running smoothly and its value contribution to the organization).

We will elaborate on this further in "Chapter 4: Delivery".

This is exactly how the economy of scale kicks in: By centralizing the right activities (infrastructure, enablement, accelerators) in your enterprise work stream, you can establish repeatable playbooks for your federated (decentralized) delivery work streams, reduce the developers' cognitive load, and let them focus on what matters – delivering business value.

Building and Prioritizing Business Cases

The great advantage of the business architecture and adoption governance framework laid out in this book is that you can strategically identify process orchestration opportunities from the top-down. This helps to integrate your business strategy with your IT strategy, and to identify gaps in ownership.

However, since the reality in plenty of organizations is still that they work in organizational silos, extensive organizational redesign can be required to address the challenges of end-to-end processes that cross team boundaries. This is in stark contrast to state-of-the-art team topologies with cross-functional, autonomous teams that are each assigned to a specific business capability. With a holistic view of your process landscape, you can more easily define transformation initiatives, drive a roadmap to assign clear ownership to teams, and set up new teams as needed. For instance, there might not yet be a team yet that owns the end-to-end loan application process. If you want to digitalize or transform that process, you need to establish one.

Having established your process orchestration program, it is thus critical to set up a structure to systematically identify transformation opportunities and prioritize your investments. When you're starting out, you'll want to begin with just a few selected domains, customer journeys, and use cases that can have a profound impact, generate traction, and maintain stakeholder buy-in.

In his book *Crossing the Chasm*[11], Geoffrey Moore provides a powerful mental model for such situations: On the one hand you have the innovators and early adopters that tend to jump on new product ideas early, but then you have to "cross the chasm" to reach the majority of the market (some of whom will be more willing than others to get on board). Specifically in the world of enterprise process orchestration, focus on identifying the innovators and early adopters to build your first successes, and only then try to bring on board the majority of the organization. A customer once described this as "riding on the success wave." At the same time, it's important to ignore the potential laggards at the beginning and make sure their negativity doesn't harm your initiative.

In short, you need to carefully select the first use cases, as they can have a big influence on your overall success. Choose use cases that will help you generate visibility for the initiative, showcase initial value, and build up learnings from which future projects can benefit. We recommend starting with a few high-value use cases of medium complexity that aren't too political. From there, you can gradually work your way up to more challenging use cases.

In this context, we are distinguishing between a push and a pull approach. **Push** describes a top-down approach through strategic initiatives that will profoundly transform whole business domains or value streams. In that case, the transformation office, together with the business process optimization group, the adoption acceleration team, and the lines of business, will identify and evaluate potential initiatives. To implement those use cases, they will often need to define new teams or ownership structures, as implementing them may not be possible in the existing structure of the organization (e.g. because end-to-end processes are transcending the different teams). In other words, the initiatives will need to be strategically pushed into the organization, while creating the corresponding structure to cater to the business needs.

Pull, on the other hand, describes initiatives that originate within existing team structures. For instance, the loan origination team can autonomously decide to leverage process orchestration to improve their business capability. With the support of the CoE, they can then implement and deploy this use case autonomously. Typically these initiatives are easier and quicker to implement and will provide value within the boundaries of the team's responsibilities. However, such initiatives usually don't have transformative power over the full end-to-end process.

Strategic adoption, thus, happens in a hybrid format: push for strategic, complex initiatives; pull for autonomous stream-aligned teams that can locally improve processes. The approach laid out below is valid for both options.

The first step to prioritize business cases involves building a pipeline of use cases for the program. In our engagements, we typically analyze and prioritize use cases based on the relative value and complexity they bring to the table. To identify the value of a use case, you can look at the following characteristics:

- **Pain points:** Start by identifying the current pain points in the process. These could include inefficiencies, high error rates, long cycle times, or lack of visibility.

- **Goals:** Clarify what you aim to achieve with process orchestration. Objectives might include improving efficiency, reducing costs, increasing compliance, or enhancing the ability to adapt to changes. This should include discussing and defining concrete metrics and KPIs, as we will explain further in "Chapter 5: Measurement". Using concrete KPIs helps you hit two targets with one arrow: selling the project internally and defining the right metrics from the start. The latter will also help the automation projects to clearly understand the goal.

- **Benefits:** Estimate the benefits of process orchestration in quantifiable terms. This could be in the form of time saved, error reduction, improved customer satisfaction, increased revenue, or other factors.

To get the full picture, you have to correlate the expected value with the complexity of the use case. Looking at individual use cases, the complexity can be determined by multiple factors:

- How many tasks require orchestration, and how complex are they?

- How much integration is needed (e.g. how many endpoints and technologies are involved)? Do APIs already exist for them? If not, how easily can you build them, or can you leverage RPA instead as a bridge technology?

- Do some of the tasks need to be performed by humans, and if so do you have existing human task management software?

Vision 67

- Has a process orchestration tool been decided upon, and is it available to the team?

- How many handoffs between teams are needed in the process?

Looking at the organizational level, the complexity is further influenced by factors such as:

- **Team structure and ownership:** Is it already clear who could drive the initiative? Is there an obvious process owner? Does it fit with a specific stream-aligned team, or would it require setting up a project team?

- **Delivery capacity:** Does the development team have the necessary bandwidth and skill set to handle the initiative, or do they need to do some groundwork in the project itself?

- **Maturity of the IT landscape:** Do the most important systems have API access? How consistent is the domain data?

- **Executive sponsorship:** Is the leadership of the domain aware of the potential of process orchestration and willing to sponsor the initiative?

Evaluating the complexity can help you to **estimate the costs** for the process orchestration solution. Costs might include implementation work, software costs, training, potential downtime during implementation, and ongoing maintenance. Whenever you have an idea about the costs, you can also do a **cost–benefit analysis** that compares the costs and benefits to determine the return on investment. This should include a high-level break-even analysis to show when the benefits will start to outweigh the costs.

In the next step, you can prioritize suitable candidates based on the estimated value and use case complexity. The business cases can relate to specific value streams, end-to-end processes, or business capabilities. You can then plot your business cases on a simple 2×2 matrix sorted by value and complexity, as shown in Figure 1.20.

Which use cases should you focus on? Of course, the ones on the right, which is where you can reap high-value gains, and especially those in the bottom-right quadrant, where you can get a quick win. Your business architecture and your list of business capabilities will be a huge help in identifying and prioritizing the best candidates.

Sometimes senior management is already aligned on which domains or use cases to begin with. If so, great. If not, however, we recommend choosing the first use

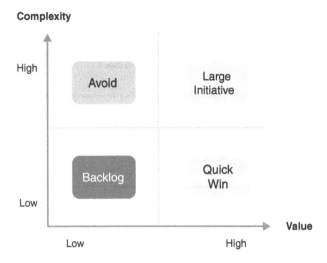

Figure 1.20 A prioritization matrix for process orchestration projects.

cases very carefully to build traction. Those use cases will also serve as a foundation to harvest real-world experience, which can be further leveraged to fine-tune the prioritization model and plan your transformation journey.

Once you've kicked things off, taking a strategic, enterprise-wide view of your transformation journey will assist you in monitoring progress. It can be helpful to sketch out a map like the one in Figure 1.21 that shows your use cases, along with their status and business value. The data can then be reviewed in monthly or quarterly business reviews with the relevant stakeholders (e.g. the steering committee and transformation office), along with the achieved value and lessons learned from the initiatives.

Amplifying Organic Bottom-Up Initiatives

With the strategic adoption pattern we've been discussing so far, the goal is to transform the business from the top down through an enterprise-wide strategy. We see this as the most effective way to truly transform your business on a value stream level, as such a transformation can never happen through local initiatives only. It also yields the biggest gains with regard to unlocking economies of scale, improving efficiency, or achieving business agility at the level required in the competitive market.

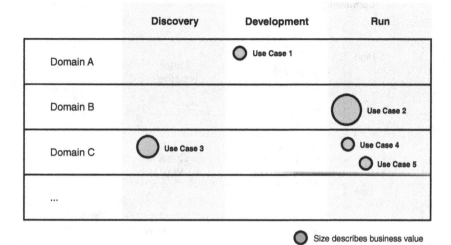

Figure 1.21 Mapping out your use cases helps you get an overview of your transformation journey.

However, we often see organizations starting their process orchestration journey in a bottom-up fashion. This happens when a specific team or business unit decides to adopt process orchestration technology for a specific use case. Often this decision is driven by IT stakeholders – especially in Camunda's case, where thanks to its open architecture even individual developers might pull to leverage its capabilities, purchasing and operating the platform independently for their current problem at hand. The business case with these grassroots initiatives is typically about saving development effort, as the requirements the process orchestration engine fills would otherwise have to be implemented manually. Sometimes, the engine is also brought in to solve a severe pain point in the current architecture, like lack of visibility in event-driven architectures, or inability to orchestrate and integrate heterogeneous endpoints in microservices architectures.

Another flavor of this adoption pattern is when projects already use homegrown state machines, legacy workflow engines, shaky batch solutions, or some other orchestration technology that's no longer cutting it, so the developers need to migrate to a more modern or more reliable solution. In this case, the project replaces one technology with another to reduce technical debt.

Such a bottom-up journey can be a low-threshold way to get started. Indeed, in our experience, it's not uncommon for there to be multiple independent bottom-up initiatives operating in parallel in bigger organizations. This presents both challenges and opportunities.

On the one hand, there's the challenge of disparate approaches operating in isolation, with no communication between the teams. Most often, these initiatives also struggle to tie their efforts to the business strategy and measure and communicate the achieved value, even though they have a positive business impact. Because they do not properly articulate the business value, they can lack the strategic focus and management endorsement necessary for genuine business transformation (although we have observed instances where bottom-up initiatives successfully evolved into top-down initiatives upon reaching critical mass adoption).

On the other hand, there is a great opportunity to build momentum for strategic adoption based on existing success stories. As you don't need to start from zero, you might be faster at defining best practices for implementing new projects. You might also be able to recruit team members to build a CoE that already has firsthand experience with the technology – and you will be able to use existing projects to advertise your initiatives.

One important aspect to understand is that even if you have achieved great results with such individual grassroots initiatives, your process orchestration efforts are flying under the radar of senior leadership. While this is sometimes a good thing, enabling you to move quickly in the early maturity stages of your organization, it bears serious risks. First and foremost, your technology decisions might be called into question, which might impact your ability to mobilize resources around the chosen process orchestration stack (we'll look at some of the other risks in the next section).

We encountered a tragic example of this at a company that had successfully automated a lot of its long-tail processes. They'd wired the functionality into their customer portal, so that, for example, every customer could trigger an address change process on a self-service basis, 24/7, getting a confirmation just a couple of seconds later. But when the company built a new customer portal, nobody on the business end had process orchestration top of mind, so they didn't even express a requirement for customers to be able to kick off this process. When the new portal was released, instead of getting instant service, customers who wanted to change their address saw a static web page saying, "please call your agent."

This unfortunate case illustrates the need for building awareness around process orchestration throughout the whole organization. By doing so, you ensure that you can secure the resources necessary for a comprehensive transformation.

Getting Started on Your Adoption Journey

Taking all of the previous discussion into account, you might be wondering: How do I get started on my transformation journey? No enterprise transformation is trivial, but it is crucial to start incrementally building up learnings and generating business value right away and not get stuck in analysis paralysis. So, in that sense, it is critical to balance a top-down strategy and agile, bottom-up execution.

Following a Wave Pattern on Your Journey

Both bottom-up and top-down activities face obstacles. The biggest risk with top-down activities is that they can be too detached from reality and disconnected from concrete daily challenges. And when you build central teams (like a center of excellence) that are too detached from project work, you can easily end up with ivory towers.

In contrast, bottom-up projects often fly under the radar of senior leaders of the organization, so their strategic potential is not recognized. This in turn can lead to a strategic direction or enterprise architecture in the organization that is not supportive of process orchestration (e.g. instead favoring proprietary and monolithic setups). Also, running multiple bottom-up projects in isolation can result in a proliferation of architecture and tech stacks, which can increase technical debt for the organization.

So, issues can arise with both. But in reality, those aren't the only two options. In fact, we advocate for a hybrid approach: top-down funding and vision, with agile and federated delivery.

Let's explore what this might look like. To start with, you secure a commitment (and funding) from top management to apply process orchestration strategically (top-down). After defining a vision with input from a diverse set of stakeholders, you select a small number of actual processes to orchestrate. These projects will address concrete pain points, and they should be tackled in an agile manner – almost like a bottom-up grassroots initiative. The teams working on these early projects will collectively gain experience, defining an architecture, selecting a tool stack, and discovering and documenting good and bad practices. All of these learnings will be harvested so that, after your initial successes, you can quickly build out your CoE – ideally staffed with people involved in those first projects. The CoE will develop a strategy to be applied across the enterprise, which then will help with the delivery of more agile projects.

When visualizing this pattern, we typically use a waveform like the one shown in Figure 1.22, alternating between a strategic business level and a very operational technical level, like we described earlier with riding the architect elevator up and down.

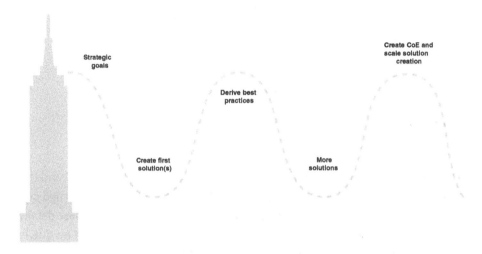

Figure 1.22 Adoption should happen in waves, making sure to cater for strategic needs but also to deliver concrete results.

Enterprise Adoption Phases

Drilling down further into the waveform, we can distinguish three phases in the strategic adoption of process orchestration in an organization: *launch*, *establish*, and *scale*. This is illustrated in Figure 1.23, with an overview of the typical tasks in each phase.

Let's take a closer look at what happens in each phase.

Launch

During the launch phase, organizations lay the foundation for their adoption journey. That includes defining the goals, scope, and strategic roadmap of the program, all of which should be aligned across the organization's stakeholder ecosystem (vertically,

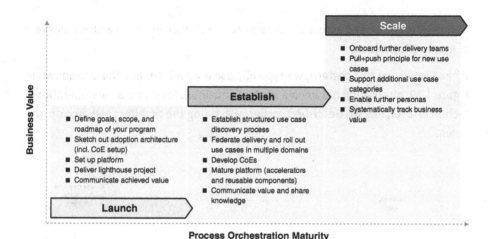

Figure 1.23 The three phases of enterprise adoption.

across the different management hierarchies, and horizontally, along IT and the different lines of business). The adoption architecture should also be sketched out: Who is driving the initiative, and which teams are responsible for what? These details should be clarified, along with a vision of a to-be state. For instance, if no CoE is established yet, you should make a plan for when and how it will be set up during the next phase of your journey (including its team structure). You will also need to decide who will be responsible for designing your architecture, running and operating your process orchestration platform (most typically this will be handled by your CoE), and setting up the platform.

The next step is to choose a team (with the support of the CoE, if you have one) to initiate the first lighthouse project. The lighthouse project serves two goals. First, it will demonstrate the business value of your initiative and generate visibility for the program inside your organization. You should communicate the successes widely to build momentum and support. Second, it will provide important learnings that you can leverage when setting up or developing your CoE, helping you define best practices and document experience from which other teams can learn.

Establish

In the establish phase, a few additional domains (typically one to three) will start to adopt process orchestration, laying the groundwork for scaling up orchestration efforts through an increasingly federated delivery model. The CoE will be heavily involved in the first projects, but will then gradually shift toward enabling the different teams. One of its main tasks will be maturing the process orchestration platform, through providing accelerators and reusable components to the teams (we will describe this in more detail in "Chapter 2: People" and "Chapter 3: Technology"). To identify new use cases, your organization should also establish a structured use case discovery process, as described in "Building and Prioritizing Business Cases". The achieved value and lessons learned from the different streams should be communicated widely across the organization.

Scale

During the scaling phase, more delivery work streams are added, expanding process orchestration across the organization. This phase enables enterprises to maximize the benefits of orchestration, improving efficiency and agility. Continuous refinement and optimization ensure alignment with evolving business needs, driving ongoing improvement and innovation. Also, the CoE typically evolves to an extent that yellow use cases are increasingly supported by providing smart low-code features, such as connectors.

Across all phases, it is crucial to establish a proactive program management practice, providing ongoing communication to all the relevant stakeholders and tracking the value of the initiative by monitoring appropriate KPIs for specific use cases (e.g. achieved efficiencies, number of use cases in production, number of business cases handled). Communication could happen through internal events such as community meetups, blog posts on your organization's intranet, or direct conversations between the CoE and business leaders. Conveying the achieved value is key in building a process mindset and generating a fresh flow of new use cases, and sharing lessons learned and best practices will help development teams succeed with future use cases.

Figure 1.24 shows an example of what your roadmap might look like, across the three enterprise adoption phases. Per a study by Bain & Company[12], you should aim to achieve a positive ROI about 12–18 months after the start of your initiative.

Questions to Assess Your Maturity

Having equipped you with some tips on successfully building your own vision, we want to close this chapter by considering how you can assess the maturity of that

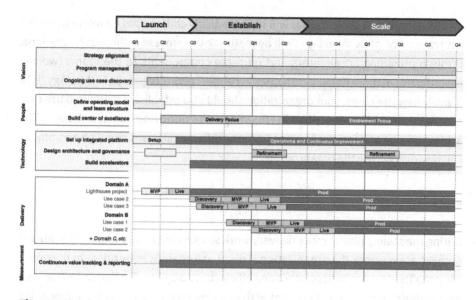

Figure 1.24 An example enterprise adoption roadmap.

vision and your readiness to get started on your transformation journey. You should be able to answer all of these questions:

- What is the scope of your process orchestration initiative, and what impact do you aim for it to have?
- Have you aligned the crucial stakeholders needed for this initiative? Is the value proposition of process orchestration widely understood among them?
- Do all relevant stakeholders have a shared understanding of where to apply process orchestration?
- Have you defined a business architecture for your process orchestration program to identify customer journeys, end-to-end processes and business capabilities to accomplish your business goals?
- Do you have a systematic approach on how evaluating use cases based on promised value vs. complexity of implementation?
- Have you set up an operating model, adoption governance and change management plan for your initiative?
- Have you developed a roadmap for your adoption journey?

- Have you identified the first solutions to be implemented, which can also serve as pilots?

- Do you have a good overview of concrete solutions that you would like to be created in the next one or two years? Why will process orchestration be beneficial for these use cases? What business outcomes do you aim to achieve?

To help with this evaluation, here is the description of the different maturity levels for vision taken from Table P.1:

- **Level 0**: Processes are not working efficiently or effectively. Some process tasks may have automated components, but those tasks are too dispersed for the effects of automation to be measured.

- **Level 1**: Focused on single, mission-critical process orchestration projects, or projects that center around a "broken" process.

- **Level 2**: Broader, scaled-up initiatives are focused on better business outcomes; measuring success remains a challenge.

- **Level 3**: Evolving toward a practice where process orchestration supports organization-wide digital transformation goals. This allows harnessing process orchestration to drive strategic business outcomes, at scale and at a rapid pace, for the entire organization.

- **Level 4**: There's a clearly defined strategy around technology, methodology, and people to execute process orchestration at scale, matched by the ability to execute that vision. A demonstrated track record of delivering strategic value to the organization through process orchestration motivates teams to deliver business transformation at scale.

Takeaways

Here are the key insights from this chapter:

- Enterprise process orchestration is most effective when it has buy-in from both IT and business leaders, to ensure alignment and strategic adoption.

- Defining a clear vision tied to corporate strategy is critical to communicate the purpose, secure stakeholder buy-in, and measure the impact of your program effectively.

- Adoption of process orchestration is a strategic play and needs to have enterprise-wide scope (or, at the beginning, business domain scope) to avoid fragmented solutions and achieve economies of scale.

- Considering end-to-end processes in the context of customer journeys and value streams is important for identifying automation opportunities and prioritizing investments.

- A good business architecture connects strategy with execution, supporting end-to-end processes by defining reusable, independent business capabilities.

- A governance model that combines a top-down vision with centralized governance and enablement but decentralized solution development is often the best option for scaling adoption.

Chapter 2: People

Process orchestration is largely about automation and technology, but we all know that it starts with people. So, in this chapter, we're going to focus on the people that create process orchestration and automation solutions. We'll look at the kinds of people and roles you need, what skills should be developed, and how you can structure your organization to support enterprise process orchestration.

In the "Introduction", we described the diversity of use cases for process orchestration and discussed how orchestrating the "red" use cases (complex core processes) requires software engineering. Because of this, we're going to start this chapter with a quick look at how software engineering ideally works today, which is very different from software engineering a decade ago. Unfortunately, these new paradigms are not consistently applied across organizations; like William Gibson famously said in his book *Neuromancer*, "The future is here, but it's not evenly distributed." We hope to encourage more organizations to apply these practices – to distribute this future more evenly – so that they can implement sophisticated process orchestration practices that will allow them to build competitive advantages.

In 2018, Nicole Forsgren, Jez Humble, and Gene Kim published the groundbreaking book *Accelerate*[1], which linked good engineering and DevOps practices to overall organizational measures like profitability, productivity, and market share. In an interview[2] about the book, Nicole commented that "The most exciting discovery came during the first year of research, when the team found early evidence that IT performance does matter. This showed that companies with high-performing technology organizations were twice as likely to exceed their profitability, productivity, and market-share goals." (You can find up-to-date numbers in the State of DevOps Report[3] produced every year.)

You don't have to be great at math to know that twice as likely is a huge opportunity – which you can also exploit in your process orchestration practice. So, let's get going!

How Software Is Being Built Today

Over the last decade, software and the way it is developed have changed dramatically and comprehensively. Let's briefly look at the facets of this change that we consider most important in the context of process orchestration and automation: structure, development methodology, operations, business models, and mindset shifts.

Focused Components That Implement Capabilities

Software systems today are smaller, more modular, and contain focused components. Monoliths are rare; instead, we base our systems on microservices, a growing number of out-of-the-box SaaS services, and other pieces of reusable functionality. This allows us to concentrate more on the capabilities of a system, rather than looking at monolithic applications, which in turn allows us not only to adjust the implementation of a capability much more easily and independently, but also to make use of new capabilities and retire outdated ones faster.

Capabilities can be developed and operated as products, and as such they can either be created internally or purchased externally. A product mindset in an organization makes this irrelevant to the consumer of a "capability as a service"; it should be the same experience either way. Getting to this state allows you to choose much more freely what you want to develop in-house – typically things that are really unique to your business or that you want to use to differentiate your offering – and what you simply consume as a service.

We didn't call this section "Microservices" because, while this is still a hot topic and a good topic to learn about, the microservices architectural style misses the main point we want to make here, which is to provide capabilities as a service. How they're implemented doesn't matter too much. If we'd been looking for a catchier title, we might have gone with "API First," which unfortunately isn't that hip a term anymore. It does express the idea of capabilities well, though: You need independent components that provide a technical or business capability via a well-defined API, independent of its concrete implementation (and of whether it is developed in-house or provided externally).

As-a-service thinking allows you to leverage services without knowing how they are operated. This frees the service consumer of a lot of responsibilities, and it works at different levels of abstraction. For example, the typical hyperscalers (Alibaba, AWS, Azure, GCP, etc.) all provide a technical basis for running applications (e.g. containers,

80 Enterprise Process Orchestration

application servers, databases) without you knowing about the underlying hardware. And with typical SaaS businesses like those pioneered by Salesforce, you can leverage business capabilities without needing to know how they work under the hood. All of this in turn allows organizations and their development teams to focus on their business problems, and not on running servers and applications. The as-as-service model thus acts as an enabler to create smaller components in a more agile way.

An interesting side effect of this shift is that the business model around software has changed. CIOs no longer buy big, expensive suites with vendor lock-in following sales pitches on golf courses; instead, even powerful C-suite executives need to make sure they have their technologists behind them when making strategic procurement decisions. Software is delivered more and more as a service itself, and subscription models derisk the use of services for customer organizations. In other words, vendors need to keep providing value if they don't want to be thrown out, and services are combined in a heterogeneous way to build best-of-breed environments.

Agile and DevOps

Agile approaches are the order of the day, even if some organizations or individuals seem to overengineer them a bit (paradoxically rendering them unagile again). The core idea is always useful: creating value through small, iterative steps instead of big bang releases. Agile software development also means including a variety of roles in the development process, breaking down the typical wall between business and IT.

The DevOps movement has also grown enormously over the last decade. DevOps aims to bridge the gap between software development (Dev) and IT operations (Ops). Its primary goals are to increase the speed of software delivery, improve the quality of software releases, and enhance overall operational efficiency. The DevOps movement brought a lot of innovation, from the basics like using version control (it's funny to think that we once had to work hard to convince customers of the importance of this) to automatic build and release cycles, or continuous integration and delivery (CI/CD). Another famous DevOps concept is "you build it, you run it," enabled via technical capabilities as a service, making sure a delivery team really cares about the solution end-to-end (from development to operations).

Process orchestration fits perfectly into this environment. It facilitates agile practices by using graphical models as a basis for discussion, implementation, and operations. It therefore helps to bring the DevOps team more into the business world, making it a true *BizDevOps* team.

People

Product Thinking

As market pressure and competition increase across all industries, organizations that have been more successful at digital transformation, including automation and software development, are finding themselves far ahead of the pack, resulting in a great deal of pressure on other organizations to catch up.

Catching up requires a fundamental mindset shift in how to approach software development, from a cost center-centric perspective that is largely organized by "IT" as an internal service provider for projects, to a more product-led strategy where business capabilities and value streams are supported by software that is owned by stable teams looking at long-term value creation (rather than focusing on project deadlines and short-term efficiencies). This approach was nicely illustrated in the book *Project to Product*[4] by Mik Kersten.

Thinking about solutions like products means focusing more on the customer journey and the long-term goals, and not so much on the short-term results of a project. Ideally, a team that understands a solution as a product will not only create the first iteration as a project, but also maintain the product over a longer period of time, improving it iteratively. This encourages making sound technical decisions, like choosing boring (but proven) technology[5].

Please note that in this book (and a lot of real-life situations) we still tend to use the term "project," for example, when discussing how to create a solution to orchestrate a process. This should not be taken to mean that we prefer the cost-centered approach, but rather that every incremental improvement of a product can be thought of as a project (like a sprint, or an iteration), no matter how small. For example, the product might be the customer onboarding value stream. A first iteration might involve setting up the orchestration technology and operating an executable process, but still pushing the tasks to humans. This qualifies as a project, but we find it essential that a product owner and the delivery team keep iterating on the onboarding process and automating the most important tasks next (where "most important" should be defined by business value contribution). Those might be tasks that require a lot of human effort, so automation will make the system cheaper to operate, or tasks where manual completion causes long delays, so automation will improve the customer experience and increase satisfaction. Or it could be tasks that are error-prone when performed manually, so automation can help reduce the risk of regulatory fines. The concrete next step often matters less than the overall approach of thinking in the long term about products. To sum it up: To run successful automation solutions, a product mindset is essential.

Process Ownership

The product mindset also sheds new light on an old problem in business process management: defining ownership for a business process. The challenge is that most end-to-end processes, or value streams if you think in those terms, stretch across multiple application boundaries as well as departmental boundaries. Organizations, however, are typically structured in functional silos (we don't personally know of any organization that centers its org chart around processes). As a result, there is most often no process owner with real power to improve a process. The result is that nobody looks at processes end to end (Figure 2.1).

Figure 2.1 Without a clear process owner, nobody has an overview.

The worst example of this that one of us experienced was at an insurance company. Asked about the process owner, they came up with a list of more than 20 people that "owned" the customer onboarding process. If there is not one process owner, there is no process ownership.

Product thinking, and an organizational focus on business capabilities, as laid out in "Building a Business Architecture to Realize Digitalization and Automation Benefits", advocates for solving this problem by assigning clear responsibilities around the business value contributions of value streams to dedicated managers, for example in the form of product owners. While those principles are established in manufacturing (like Lean Management[6] at Toyota), they are still in their infancy in information-based organizations and not yet widely adopted. Maybe there's an owner on the IT side, but ownership on the business side is lacking. Ideally, organizations should define clear and stable ownership for business capabilities and end-to-end processes that span IT and business (either through two people, or one person having ownership of both). We'd like to challenge you to tackle this opportunity head-on and hope to present a great success story in the next edition of this book!

Team Topologies

To create successful solutions in your organization, you need to start by looking at who is building and running those solutions. What teams should you have in place? How do they interact? How does that fit into your organizational topology? And how does this align with the abovementioned ideas around agile, DevOps, and product thinking?

We are big fans of the book *Team Topologies*[7] by Matthew Skelton and Manuel Pais, who give great answers to those hard questions. In essence, they make a good case for separating solution building, enablement, and platforms[8]. In that model, productive *stream-aligned teams*, which are autonomous delivery teams maintaining some value stream (equivalent to "product thinking"), require *enabling teams* as well as *platform teams* to make their lives easier. Those supporting teams remove the burden of clarifying all the hard questions around what is called the "undifferentiated heavy lifting": how to set up the infrastructure (including dev and prod environments as well as a CI/CD pipeline), what tech stack to use, how to hook it into the organization's authentication mechanisms, and so on. This reduces the cognitive load of the stream-aligned teams, freeing their brains to concentrate on the business problems and leading to business value being delivered much faster.

Looking at process orchestration specifically, we see organizations setting up a dedicated team that not only provides the process orchestration platform, but also the enablement around it – this is the adoption acceleration team, or AAT, that we've mentioned a few times already and will describe more fully later in this chapter. This setup allows the stream-aligned delivery teams to work productively and remain concentrated on delivering business value (Figure 2.2).

Diversity of Roles

Going back a decade or two, we had a world where you were either a business person or a developer on the IT side. Business requirements needed to be written down and handed over to a developer to be implemented, and you had teams led by senior engineers doing proper solution design, mixed with juniors that coded and learned. All those roles were rather binary.

This is no longer the case today. The lines between various roles have blurred: A tech-savvy business person can also develop software solutions, especially with the help of low-code tooling or supported by generative AI, and developers are much more diverse in their backgrounds and levels of experience (Figure 2.3).

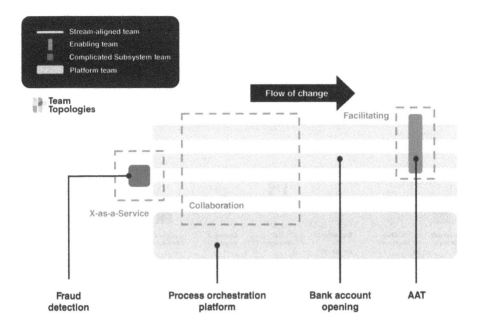

Figure 2.2 The AAT can take on the role of both platform team and enabling team for process orchestration (as defined in the *Team Topologies* by Matthew Skelton and Manuel Pais).

Figure 2.3 Today, all of these roles can participate in software development.

As organizations look to automate more, they need to allow all of those people to take part in software development in some way. We will explore this challenge later in the book, focusing on two key questions:

- How can you enable more nondevelopers to build solutions? This is basically about adding abstractions and providing a useful low-code layer.

- How can you make sure the (scarce) developers can use their talents in the most effective way? This is partly about providing good team topologies to make them productive, but it is also about allowing them to focus on building components where a developer is needed and relying on other roles to handle the less tech-heavy tasks. For example, senior developers could code pieces of software that are then used in orchestration processes modeled by business analysts (Figure 2.4). As discussed in the "Introduction", this is often much more realistic with yellow processes than it is with processes in the red category, where good engineering practices matter more.

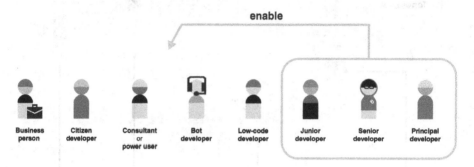

Figure 2.4 Developers create the components that enable other roles to develop solutions.

A Healthy Level of Centralization

What level of centralization makes sense is a frequent topic of discussion. This may seem to be a hard question to answer as there are two forces pulling in different directions at the same time: autonomy and independence vs. governance and economy of scale. But this is only a contradiction at first glance – looking at many real-life scenarios, we actually find the answer to be quite clear. Let's start by considering the two questions we always get asked, and our standard replies:

- **Should solutions be created by a central team?** No. Typically we advise against central solution creation, as this becomes a bottleneck quickly. However, there are exceptions to that rule, which we'll address later when talking about the AAT.

- **Should there be a central team to enable and support federated delivery teams?** Yes. We believe that a central AAT that concentrates on enabling is a game changer for success with process orchestration on a broad scale. This central function can do a great deal to reduce the cognitive load of the delivery teams (e.g. running the platform, defining the solution architecture, providing templates, etc.), which will be further described in "Zooming in on the Adoption Acceleration Team".

To summarize this rule of thumb: *You should centralize infrastructure and governance but federate delivery*.

There has been a lot of hype around decentralization in software engineering recently, most prominently driven by microservices, domain-driven design, and related methods. This leads to an objection to the AAT concept that goes something like this: "But we just untangled our monolith and moved to independent microservices and value streams so that we could speed up development by having fewer dependencies between teams. Now you're telling us to centralize things again? We don't want to do that; we don't want to have this bottleneck!"

To be honest, it's more than fair to think that because of how CoEs might have been set up in the past. But done right, an AAT blends in seamlessly with state-of-the-art software delivery paradigms, becoming an accelerator instead of a bottleneck. In that sense, the approach is well-aligned with all the recent software development paradigms mentioned in this chapter.

Looking at autonomous microservice teams (or whatever the architectural style is in your organization), the core problem without an AAT is that they must figure out many things themselves. The more freedom they have, the more of a burden this becomes. Teams have to evaluate their own tool stacks, define their own solution architectures and approaches, and, in essence, do a lot of technical work that does not implement any business logic. So, the value proposition of the AAT is actually pretty logical: If delivery teams can use an existing platform and have an architecture blueprint for how to design their solutions, they don't have to think about those fundamentals and can dive into delivering business value right away. (Of course, the blueprint needs to provide value for the teams. We'll talk about this later.) This is exactly the platform and enabling function described in *Team Topologies*[9], as mentioned previously.

We see a lot of proof for this point in the market. For example, in the blog post "How We Use Golden Paths to Solve Fragmentation in Our Software Ecosystem,"[10] Gary Nieman from Spotify describes why "rumor-driven development simply wasn't scalable." Spotify gives some more good insights in relation to its Backstage[11] open-source project. In essence, too much decentralization started to slow things down because of the resulting complexity. By centralizing services again, they reduced complexity and provided standardization, allowing delivery teams to dive into delivering business logic much faster, without sacrificing their autonomy (see Figure 2.5). A similar approach is being taken at Twilio[12]: "At Twilio, we do it by offering what we

People

call the paved path. These are mature services that you can just pull off the shelf, adopt, and get up and running super quickly."

Figure 2.5 Spotify gives a great summary of why some standardization is necessary to scale.

What you can draw from this is: Yes, you should have autonomous delivery teams, and they should work on business logic (often also called domain logic). You should try to find boundaries between business domains that make sense. But you should still provide golden paths (architecture blueprints), central enabling teams, and platforms; otherwise, those teams will drown in technology evaluations and infrastructure tasks. AATs are crucial to achieving that balance.

Having said this, let's dive into the different types of enabling teams. Then, we'll look at the various possible models of how to deliver solutions in the organization.

Centralized Teams to Facilitate Process Orchestration

In the previous section, we discussed the importance of centralizing the right activities. We are also seeing huge traction for the concept of CoEs in our customer base and the overall market. This is reflected in the numbers. In Camunda's State of Process Orchestration 2024 report[13], 93% of participants indicated that they already had a CoE for process automation, or were actively working on implementing one.

There's a good reason for this: A CoE is a game changer if you truly want to transform your business through process orchestration. To put it bluntly, **if you want to scale process automation, you need to establish a center of excellence.**

The CoE does not have to be referred to within your organization as a "center of excellence"; we have seen many different names for it, including "competence center," "capability center," "digital enabler," "process automation guild," and more. Regardless of the name, they all share the common goal of accelerating the successful use of process orchestration across the organization.

As mentioned in "Adoption Governance (aka Who Owns the Business Architecture?)" (and Figure 1.17), we use the name CoE as an umbrella term for two different groups supporting process orchestration: the business process optimization group and the adoption acceleration team. Let's look at each of these, and the relationship between them, in a bit more detail.

The Business Process Optimization Group (POG)

To achieve success with enterprise process orchestration, you need to identify which customer journeys and end-to-end processes need to be improved to meet your organization's goals. This is exactly the task of the POG, as it looks at process management from an organizational standpoint. Think of it as a business process management CoE. Leveraging process excellence best practices, the POG takes a top-down view of customer journeys, end-to-end processes, and cross-departmental interconnections. This ensures effective alignment with strategic goals, prioritization of use cases, and optimization of processes in a way that supports both operational efficiency and business objectives. As the POG focuses on improving operations, it is often a staff unit reporting to the COO and working directly with federated process owners in the lines of business.

Ideally, the POG focuses on breaking down silos and enabling collaboration across different functions. Rather than solely targeting technological or departmental improvements, this group looks at processes from a bird's-eye view, identifying pain points, dependencies, redundancies, and potential bottlenecks together with the respective owners and LoBs. The group's deep knowledge of process orchestration, automation, and process management helps them to find (and improve) the right solutions for your enterprise process orchestration program.

Key responsibilities of the POG include maintaining a process catalog, supporting federated teams in mapping and analyzing processes, and ensuring that those initiatives are aligned with the organization's broader strategic objectives. They can also drive standardization, not so much in a technical sense but in terms of modeling best practices and business capability reuse across the organization. To achieve that, they own process landscapes and internal knowledge bases around process

People   89

management, while collaborating with the process owners and subject matter experts across the organization.

A POG can be instrumental to drive a culture of continuous improvement and a process mindset across the organization. However, we still see many organizations that established a POG some years ago but never linked it to automation projects. Such ivory tower initiatives that focus more on manual processes than digital ones can be dangerous and torpedo a positive perception of process management. Make sure to get those folks on board for your process orchestration initiative – or make clear what the difference of your initiative is. Done right, this group can become a critical link between strategy and execution.

We don't go into much depth on POGs in this book, instead focusing more on the adoption acceleration team, which plays a more direct role when introducing process orchestration into the enterprise. If you want to learn more about this type of CoE, we recommend the book *Digital Transformation Success*[14] by Michael Schank.

The Adoption Acceleration Team (AAT)

The AAT is a dedicated team of experts that drives a strategic, scaled adoption of process orchestration across the enterprise. This definition is deliberately open because the exact setup of the AAT varies wildly depending on the goals, enterprise architecture, and culture of the organization. Generally, we can say that the goal is to make the adoption of process orchestration as frictionless as possible by creating awareness, providing the necessary tools, building the corresponding automation skills, and delivering value through automation initiatives.

The core difference from the POG is that the AAT has a stronger IT focus, in terms of providing the platform, technical patterns and best practices, and various other technical components needed to drive adoption. In a nutshell, the POG defines what needs to be orchestrated from a business standpoint, and the AAT enables getting it done. In the absence of a POG, of course, the AAT can also take over the task of use case discovery and identification, becoming a kind of hybrid CoE. We will go into more detail on this later in this chapter.

Where does the AAT sit in the organization? We touched on this a bit already in "Adoption Governance (aka Who Owns the Business Architecture?)". Most often, we see the introduction of process orchestration being driven by IT as an enabler for the business and the respective delivery teams in the lines of business. And this makes sense. IT can make the right technology choices and align process orchestration efforts with the general IT strategy and enterprise architecture. Furthermore, process orchestration is a horizontal function not tied to any specific LoB, making IT, as the typical provider of horizontal technology, a good place for it. Consequently, the AAT often reports to the CIO of the organization, or senior executives one level below.

Ideally, your AAT supports a wide variety of use cases (at least from red to yellow, according to our classification in "A Useful Categorization of Use Cases"), meaning some solutions might require heavy IT involvement, while others might be developed directly by the business with minimal IT involvement. Some solutions might even be based on out-of-the-box features or templates provided by the AAT or the process orchestration platform. This is visualized in Figure 2.6. In addition, you can see that some solutions might be driven by strategic intent (e.g. omnichannel initiatives in the LoB or IT modernization initiatives in IT, perhaps identified by the POG), whereas in other cases individual projects might be driving improvements from the bottom up (e.g. a LoB manager increasing their automation rates, or a development team using process orchestration to implement their current task faster).

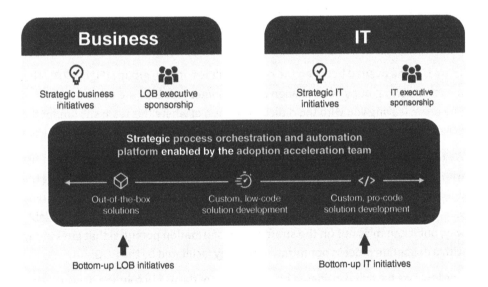

Figure 2.6 The AAT drives process orchestration across the enterprise, enabling no-code, low-code, and pro-code solutions.

So while the AAT typically sits within IT, it needs to serve the lines of business and cater for their needs, which needs to be reflected in the mindset of the AAT. Its name also reflects this team's main purpose: accelerating adoption of process orchestration by other teams. In that sense, it should have a strong focus on enablement and a strong product mindset.

It is important that the AAT and its leadership are well-connected within the business and have a comprehensive understanding of organizational processes, either through working with the POG, or – if that function doesn't exist – by covering some similar activities around value discovery and process excellence. A strategic perspective is important to drive effective, organization-wide process improvements, and this team also needs to have a clear technical understanding and be able to drive immediate and iterative value. As you can see, the AAT is not easy to staff, but it's crucial to get it right. (We'll talk more about the individual roles in this team in "Roles".)

The Relationship Between the POG and AAT

It is in the connection between business and IT where the POG and AAT intersect. The POG can work with LoB leaders and process owners to define use cases for process orchestration that are in line with the business strategy. The AAT can then enable and accelerate the delivery of solutions for those use cases. This can be a winning combination if you want to transform your organization in a profound, strategic manner.

There is some overlap between the responsibilities of both groups (Figure 2.7). This means the two groups need to align closely. Sometimes they are even merged into one team, leaving you with the difficult question of where this team sits (under the COO or CIO).

We regularly work with customers that run an AAT as their one CoE. This team sits within IT and also takes on some of the responsibilities of the POG, like helping the lines of business with identifying and prioritizing solution candidates and doing value tracking. This can work very well to get things going in a lightweight, scalable way, but it can miss out on the strategic transformation potential that goes along with a deliberate process optimization strategy facilitated by the POG.

One topic we haven't considered here is the role of the AAT in solution delivery. We'll look at a few of the options next.

Delivery Models

We'll start with what we consider best practice: an AAT enabling federated solution delivery. This model is our *greenfield choice*, which means that if there are no good

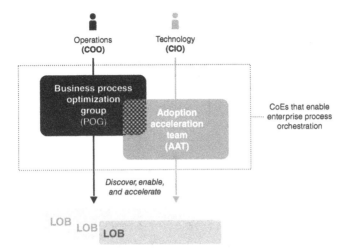

Figure 2.7 The POG and AAT centralize specific activities to enable enterprise process orchestration – while there is some overlap, the focus of each is different.

reasons not to, we try to set things up this way. It is a model that typically balances the advantages of centralization with the advantages of federation well. But of course, reality is complex, and there might be very good reasons for you to set things up differently in your organization; so, we will also look at more centralized and more federated options afterward, considering the advantages and disadvantages of each approach.

Federated Solution Delivery with the AAT as an Enabler

With this approach, you have federated delivery teams and an AAT that does not implement solutions itself, but rather enables the teams within different business units or domains (see Figure 2.8).

Advantages:

- Empowers business-driven automation. Giving ownership to the business domains and their delivery teams enables them to implement initiatives based on their current needs.
- Builds and shares experience and know-how across the whole enterprise.
- Enhances efficiency, as the AAT is building more expertise based on successful projects, helping others avoid pitfalls.

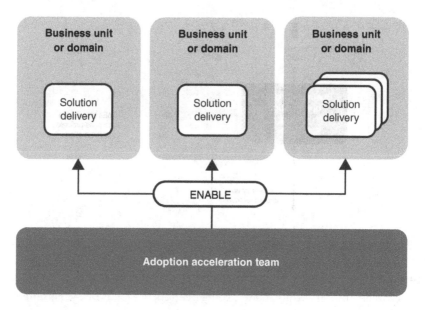

Figure 2.8 Federated solution delivery with AAT as enabler.

- Enables economies of scale through reusability. Assets and knowledge built up by the AAT can be leveraged across the different initiatives of the organization, allowing for exponential growth (the AAT doesn't become a bottleneck for solution delivery). This also reduces cognitive load for delivery teams.
- Improves governance. As one central team can influence many projects, you can avoid a Wild West setting where every project reinvents the wheel with process orchestration differently. Instead, the best approaches can be reused. Again, this reduces cognitive load.

Disadvantages:

- Centralized authorities might have a bad reputation in your organization (as mentioned in "A Healthy Level of Centralization"), so you might need to overcome that historical impediment.
- The AAT can become a bottleneck when it is too slow to react to internal requests. To avoid this, focus on a strong product mindset, good (internal) customer experience, and – once you reach a certain maturity – a federated operating model, where you shift more responsibilities to the LoBs.
- Differences between business units may not be adequately respected (But given that process orchestration technology is horizontal technology, there

are typically no big differences in process orchestration in the different organizational units anyway).

- Business domains typically need to have IT expertise in-house (or need to rely on external partners, which might generate problems with knowledge flowing out of the domain again once the partner leaves).
- Sometimes, it is challenging to "make" the domains collaborate with the AAT.
- The AAT must be obsessed with delivering value to the domains. We call this the "pull principle," where working with the AAT makes the lives of the different teams so much easier that they are automatically pulled toward it (as opposed to the "push principle," where teams feel they have to work with an AAT, whether they want to or not). This clearly isn't a disadvantage per se, but it is a challenge.

Fully Decentralized Delivery

Let's contrast the previous approach with a completely decentralized delivery approach without any AAT element (Figure 2.9). In the worst case, you have silos where domains don't share knowledge with each other. In the best case, you will have a lively community of practice (CoP), where people from different business units meet regularly to exchange experiences (see "What About Communities of Practice (CoPs)?").

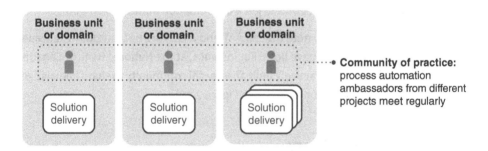

Figure 2.9 Fully decentralized delivery with CoP.

Advantages:

- No central team is required, and no separate costs are involved.
- Very flexible.

People

Disadvantages:

- Inefficient due to lack of governance. Business units often end up with different approaches, which leads to a lot of challenges during the lifetime of solutions. This can become a severe obstacle to increasing automation in highly regulated environments such as banking and insurance.

- There is no ownership of the process orchestration function, which means there is no single person responsible for fielding questions, managing vendor relationships, or taking part in industry events or conferences.

- Highly dependent on individuals' commitment and desire to exchange ideas. Often, a CoP boils down to a group of motivated individuals who drive the community in their "free time," which can potentially conflict with their daily responsibilities. An organization can address this by dedicating a set amount of time each week or month to the community, but still, this can create uncertainty because contributors often don't have a mandate to set up an enterprise strategy around process orchestration.

- There may be a lack of focus and commitment around the topic, since this is pretty much a bottom-up affair.

- Reuse is not facilitated, as nobody is responsible for providing reusable artifacts or investing the effort to make the project work (whether code or knowledge) reusable.

In essence, such a completely decentralized approach typically does not scale well. Still, it can be a good starting point to get a conversation about an AAT going.

In addition, it's important to note that an AAT and a CoP are not mutually exclusive. Best-of-breed organizations have both! For instance, at the National Bank of Canada, the AAT (they call it CoE) has actively built an internal community to share knowledge (as described at CamundaCon 2022[15]; see Figure 2.10).

Fully Centralized Delivery

Finally, let's consider the opposite side of the spectrum, where you can find more centralization if the AAT also implements and operates solutions itself (Figure 2.11). This means the business units are "only" required to capture the requirements; the AAT organizes everything else. It's almost like an internal solution integrator. As a side note, we would not call such a team "accelerators" anymore, because they actually

Early days of the CoE: building governance

- If you want to scale, you need some level of standardization
- Camunda is developer-friendly; it also means there are countless ways to do the same thing
- Who decides? Who has the authority?

Good	Could have been better
Think about standardization	CoE working on something they have no authority over

Figure 2.10 Early days of the National Bank of Canada's CoE (from CamundaCon 2022 presentation).

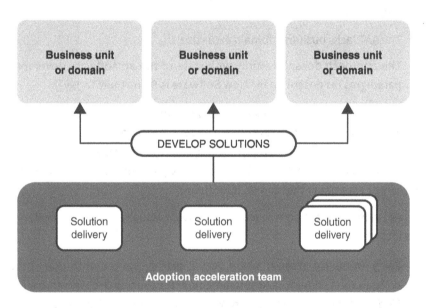

Figure 2.11 AAT responsible for solution delivery (fully centralized).

do the delivery work instead of accelerating others. For the sake of simplicity, though, we'll still talk about an AAT in this section. Also bear in mind that such a model can be an incubator to launch a federated solution delivery practice following the first successful use cases.

Advantages:

- The AAT is deep enough in the weeds to fully understand solution delivery and thus can give better recommendations.
- The AAT cannot only control governance, but also the quality of the solutions.
- The AAT can make sure solutions are built in such a way that they can be easily operated.
- Business units without their own IT capacity have a shared services model to rely on.

Disadvantages:

- The AAT quickly becomes a bottleneck.
- The need for automation solutions in most organizations is so big that the AAT will need to grow into its own software engineering unit, probably losing its focus.
- The AAT lacks business domain expertise.
- The approach doesn't comply with state-of-the-art software development paradigms (as described in "How Software Is Being Built Today").

In general, we advise against the AAT doing implementation work on a broad basis, as this simply conflicts too much with whatever software engineering function you already have. We prefer to keep a sharp focus in the AAT on enablement, letting business units do the implementation themselves or connecting them to partners (internally or externally) that can do it for them.

That said, there are exceptions when an AAT *should* actually be part of development. These include:

- **Early maturity stages:** When you're getting started with your process orchestration endeavors (if you remember the Process Orchestration Maturity Model[16] from "The Methodology Behind This Book", this is Level 0), you may simply not have the know-how yet to enable anybody. In fact, you probably won't have staffed an AAT yet either, but still, for the first few projects (say, one to five) it makes sense to have one team of people looking after the whole implementation, including go-live (relating to maturity Level 1). This team of people might become your AAT when you move on to maturity Level 2 or 3. This is a pattern we have seen be very successful in the past.

- **Strategic key projects:** When the organization is implementing important core processes with high complexity and significant top management attention, it may be strategically wise for the AAT to be part of the implementation project to ensure things don't go south, as that could damage the reputation of process orchestration and thus put the AAT in trouble.

- **Lighthouse projects:** When a new domain begins to use process orchestration, it may make sense for the AAT to be closely involved with the first few use cases. That way, the AAT can make sure the initiatives are delivered on time and on budget, as well as showcasing the potential value of process orchestration, which is very important for stakeholder acceptance. This involvement can facilitate knowledge transfer, and the CoE can gradually shift responsibility toward the domain.

- **Regular (re-)assessment of practices:** An AAT always bears the risk of living too much in the ivory tower. Therefore, it's vital to stay grounded in real-life implementation projects. While this can be done in a consulting role, it really helps to go down into the trenches, at least occasionally.

Roles

Most organizations have similar roles with the same requirements and learning paths, even if the exact names of the job profiles might differ. We list the most common ones here.

Note that people working in any CoE – be it an AAT or a POG – should generally have an appetite for innovating. This does not necessarily mean they always want to use the latest and greatest technologies, but more that they want the organization to embrace change toward a better future. They must be willing to take some risks and look at failure as an opportunity to learn and improve.

AAT Leader

The AAT leader manages the AAT. They typically report to the CIO or a senior manager (C-1) within the IT department. Sometimes, AAT leaders also report to a senior program manager, e.g., around digital transformation. Ideally, there is C-level attention and clear communication to foster recognition of the AAT's impact on the overall goals of the organization.

A good AAT leader is enthusiastic about the opportunities of process orchestration and can help challenge the status quo in different parts of the organization by envisioning a better world with process orchestration. Therefore, this person should be pretty convincing, especially when talking to senior managers or conservative (read: change resistant) parts of the organization.

Goals:

- Enable the organization to successfully conduct all process automation and orchestration initiatives.

- Support the overarching digital transformation process with adequate process orchestration technology.

- Demonstrate the success of these initiatives, mostly by looking at specific projects and their business outcomes.

- Create awareness of the potential of process orchestration in the different LoBs, thereby generating a flow of new initiatives.

Skills and requirements:

- Technical background, understanding of technology (and security).

- Able to speak "the language of the business," thereby linking technology to business potential.

- Strategic thinking.

- Communication and presentation skills.

- Enthusiasm about process automation and the benefits it brings to the table, as this can be an uphill battle in some organizations.

Enterprise Architect

Enterprise architects don't just look at IT architectures; they must understand the company's mission in sufficient detail to make informed purchases and architecture decisions across the enterprise. Enterprise architects commonly make high-level design choices on all things IT and propose technical standards, including coding standards, tools, or platforms.

For AATs, it is important to keep in close touch with enterprise architects, as they typically pursue similar goals and have a similarly central role.

A well-respected enterprise architect could also be a great AAT leader.

Rainmaker

There is a very influential role that is often forgotten when looking at enterprise process orchestration, or more generally at adopting new technologies. We call this role the *rainmaker*, as that term conveys the idea of someone who can bring about positive outcomes, much like how rain brings growth to crops and prosperity to farmers. The rainmaker's job is to drive significant change or transformation through the successful implementation and adoption of new technologies. They may sit inside or outside any of the CoEs, depending on the profile and influence of the person filling this role.

The rainmaker is often a visionary leader who has a deep understanding of both the organization's strategic objectives and the potential impact of technology on its operations. They are able to articulate a compelling vision for how technology can drive innovation, improve efficiency, and create competitive advantages for the organization. The rainmaker is adept at overcoming resistance to change by effectively communicating the benefits and addressing concerns or barriers to adoption.

In a nutshell, this person can make the business not only understand why adopting process orchestration is important, but also become enthusiastic about it. They help business departments to select orchestration candidates and can create a convincing business case for senior leadership out of any opportunity. They also are adept at communicating success and value to every executive level. Since the rainmaker is influential on both sides (business and IT), they can provide a link between the two and act as a translator.

Skills and requirements:

- Needs to have some technical knowledge to understand what process orchestration can do, but more important is that they understand the business processes, to see where orchestration can bring the most value.

- Great networker, good at making connections.

- Proficient at cross-functional collaboration across multiple domains and hierarchies.

People

- Strong communicator; comfortable with business and IT jargon, understands what type of information is important to which people and is capable of presenting the right metrics to the right people.

Business Analyst

The business analyst bridges the gap between nontechnical stakeholders and IT people and translates the desired business logic of an application from business to technical language. They need to be able to communicate well with a variety of people while also being able to structure and prioritize very strictly (a combination many people struggle with). Responsibilities and tasks vary widely depending on the organization, but business analysis is important at all stages of the software system development lifecycle.

Business analysts should be involved in any process orchestration project. As business analysts are typically not required full-time on a project, they often look after multiple projects (or products) at the same time. Many AATs also have their own business analysts, who either enable other business analysts to adopt a process mindset with BPMN or hop in and out of delivery projects to focus on business analysis there.

Skills and requirements:

- Analyzing, documenting, and managing requirements.

- Converting vague bits and pieces into structured information.

- Ability to communicate between business and IT.

- Capable of understanding processes and using the modeling standards BPMN and DMN.

- Tracking value and KPIs, e.g. in Camunda Optimize.

Solution or IT Architect

Solution or IT architects design the general architecture of a solution, which also involves defining the tool stack and procedures being used (e.g. Camunda SaaS, CI/CD pipeline, issue tracking, etc.) and respective best practices. They're often instrumental at the beginning of a project, when the first lines of code are being written, but their role becomes less important once the focus shifts to implementing more of the same.

The role of solution architect is often played by senior developers or the solution delivery team as a whole – it's vital to success, but doesn't have to be filled by a dedicated person. The more standardized your development approach is, the more solution architecture is predefined by the AAT. In those cases, solution architects might also sit within the AAT. Often, we see AATs deploying solution architects to guide the delivery teams in the LoBs throughout the project lifecycle.

Skills and requirements:

- Good overview of technological possibilities and their impact.
- Good strategic overview of the lifetime of solutions.
- Experience with different technical architectural styles.

Software Developer

Not surprisingly, software developers develop software. They write well-tested and maintainable code to produce software according to business requirements. As part of this role they may leverage different frameworks and libraries, including a process orchestration platform. Software developers focused on process orchestration can sit within the AAT or the delivery teams.

Within the AAT, software developers typically concentrate on helping out with projects, consulting other developers, or developing and documenting reusable artifacts. These developers should have enthusiasm for process orchestration.

Within the delivery teams, software developers make process models executable, connect them to endpoints, and write proper tests. In order to be productive with an orchestration platform, they need to learn the basics of the process modeling language (e.g. BPMN) as well as gaining a solid foundation in core workflow engine concepts and APIs.

In Bernd's book *Practical Process Automation*[17], he differentiated "rockstars" and professional software developers. While rockstars can perform miracles, you typically don't have many of them in the organization, and these people also bear the risk of overengineering or applying the latest and greatest technologies just to avoid getting bored. Rockstars can be a help in your AAT, but take care that they don't push the

People 103

AAT toward overengineering. Also, rockstars are sometimes not good at dealing with "normal" developers, meaning that coaching is not their strong point.

Skills and requirements:

- Software engineering background.

- Understands how the process orchestration platform fits into the organization's IT architecture.

- Embraces visual methods like BPMN (some developers are scared of visual models, for different reasons).

Low-Code Developer

Within the process automation space, you often hear about low-code developers. These may be trained software engineers who prefer to work in a low-code environment to simplify integration tasks and streamline the work, or they may have a business background and have slipped into development using tools like Microsoft Office, macros, or RPA.

Low-code developers often spend their time developing solutions in a dedicated low-code environment. They require a very constrained environment and a highly customized training course in the exact environment in which they will be working.

For many companies, the key to scaling their process automation efforts is enabling these developers to model executable workflows. Low-code developers are typically part of the solution delivery teams, not part of the AAT itself. They may also be called business technologists, as this name reflects that they might work outside of IT departments.

Skills and requirements:

- Experience with BPMN.

- Experience with low-code platforms.

Note that low-code developers are not citizen developers. Citizen developers are typically end users with some IT affinity, not developers working on solutions all the time. Their aim is to solve an active pain point with a technology they can master. Solutions implemented by citizen developers are often outside the scope of the processes we cover in this book, but of course, there is a gray area in between.

Operations Engineer

Operations engineers look at running process solutions (or more generally, applications) in production environments from a technical point of view. Some operations engineers understand how to provision machines (e.g. Terraform, Kubernetes, etc.) and how to run software on them (e.g. Docker, Kubernetes, etc.). Others focus on technical operations, meaning they can monitor applications and resolve issues when they occur. They can work in the front row of support, relying on developers whenever a problem goes deeper into process or application specifics. Very often, operations engineers work on call to provide 24/7 support for critical applications. Consequently, they tend to look more for stability than fancy features and often provide a good balance in any delivery team.

If your AAT operates software, you will need at least two operations engineers. Maintaining an on-call rotation and providing sufficient support coverage is not feasible with fewer people, unless you weaken the business requirements around incident resolution times.

The AAT might also have at least one operations engineer to consult with delivery teams and make sure that operational concerns are not left out of best practices.

Skills and requirements:

- Knows how to run software applications reliably.
- Can read and understand technical logs.
- Knows BPMN and process orchestration basics.
- Able to collaborate with InfoSec teams to meet security standards (sometimes InfoSec experts can be provisionally part of the AAT, e.g. during the initial platform setup).

Product Owner

If your adoption acceleration team provides an internal platform or artifacts to accelerate solution development (such as connectors, reusable libraries, templates, etc.), someone must take ownership of these components. As we'll explain later, adopting a product mindset is critical for success, and the key role to drive this is the product owner. This person is responsible for prioritizing and managing the

People 105

development of your process orchestration and automation platform, as well as surrounding accelerators and related artifacts. Their responsibilities include defining requirements, managing vendor relationships, overseeing the product backlog, and more.

Skills and requirements:

- Strategic alignment: Maintain a strategic focus and ensure the roadmap aligns with business goals.
- Effective communication: Engage with a wide range of stakeholders, combining strong communication skills with analytical thinking.
- Prioritization: Balance diverse inputs, making tough decisions on what to pursue and what to let go.
- Adaptability: Switch seamlessly between high-level vision and detailed, practical issues.

A product owner must excel at managing the big picture while simultaneously addressing granular features and issues. Strong communication and analytical skills are vital to succeed in this role. While it is sometimes filled by the leader of the AAT, as your initiative grows, separating these responsibilities may improve focus and scalability.

Zooming in on the Adoption Acceleration Team

Because of its strategic relevance for your process orchestration initiative, let's dive a bit more deeply into the AAT and how to set it up.

The Scope of Your AAT

Your AAT should at least own the process orchestration topic, with all its related facets; for instance, also advising on how integration is typically done, how humans are pulled into processes, and how executable processes can be automatically tested. As an example, Figure 2.12 illustrates how the AAT at Provinzial, Germany's second-biggest public insurance company, defined the typical specifications of a process model (e.g. service task, user task, and data warehouse integrations as well as DMN, modeling conventions, etc.).

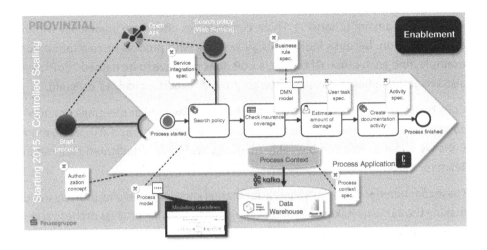

Figure 2.12 How to design an executable process at Provinzial, as defined by its AAT (taken from Provinzial's CamundaCon 2023 presentation[18]).

Ideally, your AAT will look after all process automation technologies holistically, so in addition to process orchestration it will also be in charge of RPA tools, business process management suites, and low-code tools. Sometimes, AI is also looked after here. For example, we saw one "process automation CoE" at a bigger customer looking after Camunda, Pega, UIPath, and Mendix. The big benefit of this is that the people in the AAT will understand the differences between those tools as well as their respective sweet spots. The AAT will therefore be able to provide guidance on which tools and technologies to choose for specific use cases, which is much more beneficial than having two different competence centers being at war with each other. This way, the AAT can effectively drive vendor rationalization efforts as well. (That said, we have also seen customers benefit from having different CoEs for different tools, typically because a healthy friction between them drives innovation.)

Take care not to widen the scope too much beyond process automation, however, as, for example, a "digital transformation CoE" can easily end up with too many topics and tools to look after to work effectively.

What About Communities of Practice (CoPs)?

A community of practice is "a group of people who share a common interest, passion, or profession and come together to learn from one another, share experiences, and collaborate on solving problems or advancing their collective knowledge and skills in a specific domain" (ChatGPT). Those communities often form organically within an organization, because individuals all working with process orchestration, for example, find each other. Of course, a CoP does not have to be named "CoP"; we also see other names in use, like "interest group," "expert exchange," or "guild."

CoPs typically organize communication channels, like regular meetings or knowledge forums. While they may start out as something as simple as a Wiki page, most CoPs we know of also run biweekly meetings and have a dedicated channel in Teams or Slack.

These communities are highly valuable for sharing knowledge, helping projects avoid making the same mistakes over and over again, and driving process orchestration maturity. But here's the catch: A CoP requires some organization, and typically there is no one individual who's responsible for this, and no official mandate or budget. In other words, the functioning of the CoP is dependent on the commitment of certain interested individuals, and if their priorities or duties shift, the whole CoP may be at risk.

This is why we advise having a dedicated role to organize the CoP. Not only is it a lot of work, but it also requires continuity and passion. The ideal place for such a task is the AAT. This also means that CoEs/AATs and CoP are not mutually exclusive. In fact, ideally they come as a pair.

What Should Your AAT Look Like?

AATs can differ in many ways. They can be sizable teams with more than a dozen people, but we've also seen successful AATs with only two people. It all boils down to your organization's size, your strategy, and what will help with your target operating model. That will determine the appropriate size, staffing, and activities for your AAT.

Let's first explore what a mature AAT will look like, before diving into the journey to build it. The setup that our customers with the highest level of process orchestration maturity deploy tends to look like this:

- A centralized team that helps delivery teams with all things process orchestration, comprising four to eight people filling the following roles:

  - AAT leader.
  - Software developers.
  - IT/solution architects.

- ○ DevOps engineers.
- ○ Business analysts (BPMN & DMN experts).

- The rainmaker may also sit within the AAT, but more often than not they provide external support.

- The AAT team see themselves as enablers, and the organization pulls their offering. Delivery teams love to use their help because it makes their lives easier and their projects more successful.

- The AAT provides a set of artifacts (best practices, reusable components, and some templates) and a process orchestrations infrastructure (in the case of Camunda, for example, either a self-managed Camunda installation provided via self-service to the organization, or simply relaying the Camunda SaaS offering).

Delivery teams and AATs can be augmented by other centralized IT resources or third-party partners (e.g. outsourcing operations). This is visualized in Figure 2.13.

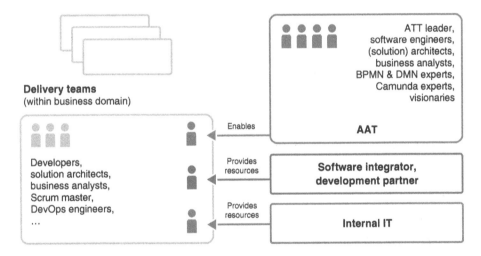

Figure 2.13 Delivery teams receive support and resources from the AAT and other internal and external actors.

The best AATs we have seen have a product mindset (see "Product Thinking"). They view themselves as building an internal product, like a framework, tooling, or a platform, and they see developers, operations teams, SecOps, and other stakeholders as internal customers. So, just like product design software vendors do, they always

People

source their ideas from those customers and validate their decisions with them, making it easy for customers to provide feedback or request functionality and making sure they know to which they will be listened to. Remember: You're building it *for* those folks, and not because you know better. A good reference here (although it focuses more on the platform side of the AAT) is the article "What I Talk About When I Talk About Platforms"[19] on Martin Fowler's blog.

The setup pictured in Figure 2.8 is our greenfield choice. (Remember: If there are no good reasons not to use the greenfield choice, we try to set things up this way.) But as we mentioned earlier, reality is complex, so there might be good reasons to use a different setup in your organization. For example, some company cultures are built around strong rules and enforcement, so it would alienate employees if the AAT were just sitting there waiting for people to ask for help. Still, it's helpful to keep this greenfield recommendation in mind and make deliberate choices about where to deviate from it.

The Business Case for the AAT

In our experience, the higher up an AAT reports in an organization, the more effective it can be. In that sense, it's mandatory to get management buy-in and sufficient funding for your AAT initiative. That's why articulating the associated business impact is crucial. There are two dimensions to this:

1. Why process automation and process orchestration?
2. Why a center of excellence or AAT?

In other words, you have to make a case for what you want to do (process orchestration) first, before you can argue why the AAT will make you more successful in adopting it.

In general, the AAT will help you harvest the value proposition of process orchestration at scale in your organization. This is less about *what* you achieve through successful orchestration initiatives (for example, improved process cycle times) and more about *how* those initiatives are being delivered. An AAT will help teams to become more efficient and agile, while also improving the (internal) customer experience for your developer community (e.g. by helping them reduce their mental load through the technical advantages provided by the AAT). But of course, the AAT can also help in finding the right opportunities and business cases for process orchestration and expressing their value.

The strategic impact of the AAT on the business is unfortunately tough to quantify, as there are a lot of factors that contribute to it. On the other hand, simple metrics around the number of people trained in process orchestration or the level of adoption within the organization hint at the value an AAT is delivering but are not directly connected to its business impact; they are only what is known as proxy metrics. This trade-off is illustrated by the AAT value pyramid in Figure 2.14, which we adapted from the paper "Managing Value in Use in Business Markets"[20] by business researchers Michael Kleinaltenkamp and Katharina Prohl.

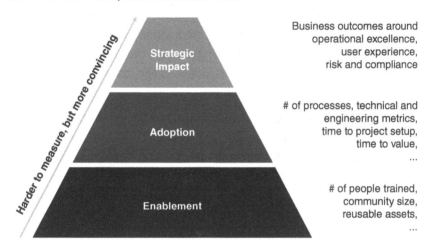

Figure 2.14 The AAT value pyramid.

In general, successful AATs are better at communicating their value at higher levels of the pyramid and translating this into business outcomes. In order to help you do this, let's dive into the concrete advantages that an AAT provides. Foremost among these are:

- **Increased developer productivity:** Having an AAT that takes care of best practices, project templates, getting started guides, governance, and other materials will drastically improve the productivity of delivery teams. Just think of the time and effort required to start an automation initiative from scratch: evaluating a tool, deciding on an architecture and approach, burning your fingers with the first mistakes you make, etc. In our experience, it can take teams two to six months to go through this cycle, which an AAT can significantly accelerate. As Deepak Tiwari, Managing Director at EY, put it in a CamundaCon Q&A[21]: "CoEs [i.e., AATs] usually have visibility across other projects across the organization. They may have seen pitfalls the delivery

People

team may not have been exposed to (better to learn from others' mistakes than your own)." Beyond knowledge sharing, AATs might also provide technical accelerators such as connectors or an internally managed platform to reduce the cognitive load for delivery teams. We will discuss this later in more detail.

- **Efficiency and cost savings:** Of course, increased efficiency of your development teams will save effort and thus make completing projects quicker and cheaper. While this will typically not lead to a reduced headcount (after all, we're still facing a talent shortage), it means that you can improve your developer productivity and automate more within your existing setup, leading to further efficiencies and cost savings. An AAT can, for example, also make sure that licenses for tools are efficiently used and standardized, helping with the process of vendor rationalization.

- **Improved quality and reduced complexity:** Documenting best practices and making sure there is knowledge exchange between teams will result in teams consistently producing higher-quality (for example, more maintainable) solutions and delivering results on budget and on time. An AAT will also help provide the right technology, thereby allowing a best-of-breed approach and reducing complexity for agile delivery teams. Just looking at the sheer size of the CNCF Cloud Native Landscape[22] illustrates the challenges that delivery teams face here – how are they supposed to keep track of all the different tools? An AAT helps improve time to value significantly by shaving off the evaluation time for the respective teams. Additionally, the AAT can help avoid obscure or suboptimal technology choices made by inexperienced teams or playful individuals that will cause maintenance efforts later on.

- **Process mindset and stakeholder enablement:** Typically, the adoption of process orchestration at scale corresponds with a wider transformation of how an organization thinks about processes and how business and IT teams collaborate. As a survey by McKinsey[23] pointed out in 2022, the more parts of the organization are involved, the more automation initiatives are likely to succeed. CoEs can help build this process mindset by providing the right tools and frameworks to enable every stakeholder, including citizen developers, to take part in process orchestration – from modeling to development, operation, analysis, and continuous improvement. It can also encourage stakeholder buy-in and provide strategic alignment across domains and hierarchies by building a mutual vision of what to achieve through process orchestration.

In summary, as an IT executive at one of our customers put it: "Process orchestration allows us to create solutions more quickly, making the resulting systems more reliable, and the AAT ensures the organization is leveraging all of that in the best way possible."

Building Your AAT

To formally set up your AAT and maximize its impact on your organization, you will need management buy-in and sufficient funding. This typically happens either through a buildup of enough bottom-up pressure (i.e. more and more teams articulating the desire to use process orchestration) or through a strategic top-down initiative to drive process orchestration at scale.

In the previously mentioned Q&A[24], Deepak Tiwari also excellently summarizes how to get management buy-in for funding a CoE or AAT:

1. **Think "big"** (and make the stakeholders think big). Show the "big picture" – [describe] strategic benefits, visualize your target operating model, paint a clear picture of the future state and an implementation roadmap to get there.

2. **Start small.** Ask for small funding in the beginning. A 90-day go-live plan is a good idea. Pick a high-value but low-effort use case for a pilot "lighthouse" project. Get a meaningful win that will help consolidate business sponsorship and build momentum.

3. **Finish strong.** Maintain executive sponsorship and commitment throughout the duration of the program by focusing on benefits realization.

After those phases, Deepak suggests **scaling** and **continuously improving** your CoE. We typically use the following four phases to describe building an AAT, as visualized in Figure 2.15:

- **Initial:** Organizations that are just getting started with adopting process orchestration don't have an AAT yet. There might be a CoP established to facilitate knowledge sharing and start the journey toward an AAT, or a strategic plan to scale process orchestration and create an AAT.

- **Forming:** The AAT starts to exist as a dedicated team within the organization and begins developing guidelines and infrastructure. It either focuses on enabling from the beginning or is deeply involved in the first solution delivery projects itself.

People 113

- **Scaling:** Now it's time to scale the adoption across the enterprise and evolve the AAT accordingly. Experience from more and more projects improves the maturity and credibility of the AAT. The AAT needs to improve at capturing metrics and communicate the business value of process automation and of itself to secure funding. Typically, in this phase we see stronger centralization of governance, enablement, and infrastructure and increasingly federated delivery in the business domains.

- **Maturing:** The AAT is established and helps with the strategic application of process automation and orchestration throughout the organization. It's continuously improving its offering across the board.

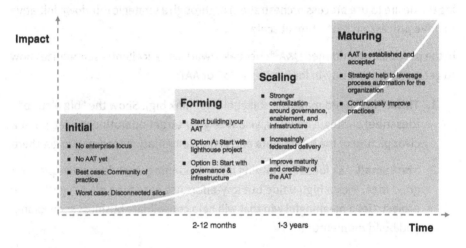

Figure 2.15 The four phases of building an AAT.

Keep in mind that this is an iterative journey and you need to get there step by step, focusing on incrementally delivering value, ideally from day one.

AAT Tasks

Now let's dive a bit more deeply into how an AAT provides its value. What activities does an AAT normally perform, and which activities is it better to avoid? Let's start by going over the core activities of an AAT, including the typical resources an AAT provides (Figure 2.16).

We've grouped the tasks into four main categories: enablement, communication, tools, and solution delivery. Let's go over these one by one.

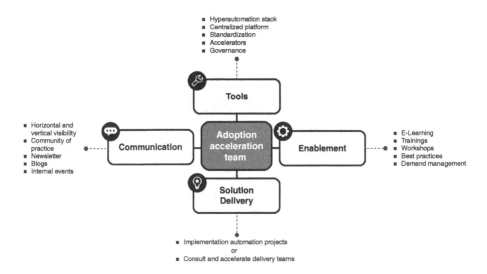

Figure 2.16 The core activities of an AAT.

Communication

The AAT needs to **evangelize process automation**. This can be done in many ways. You can hold **internal events** like lunch and learn[25] meetings, tech days, success story presentations, vendor pitches, or roadmap discussions, many of which your process orchestration vendor can also support. Also, hackathons are a great way to spread the word in a fun and engaging way. And don't forget about the power of **good branding**, perhaps coming up with something a bit more fun than a "process orchestration CoE." At one customer, we saw "Process Samurai" stickers on various laptops throughout the firm, and others had their own great T-shirts. Keep in mind that the branding should fit your company's culture (at Camunda, humor always works well!).

Additionally, you can leverage **external events** like industry conferences or vendor events (for example, CamundaCon[26], Camunda days[27], or regional meetups[28]). Surprisingly enough, good external presentations often get more internal attention than internal events. We frequently connect different business units within a single customer that don't yet know each other through Camunda events.

Apart from events, you can write about your experiences. **Case studies** are a good way to communicate value, and many AATs write extensive internal case studies for all projects. Emphasize the benefits and point to quick wins. The better you are able to **quantify the achieved value**, the more convincing those case studies will be. You can also participate in vendor case studies (e.g. Camunda case studies[29]), typically revealing fewer details but getting more exposure. Most AATs run a regular **newsletter** too, or maintain a news section in their wiki that people can subscribe to.

The AAT should also try to **foster internal communication**. By hosting regular coffee meetings, reviews, open spaces, or other kinds of workshops, the AAT can give the impression of being approachable and caring.

Part of this is also to make sure the right technical foundation is in place to form and **manage a community of practice**, where all professionals involved with process automation can easily meet and exchange ideas. Typically, companies provide a **forum** or **Slack channel**, a **blog** or **Wiki** section, or regular speaking slots at company-wide meetings.

AATs typically also **manage vendor contacts and licenses** (together with their procurement, of course). Centralizing this not only makes collaboration with vendors more efficient, but can also help ensure the right configurations of the tools are applied and licensing is optimized for all use cases. For instance, Camunda allows licenses to grow without going through a complete sales and legal cycle every time, e.g., with agreed adoption paths or frame agreements.

We want to emphasize that good vendor support is vital for organizations to succeed, so vendor management is actually a more essential activity than most anticipate. A thorough understanding of the vendor's offering – not only with respect to features, but also customer success, support, and enabling services, as well as the vision and roadmap – is crucial for effectively improving your level of process orchestration maturity.

Enablement

The main goal of an AAT is to enable others in the organization to successfully implement process orchestration solutions. This can happen on many levels:

- **Consulting:** The AAT can be the go-to place to ask questions about process automation in general, methods like BPMN or DMN, or specific tools like Camunda. In a minimal form, the AAT is just **approachable for questions**. In a more structured way, this could include offering defined **consulting packages**: anything from a virtual coffee chat for projects thinking about using process orchestration or a half-day orientation **workshop** up to a five-day PoC session. Many AATs also stay close to projects, e.g., by conducting regular, proactive **check-ins** or **reviews**. In mature organizations we often see a quite broad offering, which to some extent reminds us of our consulting offerings, including out-of-the-box **training courses**.

Instead of relying on rigid rules stating that people have to attend mandatory training courses, try to **build a learning culture**, where learning and training are seen as not only valuable and helpful, but also fun.

Note that it might also make sense to include vendor offerings (e.g. in-person training, or free **e-learning courses** from Camunda Academy[30]) in your own offering. In this case, the added value of the AAT is often in curating the important content and establishing a link between the vendor's generic world and the organization's specifics. This also results in a much more realistic workload, as it is hard for an AAT to develop and maintain too much material on its own.

- **Best practices:** Successful AATs document their best practices, at least in a basic way. You might find some inspiration in the Camunda Best Practices[31], but the advantage an AAT has is that it can tailor the best practices to the organization, eliminating choices that aren't relevant. A good example of this is the solution architecture for automation projects, where it might be sufficient to define one common architecture for pro-code and another for low-code environments. This architecture can then include company specifics like which version control system is used, how a project can be hooked into CI/CD, and so on. (You don't need to call these best practices; it can simply be your process orchestration **documentation**.)

  AATs might share those best practices in a **knowledge base**, capturing frequently answered questions (**FAQs**). This might simply happen in your company's Wiki (e.g. Confluence), but of course, you can also use an internal forum or specific tools if there is enough internal traffic.

- **Demand management:** One big challenge in organizations is determining which projects will benefit from process orchestration. This includes identifying the candidate projects, describing the role process orchestration will play, budgeting, developing a business case presentation, defining KPIs, and finally prioritizing and planning those projects. The AAT can play an instrumental role in the whole process to support business initiatives with the insights required.

Many AATs have a low-touch entry point for initiatives to get in touch (one of our customers calls this the "Front Door"). Projects are then quickly assessed (e.g. with a virtual coffee chat and templates to capture the important information), and recommendations can be given. The AAT can give an indication of whether or not process orchestration might be helpful in this project, and if so help show the value it can bring. It can also help to define the required roles to develop a solution and perhaps recommend development partners (both internal and external).

AATs in more mature organizations even start one step earlier and sit down with leaders of their business domains to proactively think about the potential of process orchestration for various use cases. Done well, this can reveal big **strategic opportunities** to **save money, earn more money**, or **reduce risk** through the benefits process orchestration brings to solution delivery.

In general, this task might also be done by your POG instead of the AAT.

Tools and Infrastructure

As part of the enablement practice, or in addition to it, many AATs provide guidance on the tool stack or additional reusable artifacts. Increasingly, AATs provide a shared platform for process orchestration. This might involve defining any or all of the following.

The Hyperautomation Stack

A process automation AAT typically owns the full hyperautomation technology stack[32]. This means the AAT knows about a variety of tools from different categories and can give recommendations on which tool to use for a specific use case (we've sketched out a decision map for this in "Selecting the Right Process Orchestration Technology"). Typically, the AAT also has knowledge of how to combine those different tools, because, for example, you might want to orchestrate the overall end-to-end process with Camunda but integrate certain legacy systems via RPA within single tasks[33].

In most organizations, AATs **recommend and provide specific tools** to be used, potentially as an internal platform as a service. Depending on your organization's culture, this recommendation may be seen as a suggestion that can be ignored, or as an official standard that everybody has to follow. In addition, the AAT can **recommend the way tools should be used** in projects – for example:

- SaaS vs. self-managed (provided as an internal platform as a service).

- The programming language used (e.g. Java and Spring Boot).

- How tests should be done (e.g. unit testing with JUnit, behavior-driven testing with Cucumber, integration testing with Selenium, etc.).

- The CI/CD pipeline (e.g. with Jenkins or GitHub Actions).

This can go even further. For example, we've seen AATs that run **architecture workshops** and **architecture reviews,** and others that help projects that need high scale to do **load tests, benchmarks,** or **performance tuning**. In particular, activities that require deep expertise around a tool but are often unrelated to the business problem can be best supported by an AAT.

Accelerators

If the tool stack is standardized, the AAT can provide resources to make delivery teams more productive. There are many things that are quite similar in various projects, and in these cases it's simply easier to reuse the existing know-how and code. Good examples are:

- Project templates (e.g. a Maven Archetype or simply a template project to be copied).

- Frameworks that help with harmonization or standardization (e.g. build tools, Maven parent POMs, Maven BOMs, etc.).

- Installation scripts.

- Connectors, including company-specific connectors for common systems (e.g. Mainframe or some bespoke core business system) or sometimes just reusable job workers and element templates.

- Security configuration (e.g. SSO or LDAP integration and configuration).

- Plugins (e.g. for pushing audit data of the orchestration platform into the data warehouse).

- BPMN patterns for typical problems (e.g. maker-checker).

One specific form of accelerator is **internal marketplaces or portals,** which can be used as catalogs to find and leverage reusable artifacts – something that tends to become a big problem once adoption is scaled. While many AATs in the past organized this via Wikis, some have their own portal software (e.g. API portals). Camunda also provides a marketplace component that can be leveraged for this,

People

as well as for sharing artifacts only internally. Such an internal marketplace would most likely be curated by the AAT and augmented by the contributions of the internal community.

Solution Lifecycle

Many AATs define what the solution lifecycle should look like. This might depend on the type of solution (pro-code vs. low-code), but typically, it aligns process development with the general **software development lifecycle (SDLC)**. So, for example, the AAT recommends how to version control your sources (e.g. using GitHub), what stages deployments should go through (e.g. dev, int, pre-prod, and prod), how to deploy process models to production (e.g. with the BPMN being part of the deployment artifact deployed during startup), and what the CI/CD pipeline should look like (e.g. predefined GitHub Actions).

As part of the solution lifecycle, some organizations also establish **quality gates** or **approvals**. For example, a BPMN process model requires a review by the AAT before it can go live, or there may be a definition of done (DoD) that includes specific process-related checkpoints (e.g. that there is basic test coverage).

KPIs/Value Tracking

The AAT can support projects in identifying useful key performance indicators. In our experience, many project teams are unsure of which KPIs they should track and how to connect those to business goals. However, doing this is essential to prove the business value of process orchestration, identify bottlenecks and improvement opportunities, and track continuous improvements over time. The experts within the AAT can provide assistance with this.

Solution Delivery

An AAT can also be involved with certain aspects of solution delivery, such as:

- **Evaluating the automation pipeline:** Organizations need to decide which projects process orchestration will be beneficial for and **prioritize** those projects so that (typically rare) resources can be distributed properly. The AAT cannot only consult with the initiative stakeholders on the benefits of process orchestration and help with early estimations to make the business case, but often also **see opportunities** others have missed because they are not as familiar with process orchestration. For example, the AAT knows that you can easily change processes running on the orchestration platform later and that this will enable experiments with new technologies like AI.

- **Orchestrating partners:** The AAT can **coordinate with external partners** (software integrators, consulting companies, training providers) to **staff projects** or to find enablement support. Many AATs work with a curated set of people at dedicated partners who they know are familiar with not only process orchestration and the tool being used, but also the specific needs of the organization. Of course, this can also work the same way with internal people, especially in bigger organizations.

- **Implementing automation projects:** Some AATs also do real implementation work themselves. As discussed earlier, we generally advise against AATs doing implementation work on a broad basis, but there are valid reasons for exceptions (see "Fully Centralized Delivery").

Governance

Finding a healthy level of governance is not easy and requires balancing contradicting requirements. Forces advocating for more centralized governance in the context of process orchestration typically include:

- **Standardization and consistency:** Centralized governance allows for the establishment and enforcement of standardized processes, coding conventions, and best practices across the organization. This ensures consistency in software development, making it easier to maintain and manage codebases.

- **Security and compliance:** Centralized governance allows organizations to enforce security policies and data protection measures as well as to ensure compliance with industry standards and regulations.

- **Quality assurance:** With centralized governance, there can be a focus on quality assurance processes, including code reviews, testing standards, and quality metrics. This helps ensure that software products meet the required quality standards.

Forces advocating for more decentralized governance typically center around:

- **Agility and flexibility:** Decentralized governance allows for greater agility and flexibility in responding to changes and adapting to evolving requirements.

Teams can make decisions independently and respond quickly to emerging opportunities or challenges without waiting for central approval.

- **Empowerment and autonomy:** Decentralized governance empowers teams by giving them autonomy over decision-making processes. It minimizes bureaucratic hurdles and eliminates the need for decisions to go through a centralized approval process. This can lead to increased motivation, creativity, and a sense of ownership among team members, fostering a more innovative and dynamic work environment.

- **Local expertise:** Decentralized governance allows decisions to be made by teams or individuals who possess local or specialized expertise. This is particularly beneficial when dealing with projects that require domain-specific knowledge or expertise that is distributed throughout the organization.

- **Innovation and experimentation:** Decentralized governance fosters a culture of innovation and experimentation. Teams can try out new ideas, technologies, or development methodologies without being constrained by rigid central guidelines, leading to more innovative solutions.

For most organizations it makes sense to aim for somewhere in the middle to get the best of both worlds, as we described in "A Healthy Level of Centralization", with the sweet spot being a central AAT that enables federated delivery teams and provides a platform, taking care to ensure the right level of governance in the platform and corresponding getting started guides, templates, and examples. For instance, most organizations provide a prebuilt integration into their single sign-on (SSO) environment, as this is crucial for every project and no creativity is required here. On the contrary, this should not become a hurdle and should just work out of the box. At the same time, the AAT might leave delivery teams the freedom to choose which libraries to use to connect their REST services.

In general, we are fans of the idea of golden paths[34]: Using a solution template, for example, should be such a great experience that delivery teams will not see this as annoying bureaucracy, but as help they would never want to work without.

Of course, organizations are all different, so the approach to governance must be **aligned with your company culture**. For example, if your organization embraces microservices, heavily hyping the autonomy of development teams, any central guidance should be approached cautiously (while still ensuring that governance guardrails, however strictly or loosely they are designed, are respected). In contrast, if your organization is used to very rigid central governance, giving too much freedom to development teams might be a burden on those teams, which are not used to making their own decisions.

In summary, the path to getting to the sweet spot of governance might be very different for each organization.

AAT Anti-Patterns

As we all know, failure is the best teacher, but unfortunately those stories are seldom shared openly. So, we also want to describe some typical problems we've seen with our customers.

For instance, we saw one organization where the **delivery teams tried to avoid working with the AAT**. They developed autonomously and even procured their own licenses. The main reason cited was that **the AAT significantly slowed down delivery work** by adding bureaucracy and applying too-restrictive guidelines (e.g. mandatory quality checks that weren't helpful for the teams). In this case, the AAT was detached from the real challenges of delivery teams "on the ground" and created governance guidelines that were not only unhelpful but actually an obstacle – a typical ivory tower example.

To avoid this situation:

- **AATs need to establish a continuous feedback loop** with all delivery initiatives (and potentially a CoP) to continuously evolve their offerings and align them with project needs. This is all about mindset. As mentioned previously, the AAT needs a product mindset and should be obsessed with providing value for the stakeholders in the organization.

- **The AAT model needs to evolve according to the needs of the organization.** While it might make sense to have stricter governance guidelines in the beginning, it might also make sense to provide more autonomy to enable scaling in later maturity stages (our customer Provinzial called this "managed autonomy" in their CamundaCon 2023 presentation[35]).

Another anti-pattern we've seen is **spending too much time on activities that don't have an impact** on the organization. This often comes up in a pair with "planning over doing" or "paralysis by analysis." The effect is that AATs jeopardize their credibility, and people do not perceive them as valuable.

Instead, the AAT should:

- **Incrementally deliver value right away.** Of course, this should be done with a goal in mind, but the focus should be on going step by step and not getting bogged down by initiatives that provide value only after a significant amount of time has passed, with the risk of not being helpful at all in real life.

- **Adjust the plan** to accommodate any learnings along the way.

This plays into the next anti-pattern: **Doing too much too early**. This can also be dangerous. For example, we have seen customers that wanted to build their own bespoke platform, provide lots of best practices around its usage, share reusable patterns, and so on. That all sounds good – but the problem was that they started when they didn't yet have any experience. Solution delivery teams, detached from the AAT, adopted the best practices early on, but they turned out not to work very well. This led to a lot of work being required within the AAT to fix problems or develop important features, very often in a firefighting manner, especially when the first project went live. After only a handful of projects, the team was completely blocked, ending up with a half-baked, relatively unstable platform and not enough capacity to enable projects.

Instead, the AAT should:

- **Harvest real learnings**, distill best practices, and **derive feature requests** for any software components they provide. The real-life context helps the AAT to provide meaningful artifacts.

- **Develop internal platforms incrementally** together with real-life projects.

Last but not least, we've seen AATs struggle because they **lack a mandate** within the organization. This can lead to too little capacity to do impactful work and a shortage of credibility within the organization. To avoid this, it is crucial to **have sufficient authority and funding**. This is achieved by creating and sustaining stakeholder buy-in, especially with your internal sponsors. To that end, it is critical to monitor and report on the business impact, not only to the sponsors, but also across the business, to generate interest in new initiatives.

Figure 2.17 shows a summary of some typical AAT anti-patterns and how to address them.

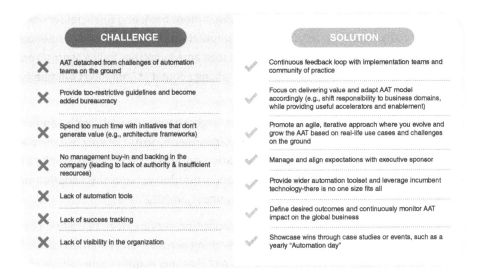

Figure 2.17 Common AAT challenges and how to solve them.

Real-Life Examples

To give you a starting point to dive more deeply into the topic, here are some publicly disclosed examples of successful and effective AATs (often simply called CoEs by the respective organizations), in alphabetical order:

- **Atlassian**, a leading provider of collaboration tools for software development and project management, has established an AAT to support the automation initiatives of federated delivery teams by providing an internal platform, accelerators, and enablement, as well as bringing the community together for knowledge sharing. The teams have already built more than 16 apps using process orchestration, with more than 100 million decisions being made and 65 million process instances being created yearly. They talked about it at CamundaCon 2024[36].

- The **City of Munich** ("Landeshauptstadt München") enables citizen development empowered by a Camunda-based workflow platform and an AAT in the IT department in order to boost the digital transformation of the administration in a scalable way. They talked about it at CamundaCon 2023[37].

- **Desjardins**, a Canadian financial service cooperative, set up a team to provide governance, enablement, and accelerators to use Camunda in their hyper-automation toolkit. They talked about it at CamundaCon 2022[38].

- **Goldman Sachs**, the multinational investment bank and financial services company, built an enterprise process automation platform on top of Camunda to enable automation at scale. You can read about why they built a platform on the Camunda blog[39] or listen to them talking about it at Camunda Community Summit 2022[40].

- **National Bank of Canada** is the sixth-largest bank in Canada, with approximately 25,000 employees. Within this organization, an AAT of only two people has built and shared process automation expertise, set up a community of automation experts, and created standardization around the adoption of Camunda. They talked about it at CamundaCon 2022[41].

- **NatWest**, a UK-focused banking organization serving over 19 million customers with business operations stretching across retail, commercial, and private banking markets, has built an AAT that successfully scaled across the enterprise, with more than 4,000 Camunda users as of today. They talked about it at CamundaCon 2023[42].

- One of the largest commercial banks in Germany, Norddeutsche Landesbank (**NORD/LB**), set up an AAT to drive the adoption of process orchestration at the enterprise level. They talked about it in a process automation forum[43] (available in German only).

- **Provinzial**, a leading insurance company in Germany, has successfully adopted Camunda for end-to-end process orchestration across all domains, with over 220 processes and 270 decision tables in production. With their AAT, they are now advancing toward hyperautomation with AI integration. They talked about it at CamundaCon 2023[44].

Defining Your Target Operating Model

Defining the right target operating model is key for successful adoption of enterprise process orchestration. This model encompasses the team structure, processes, and capabilities that an organization aims to achieve to effectively deliver process orchestration solutions. While the target operating model also includes other aspects than people, like workflows and tools, we see the people-related aspects as the most important, which is why we're talking about it in this chapter.

Key Dimensions to Define Your Operating Model

Based on our discussions of the target operating model with many customers and prospects over the years, we've derived a set of eight dimensions you can use to evaluate the current state of your operating model and define your target state:

- **Solution delivery:** What solution delivery model is used in your organization? Does your AAT provide some form of centralized enablement for building solutions? Do teams need to actively request it or is it provided broadly? Alternatively, is the AAT building solutions itself?

- **Enabling function (AAT):** Does your organization have an enabling function like the AAT? If so, what's the scope of the AAT? Is it focused on a single tool (e.g. Camunda), a wider category of tools (e.g. process orchestration), or some even broader topic (e.g. digital transformation in general)?

- **Infrastructure:** Does the AAT provide infrastructure (for example, add-ons or Camunda Connectors) instead of simply recommending a tool? Does it operate software and offer it via an internal SaaS model? Maybe it even provides the infrastructure to build, deploy, and run complete solutions.

- **Governance:** Is the AAT seen as an enabler that helps with projects or as a police force that mostly enforces guardrails? Are stacks standardized and obligatory, or documented as best practices you can choose to follow or not?

- **Process overview and value tracking:** Is your AAT the go-to place in the organization to gather an overview of business processes, probably providing some kind of process architecture or process landscape? Does it manage the automation backlog and proactively measure the value of automated processes within the business domains? Or are these the responsibilities of the business domains or another centralized unit like the POG?

- **Supported use case complexity:** Does the AAT focus on your core business processes that typically have a high degree of complexity and criticality and deliver a lot of value? Does it focus on the long tail of simpler processes that can potentially be implemented by citizen developers? Or does it cover the whole diverse set of processes, enabling it to see the sweet spots of the different tools being used?

- **Depth of enablement:** Does your AAT offer best practices, workshops, and training? Does it provide a specific learning and upskilling path for your organization?

- **Communication:** How much does your AAT invest in communication to create awareness about process orchestration? For example, does it work to build an internal community, do internal case studies and presentations, or even create sophisticated marketing materials?

Figure 2.18 provides an overview over those dimensions (you can access this graphic as a Google Slide[45] to visualize your own AAT design easily).

Figure 2.18 The target operating model dimensions.

Considering these dimensions can be a big help in making key decisions around your target operating model. For example, our greenfield recommendation looks like Figure 2.19, where the black dots indicate the target state for each dimension.

This setup describes an AAT that:

- Fosters deep and strategic internal enablement, but does not implement solutions itself.
- Provides a wide array of process automation tools, including a platform like Camunda, testing tools, RPA tools, and more.
- Proactively guides delivery teams in their adoption of process orchestration (depending on the needs and skills of those teams).
- Hosts a centralized process orchestration platform as an internal SaaS offering, which is augmented by accelerators (e.g. integrations into the data warehouse, user task management, SSO, etc.).

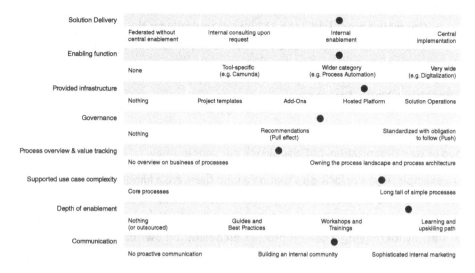

Figure 2.19 Our greenfield target operating model.

- Provides sensible governance through a helpful reference architecture that matches the requirements of the internal teams.

- Encourages process remodeling and value tracking to improve and measure the achieved value (may also be driven by a POG).

- Enables low-code developers to implement the long tail of use cases with low or medium complexity.

- Provides a training curriculum that is tailored to the organization's needs, leveraging internal and external resources.

- Has built a strong internal community from which it learns while also continuously showcasing successes to the wider organization (business and management stakeholders).

Clarifying the target dimensions will help you set up your AAT. Things you'll want to consider include:

- **Vision and mission statement:** Paint a target picture of your AAT to get internal buy-in.

- **Roadmap:** Build an action plan to bring the vision to life.

- **Staffing:** How many people will be in your AAT, and what are their roles and responsibilities? (The more centralized activities you have, the more personnel you need in your AAT.)

- **Operating model:** Will the AAT be run centrally for the whole organization, federated within business units or domains, or some hybrid in between?

Sketching Your Journey

The operating model dimensions are a wonderful tool to not only discuss the status quo of your organization, but also sketch out your journey.

For example, if you're facing a situation where there are a handful of different grassroots initiatives in place, resulting in different teams using process orchestration technology operating in fragmented silos without central ownership, you might want to start by identifying a central process orchestration **owner** or **champion**. This should be someone who has been involved in prior process orchestration projects. Most often, they are already widely regarded as an expert and informally consulted with technical questions. This person doesn't have a formal mandate and is typically driven by personal motivation, so the champion is actually not formally designated but informally grows into that role. This can be a great incubator for setting up an AAT.

This champion can build a **community of practice**. Building a CoP will help you bring together different users in the organization so they can learn from each other's projects. It will also help create visibility within the organization, showcasing successes and generating a snowball effect where success breeds success. That way you can start to make an impression on the enterprise level, even if you don't yet have a formal mandate or budget for any CoE.

We often see the CoP as an interim solution for organizations where an AAT does not have funding yet but there are motivated individuals who want to push process orchestration forward, probably working toward making the case for an AAT.

You can see this stage visualized in Figure 2.20.

The advantages of process orchestration are proven with those first projects, but new projects cannot easily benefit from earlier experiences, despite informal conversations among community members.

This is an ideal breeding ground to form your AAT, often staffed with people who were part of the initial solution delivery teams. The AAT concentrates on enablement and governance and will probably not be part of new solution delivery projects. We see typical team sizes of two to eight people at this stage.

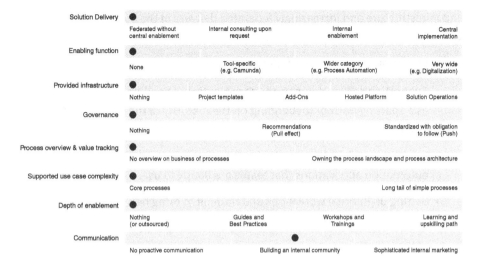

Figure 2.20 The operating model of an organization that has not yet established an AAT.

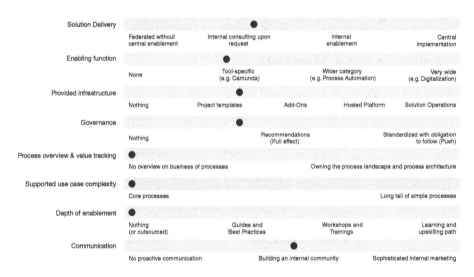

Figure 2.21 The operating model of an organization that is just forming its AAT.

Plotted along our eight dimensions, the operating model during this formation stage looks like Figure 2.21.

Now it's time to scale the adoption across your enterprise and evolve your AAT accordingly. Typically, at this stage we see more centralization of governance, enablement,

People 131

and infrastructure and increasingly federated delivery in the business domains. We also see more solutions being implemented in parallel.

The activities of the AAT now include:

- Supporting delivery teams through consulting or providing proactive guidance as a sparring partner (depending on the maturity of the internal customers), but doing less implementation work.
- Establishing a helpful governance and reference architecture around process automation applications that teams are happy to use.
- Setting up internal workshops and training to bring new users up to speed.
- Advising teams on process refactoring and starting to track the business impact of the initiatives.
- Growing the community and leveraging it as a feedback instrument for the AAT.
- Opening the scope toward wider automation tools or joining forces with other existing CoEs to better serve the evolving needs of the organization.

You can see this plotted in Figure 2.22.

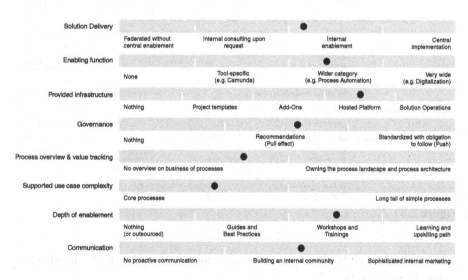

Figure 2.22 The operating model of an organization with an evolving AAT.

The roles are similar to those in a mature AAT, with the size typically ranging between four and eight people:

- AAT leader
- Software developers
- IT/solution architects
- DevOps engineers
- Business analysts (BPMN & DMN experts)

These snapshots are examples that indicate the journey. Exactly where the dots are placed will depend on many factors; the important thing is to move the right dots at the right time in the right direction. The goal is generally to arrive at what we sketched out as our greenfield target operating model at the beginning of this section.

It can be helpful to plot your current state alongside the next or final target state, to help you visualize the steps required to get there. For example, Figure 2.23 shows the current state (white dots) along with the target state (black dots).

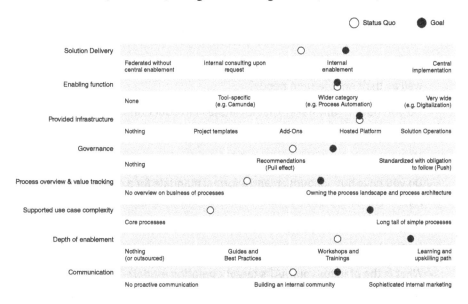

Figure 2.23 Plotting the current and target state together can help you plan your next steps.

Ideally, you will use this as a communication and discovery tool, helping you assess your current level of maturity and keep track of where you are in your process orchestration journey.

Questions to Assess Your Maturity

For people, we describe the five maturity levels as follows (see Table P.1):

- **Level 0:** IT team is not set up to centralize projects or resources.
- **Level 1:** Disparate process orchestration projects are implemented in a decentralized manner (the "sprouting mushrooms" approach).
- **Level 2:** AAT seeks to empower business roles to understand their process orchestration projects.
- **Level 3:** An AAT or distributed team focused on repeatability, enablement, and scale has been established.
- **Level 4:** A global AAT acts as a SaaS platform within the organization, providing enablement, training, and internal consulting and developing connectors for process orchestration technology solutions.

Questions you should ask yourself to assess your maturity include:

- Which delivery model have you chosen for your program?
- Do you have a clear understanding of the people and roles in your program as well as their enablement needs?
- Do you have a rainmaker that facilitates introductions to the business and advocates for your program?
- Have you established a community of practice?
- Do you have buy-in, budget, and a formal mandate for a center of excellence / AAT?
- How are you identifying new use cases? Are you leveraging your AAT or POG for this?
- What is the plan for your AAT's target operating model?
- Have you developed a roadmap to incrementally develop your AAT?
- How do you set up internal communications?
- Which tools and accelerators do you provide?
- Are you providing process orchestration as a service (either through SaaS or your internal platform)?
- How do you enable the different teams?

Takeaways

Here are the key insights from this chapter:

- Process orchestration should be embedded in modern software development practices like Agile, DevOps, and product thinking.

- Establishing dedicated teams, such as the Adoption Acceleration Team (AAT) and Process Optimization Group (POG), is crucial to scale adoption, achieve economies of scale, and accelerate projects.

- Enterprise process orchestration requires clearly defined roles, appropriate skills, and effective team structures.

- A federated delivery model, where a centralized team like the AAT enables autonomous delivery teams, balances autonomy and governance for scalable adoption.

- When setting up an AAT an organization must consider multiple dimensions, including its scope, provided infrastructure, enablement program, and degree of involvement, as well as the delivery lifecycle, value tracking, and more.

- Assigning ownership of end-to-end processes across business and IT domains is critical for aligning efforts and ensuring accountability.

Chapter 3: Technology

Even if we keep stressing that process orchestration, and in fact any kind of organizational transformation, requires more than just technology, technology still plays a vital part in such an initiative. So, this chapter provides a detailed look at the technology you need to successfully leverage process orchestration.

We'll start by exploring enterprise architecture and showing how process orchestration can be the glitter glue for business capabilities to form end-to-end processes. We'll also take a quick look at modern architectural styles, like microservices, and see how domain-driven design (DDD) influences all of this.

Next, we'll examine the tool stack you need to achieve end-to-end process orchestration – most prominently, the process orchestration platform. We will discuss the technical capabilities it brings and what additional capabilities you will need around it. As the whole automation software market is quite dynamic and includes many subcategories, we'll also provide an overview of adjacent tool categories, such as robotic process automation tools, and explain how they relate to process orchestration.

The primary goal of this chapter is to equip you with the knowledge to sketch out your own architecture and tool stack.

Implementing Your Business Architecture

Let's quickly recap the process for implementing a business architecture, as introduced in "Building a Business Architecture to Realize Digitalization and Automation Benefits". First, we zoom in on one business area (Level 1), pick a customer journey, and model value streams that show how we can fulfill the customer journey (Level 2). Next, we define the strategic end-to-end processes that need to be completed along the way (Level 3) and the business capabilities the organization needs to have in order to complete those processes, and thus the value streams as a whole (Level 4).

We often use the illustration in Figure 3.1 to communicate this vision.

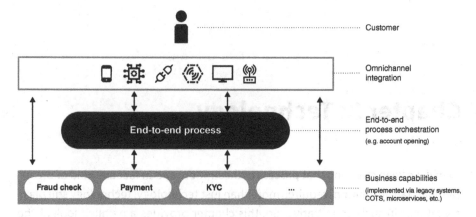

Figure 3.1 High-level business architecture diagram.

You can see that the end-to-end process is an elevated concept in this drawing, even if it might be a business capability at the same time (and should therefore be additionally visualized on that layer). You might recall this discussion from "Strategic End-to-End Processes", in Chapter 1, page 42. We actually take a pragmatic route here and use this visualization to emphasize the important role of end-to-end processes and their relationship to customer journeys, and skip the business capability covering the end-to-end process for simplicity. If you don't like it, don't use it, and just talk about business capabilities instead; but if you want to promote the idea of end-to-end processes as first-class citizens it might help you. In reality, both approaches are valid – they're just different perspectives on the same reality – and it may be wise to adjust your communication strategy to the audience you are talking to.

As we discussed in "Chapter 1: Vision", the business architecture is powerful for various reasons. One is that concentrating on end-to-end customer journeys ensures that you don't get lost in internal details that don't matter to your customers. Another is that this approach allows for modularity and flexibility, so you can easily adjust how your processes work, add new requirements, and automate and improve them step by step. It also allows you to introduce completely new business models or customer journeys as needed.

Implementing Business Capabilities

Business capabilities (see "Business Capabilities") refer to business functions within your domain. For example, doing a fraud check, verifying an address, or billing a service are business capabilities. Business capabilities describe what can be done in business terms. In other words, they describe the *job to be done*[1], meaning the required business outcome, independent of the implementation details. This abstraction is precisely what makes thinking in terms of capabilities so powerful.

That said, of course, every business capability needs to be implemented somehow. There are different ways to do this, as shown in Figure 3.2.

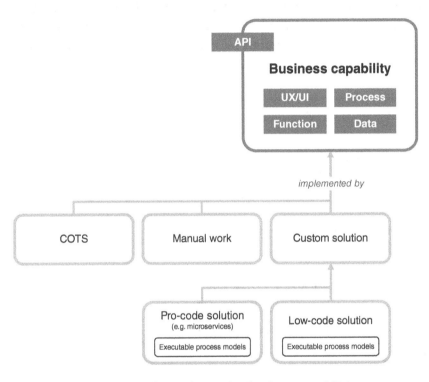

Figure 3.2 Different options for implementing business capabilities.

One option is to purchase a commercial off-the-shelf (COTS) solution, to be used either on premises or in the cloud as SaaS. For easy integration the capability should offer an API, typically using HTTP/REST or messaging protocols, depending on the standards defined in your organization (for some legacy systems, RPA is used to make the system invokable). Alternatively, a capability could be supplied by humans working manually on tasks; then, your API might simply mean that you define what teams need to receive what information when and how (e.g. an email containing all the required customer information as bullet points). A third possibility is to develop custom solutions. These solutions might be software applications or microservices, or you might leverage low-code tools to implement simple capabilities. In any event,

Technology 139

it is likely that your business capabilities will also contain business processes, or at least some long-running integration processes (as introduced in "Understanding Process Types That Can Be Orchestrated"), that need to be orchestrated. That means you will probably use process orchestration technology to implement those business capabilities.

To give an example, let's look at the billing capability of a company required to collect money. This can be implemented via an off-the-shelf ERP system, an email to your accounting team, or a dedicated microservice you developed in-house. In the case of a microservice, the billing process will most probably be expressed as executable BPMN (see Figure 3.3).

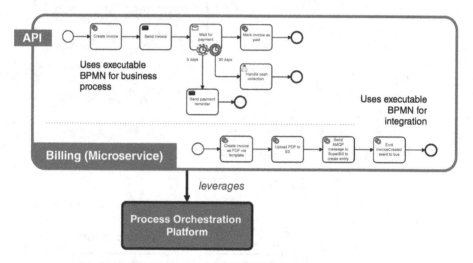

Figure 3.3 When implementing a business capability as a microservice, you might leverage process orchestration for business or integration processes.

Technical Capabilities, Platforms, and Enabling Technologies

For digital success, you need to be able to implement business capabilities efficiently on a broad scale across the enterprise. There are two key requirements for this:

1. You need to be able to leverage SaaS services for capabilities where you don't differentiate. This is easier said than done as many organizations have legacy systems implementing functionality that could easily be handled by SaaS services nowadays. Ripping out and replacing these systems is not a simple process, but it is one where process orchestration can help (as we explained

in "Technical Use Cases of Process Orchestration"). That said, the biggest roadblock here is often the mindset of people that don't embrace change.

2. You need to provide technical capabilities to the organization that teams can leverage to efficiently implement their applications, microservices, functions, or whatever the deliverable is that you favor in your organization. This will reduce the delivery teams' cognitive load and make them faster, more efficient, and able to produce higher-quality outputs. The most efficient and scalable way to achieve this is to provide technical capabilities as a service internally (Figure 3.4).

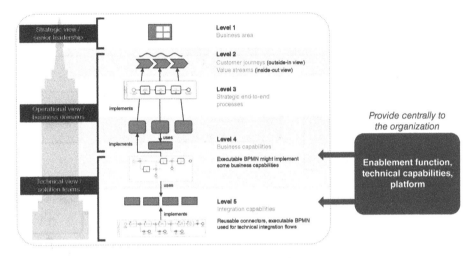

Figure 3.4 You need to provide technical capabilities, platforms, and enablement centrally to efficiently implement the business architecture.

We will dive deeper into questions around team autonomy, federated development, and avoiding bottlenecks later in this chapter, but for now we want to simply acknowledge that it is important to have technical capabilities that enable building applications or services. Those technical capabilities might include tools such as databases, middleware (e.g. Apache Kafka, messaging, API gateways, etc.), platforms (e.g. Camunda), frameworks, and so on. The cloud services that hyperscalers offer are also in this bucket (e.g. the technical capability to store documents, as implemented in AWS S3 or Azure Blob Storage). As with business capabilities, the description of the capability is abstracted from how it is implemented (or provided) and just indicates what purpose it serves.

As discussed in "Zooming in on the Adoption Acceleration Team", technical capabilities should be provided by a shared services team like a center of excellence.

Business Orchestration and Automation Technology

Looking at process orchestration and automation, there is a cluster of technologies that are important to stitch together to effectively build solutions. This is what the analyst firm Gartner called BOAT[2], an acronym for *Business Orchestration and Automation Technology*, and their counterpart Forrester named *automation fabric*[3]. Both analysts' visions are quite close to what we see our customers building, which is sketched in Figure 3.5.

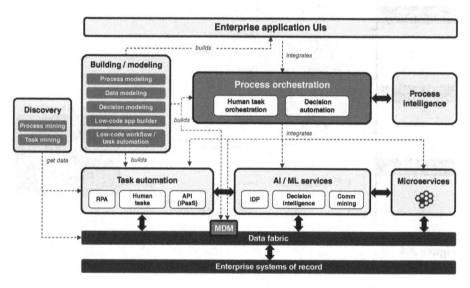

Figure 3.5 Technologies around process orchestration required to digitalize your business.

Starting at the bottom of the illustration, you can see your existing systems of record. The data fabric layer is responsible for making data stored in those systems easily available and accessible to be orchestrated. In that context, Master Data Management (MDM) systems should provide a consistent view of important core business entities like customers or products. This foundation allows you to leverage data in task automation, AI/ML services, and microservices.

Task automation includes RPA and human task management, as well as integration services via API. You can leverage AI-powered services such as Intelligent Document

Processing (IDP) to not only do Optical Character Recognition (OCR) on documents, but also understand their meaning. Decision intelligence and communications mining services can also be useful.

At the heart of this stack is the process orchestration platform, which can integrate with the various services beneath it to orchestrate and automate processes across all the different endpoints. If the services in the layer below are the hands and feet of a human body, the process orchestrator is the brain making them do the right things at the right time.

You'll also need modeling capabilities to build artifacts like process or decision models, low-code applications, and user interfaces. The building of your solution might be informed by process or task-mining tools that can derive information about how the process is currently running from existing log files. AI can, of course, also help you efficiently design all the required models.

Finally, process intelligence makes sure you gain insights into what is going on with your processes, and of course you need a user interface layer to make sure humans can interact with all of it.

In real life, we typically see a best-of-breed approach using different tools to implement all aspects of that map. A real-life customer scenario from a German state bank (Norddeutsche Landesbank) is shown in Figure 3.6.

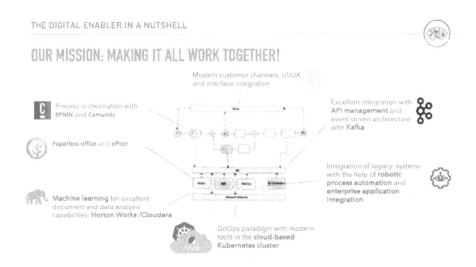

Figure 3.6 Example customer architecture.

Composable vs. Monolithic Platforms

Going one step back, there are actually two primary strategies to define such a process orchestration technology stack:

- A monolithic product that integrates the entire stack.

- A product with composable components.

This decision is not necessarily about choosing between "all-in-one vendors" and "various suppliers," as some vendors offer a complete stack that remains flexible enough to be composable. The key difference is that monolithic products have tightly integrated components, whereas a composable stack features loosely coupled components that can be replaced with products from other vendors.

The strengths of each strategy are clear. A monolithic stack can be easier to handle initially, allowing rapid development of process applications due to preconfigured components that just need assembly. However, using this stack requires proprietary knowledge tailored to it, and technical debt can build up due to its lack of flexibility.

In contrast, a composable stack typically offers more flexibility, enabling the development of process applications that better meet individual needs. The components in a composable stack are optimized for their specific use cases (e.g. a BPMN modeling tool for process modeling), often outperforming their counterparts in a monolithic stack that tries to do everything but may do nothing particularly well. Additionally, this approach allows for a more adaptable project methodology, making it easy for you to integrate process models into your software engineering approach and existing best practices around software deployment (e.g. CI/CD). Thus, a composable stack integrates seamlessly into your organization's IT infrastructure.

Typically, the philosophies of the respective vendors also differ. Vendors of monolithic stacks often promote the idea of eliminating the need for software developers, while vendors of composable stacks aim to actively involve developers in process automation. This results in open architectures, robust software development kits (SDKs), and developer-focused documentation.

It might not come as a surprise to you that we are big fans of composable stacks, as it is impossible to imagine running your core processes without pro-code developers. As visualized in Figure 3.7, while those stacks typically include

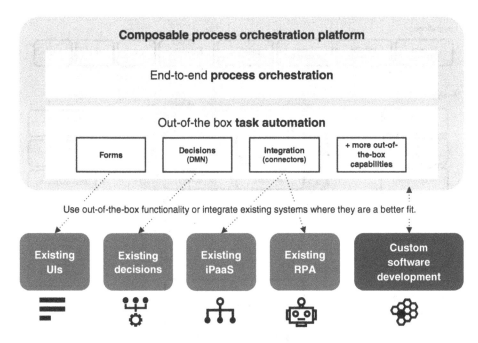

Figure 3.7 Composable platforms are integrated, yet flexible.

integrated components for the important capabilities, they are flexible enough that you can easily replace any component, either with more powerful third-party components or, more often, with tools that are already used and established in-house.

Components Required for Process Orchestration

Going one level deeper, Figure 3.8 shows an overview of the different components you may need to support your process orchestration platform itself. It groups them into six categories: the core process orchestration capability, accelerators, integrations, analytics, InfoSec, and DevOps.

You'll rarely need *all* of these components, and typically you'll define a roadmap to fill in certain areas iteratively. For example, business intelligence (BI) integration can come at a later stage, and encryption might not be important in your first processes if they don't include sensitive data. That said, let's take a look at the various supporting components in each category that might be required.

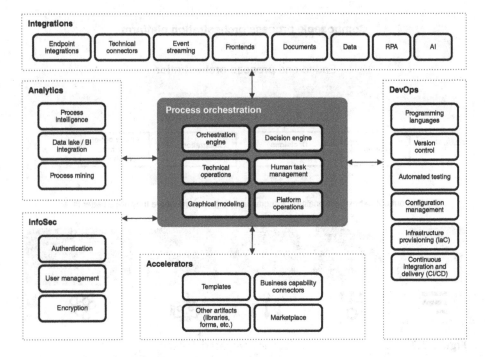

Figure 3.8 Components required for process orchestration.

The Core Process Orchestration Capability

The process orchestration capability is supported by several concrete components. We'll use the platform we know best (Camunda) as an example, but similar tools should provide comparable components:

- **Process orchestration engine (aka workflow engine):** This is the heart of the platform. It is responsible for defining, managing, and executing the sequence of tasks or steps that constitute the automated process. It ensures that tasks are executed in the correct order and handles dependencies between different steps. In Camunda, this engine is called Zeebe.

- **Decision engine:** Most orchestration platforms can also execute decision logic in the form of decision tables in DMN, which allows decisions to be automated based on predefined rules and conditions. This is especially useful for scenarios where the automation needs to adapt to changing circumstances or business people want to understand why certain decisions are being made. In Camunda, the decision engine is integrated into Zeebe.

- **Human task management:** As processes need to be able to involve people, they also need a way to manage human tasks. In Camunda, this comes in two layers. First, the task management is headless API-based functionality, so that you can query and filter all currently open tasks to show them in your own UI, for example. You can also react to events to push tasks to other systems where they are managed. Second, Camunda provides a Tasklist application[4] and forms[5], which can be used to involve people in processes. The forms can also be embedded in custom UIs using form-js[6]. If you need to build more complex UIs, you will need to connect additional UI technology.

- **Technical operations:** The platform provides tooling to discover, analyze, and solve problems related to process execution. In the case of Camunda, that's Operate[7]. Imagine there is a problem with the service call to the CRM system. You first need monitoring that will recognize that problem, e.g., because incidents are piling up. You will also want to send alerts or integrate with your existing application performance monitoring (APM) tool, so the right person gets notified quickly. In addition to alerting, the tool should support root cause analysis to help you understand the problem at hand (say, if some endpoint URL has changed) and fix the issue (for example, by updating a configuration option and triggering a retry) – and it should be able to operate at scale, because there may be a large number of affected process instances. Developers can also use these tools to play around during development.

- **Platform provisioning:** Platforms need to provide easy ways to be provisioned and operated. Nowadays, this typically means leveraging Kubernetes. Camunda provides Helm charts and a Kubernetes operator to make the most of the environment, but there are also simple ZIP files allowing you to run the platform in other environments.

- **Graphical modeling:** Good BPMN modeling tools are essential to initially design process or decision models, and to add all the necessary details to make them executable. They're typically ubiquitous in the organization and used by a wide variety of stakeholders, from business people to software developers. Good graphical modeling tools also provide collaboration features for discussing or sharing models. Ideally, those tools are provided as web applications so they're easily accessible to a large range of people. Camunda offers both a desktop modeler and a web-based modeler[8] to provide maximum flexibility, as (for example) developers might prefer a tool that works on local files.

Technology 147

Accelerators

In addition to the core platform, accelerators are important to make projects faster. Some of these are provided out of the box by the platform vendor or its community, but accelerators can also be organization-specific, built for example by the AAT (see "The Adoption Acceleration Team (AAT)"). Typical types of accelerators include:

- **Templates:** There are many possible valuable templates. First and foremost, you might find project templates that ease the task of setting up a solution (e.g. a Maven Archetype or a template project that can be copied and serve as the basis for Java-based solutions). Experience shows that this simple technique can help both to avoid blank paper syndrome with projects and to ensure that company standards are met. As part of this effort, you might also have supporting frameworks or libraries that help with harmonization or standardization (e.g. build tools, Maven parent POMs, Maven BOMs, etc.). Other useful templates might include installation scripts, sample frontends, and even example projects or reference architectures for typical problems. The templates are commonly provided by the AAT and customized to your organization, or you can use templates from your vendor as a basis.

- **Connectors:** Connectors are a great way to accelerate projects, as they bundle glue code for integration in a reusable way. Technical protocol connectors (e.g. for REST or Apache Kafka) allow you to productively implement connectivity, but more powerful are business connectors that have a high level of abstraction in the form of business capabilities. For example, you might have a "Fraud Check Connector" that lets your business people configure relevant inputs in the process model, hiding all the technical details (e.g. that technically it's a REST call underneath).

  Increasing the level of abstraction for a connector allows more roles to use that connector in process models. This also enables some level of low code for some processes, which in turn increases flexibility, as such processes can be more easily understood and changed. You can think of it as separating the coded parts (the connector) from the domain logic (the process). The connectors might be provided by the AAT, and federated solution projects can simply use them as needed.

  The abstraction of connectors can also form a hierarchy, as the example in Figure 3.9 shows. The REST connector is a basic protocol connector. Alongside

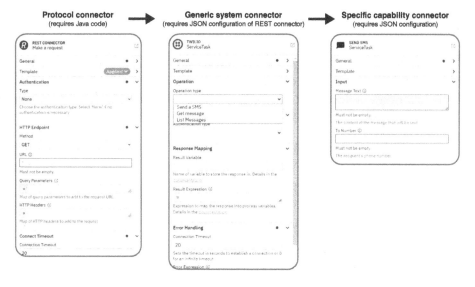

Figure 3.9 Connectors with different levels of abstraction.

this is a generic Twilio connector that uses REST underneath. Finally, there's a connector to send a text (aka SMS), reduced to only the configuration fields important to business stakeholders; in the background, this connector uses Twilio, which technically means it uses REST.

- **Marketplace or registry:** If you have templates and connectors, you have to make sure other people can find them. A tool that provides a searchable inventory is very helpful here: as experience shows, a normal Wiki can quickly get overwhelmed with the amount of content. In the case of Camunda, for example, there is a Marketplace component[9] that is directly integrated with the modeler, so that you can easily search for and use connectors. This can also be operated privately for your organization.

- **Other artifacts:** Organizations can provide further accelerators for all of the other platform components we mention in this chapter, ranging from process endpoints (e.g. user task list integrations or glue code for software endpoints) to DevOps tools (e.g. templates for CI/CD pipelines) or InfoSec integrations (e.g. SSO/LDAP connections). Considering the needs of your delivery teams and providing the right tools through your AAT can get you a long way in improving time to value. You can also leverage best practices like inner-sourcing[10] to share and reuse artifacts created by delivery teams and make them accessible to others.

Integrations

Some capabilities that are interwoven with process orchestration are normally provided by other tools. A good example is that many processes need to store and manipulate data or documents stored in databases or document stores. Common adjacent tool categories include:

- **Endpoint integration APIs and connectors:** The automation solution itself needs to provide an API, but it must also integrate with other systems via their APIs, which we typically call endpoints. Connectors can be provided for this, but it's crucial that the platform is flexible enough to integrate other technologies too, for example, by using normal programming code (say, Java).

- **Event buses or streaming platforms:** Many big organizations use event streaming technology within their enterprise architecture (e.g. Apache Kafka or AWS Kinesis). It's vital to connect those platforms with process orchestration, because events from a stream might influence processes, and certain steps in a process might lead to new events being emitted. Technically, this is often easy to do, and out-of-the-box connectors might already do the trick. Otherwise, some glue code can be developed. The goal is that you can easily react to events in your processes and emit new events from your processes (Figure 3.10).

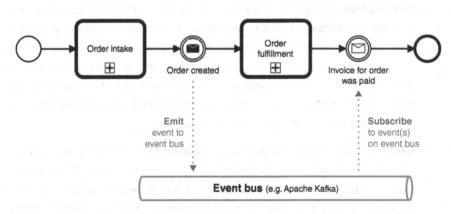

Figure 3.10 Connecting your process orchestration platform with your event bus.

- **Frontends and end user interfaces:** The user interface that can be used by external users (customers) or internal users (e.g. clerks) is the frontend of the automation solution, providing a way for users to interact with and control the automation process. There is often a big difference between customer-facing UIs and internal ones. Sometimes, the UI is a command-line interface (CLI). Tasklist applications (also known as todo lists), as mentioned previously, can also be part of a custom frontend. Generally speaking, there's a lot of flexibility here: You can use your organization's existing task management software, so that your clerks can keep working with the interface they already use now, or you can create new, custom frontends in any UI technology, either by leveraging typical UI development frameworks (like React.js, Angular, or Vue.js) or by using a low-code UI builder.

- **Data:** Depending on the nature of the automation, a database or other data storage component may be required to store and retrieve information during the execution of the automated process. The process orchestrator persists only minimal data along with process instances, like references or control data that is required to decide about the orchestration flow (see Camunda's best practice guide to handling data in processes[11] for more on this topic). Real domain data needs to be stored outside of the orchestration engine. For that, a database is typically run next to the orchestration engine.

- **Documents:** Many processes interact with documents. The documents may be the driving force (e.g. customer application forms), or they may be summarizing the results (e.g. a case folder), or a mix of both. Documents, like data, should be stored in appropriate systems (a document management system, AWS S3, SharePoint, etc.) and referenced from the process. Still, they often need to be shown on the frontend to people working with the process.

- **RPA:** Robotic Process Automation is often mixed up with process orchestration. But as we touched on earlier in this book, RPA is actually about task automation; that is, automating the execution of a single task in an application that does not provide a proper API. As such, RPA can very well be combined with process orchestration, as the orchestrator will then coordinate the overall process and delegate to RPA for specific tasks. This design also allows you to evolve solutions from manual work to RPA-based automation to true API-led integration – a journey nicely described by Deutsche Telekom[12] at Camunda-Con Live 2020 (Figure 3.11).

- **AI:** Artificial intelligence, and especially generative AI, will have a huge impact on processes of all sorts in the coming years. As we mentioned in "Enabling Artificial Intelligence", we believe that for many use cases AI can best be introduced through orchestration. The clarity around the process flow makes it

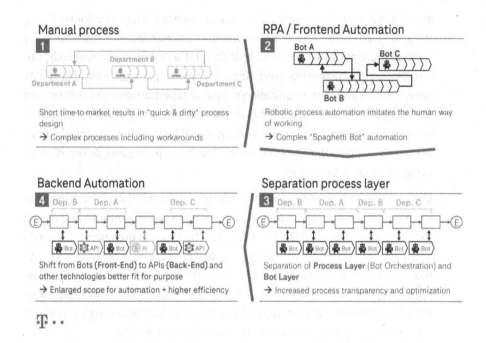

Figure 3.11 Deutsche Telekom's journey from manual process to RPA to orchestrated bots to true API-based automation.

easy to add new AI-based tasks (AI agents) and replace existing ones with AI, perhaps using A/B testing. Technically, the use of AI as an endpoint in a process just requires an API call to the AI platform. We will dive deeper into the topic in the next section "Operationalizing AI for Autonomous Orchestration with Guardrails".

Analytics

Having access to process data is essential for process orchestration because it enables performance monitoring and continuous improvement and provides your business with a real-time view of how your processes are performing. Useful tools in this category include:

- **Process intelligence solutions:** As well as monitoring technical operations and fixing problems that occur at runtime, business stakeholders also need to monitor and improve processes. These people are typically interested in the overall process performance and its business impact. They might also want notifications around performance indicators like cycle times or waiting time; for example, they need to be notified if a process instance is taking too long and thus will miss its SLA.

To optimize the overall process, analytics capabilities can provide a clear view of which process paths are used most often, which paths are slow, which data conditions often lead to cancellations, and so forth. This information can be derived from the audit data that a workflow engine stores when executing process instances.

Process intelligence tooling (e.g. Camunda Optimize[13]) has a clear business process focus and allows the use of graphical process models for everything from analysis to communication.

- **Business intelligence tools:** Most organizations also have generic business intelligence capabilities in use, often centered around data warehouse (DWH), BI, or data lake tooling. The difference from process intelligence is the focus on looking at all data, including object data and events. It is of course also interesting to push audit data from the process orchestration platform to those tools, so it can be put into the context of all the other data; e.g. if you want to cross-reference your process data with financial data to calculate the cost per process instance. If you are interested in how this can be achieved in the context of Camunda, please refer to the best practice guide to reporting about processes[14].

- **Process mining tools:** Process mining is a data-driven methodology that involves the analysis of event logs from information systems to gain insights into executing business processes that were not explicitly visible before. By visualizing the actual paths, deviations, and bottlenecks within processes, process mining can help you identify inefficiencies or problems as well as areas where there is automation potential.

In theory, process mining could serve as a great starting point for process orchestration initiatives. In practice, we don't see that happening often, perhaps because process mining typically looks at log files from core systems like ERP systems to get an overview of how the process is working, but is not wired with applications at runtime. Process mining is also applied by different groups in an organization and rarely connected to automation initiatives. Process tracking, as described in "Derisking Your Start with Process Tracking", might be a better approach to use as a basis for automating processes.

Technology   153

InfoSec

When introducing process orchestration within an organization, ensuring robust information security is paramount. Process orchestration involves coordinating and managing multiple processes and workflows across various systems and departments, which can introduce new security challenges. At the same time, looking at processes holistically provides a great opportunity to understand the associated risks and assess them by examining the CIA triad: confidentiality, integrity, and availability. This can happen very early in the requirements and design phase, making sure security is built in right from the start.

This section outlines key InfoSec considerations to address during planning and implementation of process orchestration:

- **Access control and authentication:** You need to establish clear roles and permissions for users involved in process orchestration. Different roles may require different levels of access to data and system functions. Implement role-based access control (RBAC) to enforce these permissions and minimize unnecessary access. There will be a difference between end users (e.g. clerks) participating in human tasks, developers, operators, and business executives. You should also use strong authentication methods, such as multifactor authentication (MFA), to guarantee that only authorized personnel can access the orchestration system. Ensure that credentials are managed securely and are not shared or stored inappropriately. Keep in mind that an executable process entering data in a system might have elevated privileges compared to a human entering the same data in the system.

- **Data protection:** Encrypt sensitive data both in transit and at rest. This ensures that data exchanged between orchestrated systems remains confidential and protected from unauthorized access. Apply data minimization principles to collect and process only the data necessary for orchestration tasks. This is also known as **privacy by design** – having a clever data design that can perhaps avoid putting sensitive data into the process orchestration platform in the first place.

- **System integration and interfaces:** When integrating with other systems through APIs, ensure that these APIs are secure. Use secure coding practices, authenticate API requests, and validate inputs to prevent vulnerabilities such as injection attacks. You should also perform server-side validation of any API inputs to make sure that no malicious payloads can be inserted.

- **Compliance and regulatory requirements:** Ensure that the process orchestration platform complies with relevant industry standards and regulations, such as ISO/IEC 27001, SOC 2, or TISAX level 2. Implement policies and controls to meet these requirements and regularly review compliance status.

In addition, there are many generic requirements that apply for any type of automation solution within your organization – including, of course, the process orchestration solutions. As our experience shows that these are not at the front of everybody's mind, we'll briefly repeat them here:

- **Security by design:** Design the solutions built with the process orchestration platform with security in mind from the outset. Incorporate security features and controls into the architecture to address potential threats and vulnerabilities. Adopt a secure-by-design approach that includes ongoing evaluation and enhancement of security measures as part of the orchestration lifecycle. Stay informed about emerging threats and update security practices accordingly.

- **Third-party risk management:** Assess the security posture of third-party systems and services that interact with your orchestration platform. Ensure that any external systems comply with your organization's security standards and have appropriate security controls in place.

- **Audit and monitoring:** Leverage the logging and monitoring capabilities of the process orchestration platform. Track access, changes to, and interactions with sensitive data to detect and respond to suspicious activities promptly.

- **Regular audits:** Conduct regular security audits and reviews of the orchestration system. Evaluate the effectiveness of existing security controls and identify potential vulnerabilities or areas for improvement.

- **Business continuity practice:** Develop and maintain an incident response plan tailored to the process orchestration environment. This plan should include procedures for detecting, reporting, and mitigating security and other incidents. Also ensure that there is a clear process for coordinating responses to those incidents. This includes communication protocols and responsibilities for internal teams and external stakeholders.

- **Documentation and training:** Maintain thorough documentation of security policies, procedures, and controls related to process orchestration. Provide training for employees on security best practices and the specific security measures in place for the orchestration system.

Technology

By addressing these security considerations, organizations can better safeguard their orchestrated processes, protect sensitive information, and mitigate potential security risks. Ensuring that these aspects are thoroughly reviewed and integrated into the orchestration strategy will contribute to a more secure and resilient organizational infrastructure.

DevOps

As most process orchestration solutions are software projects too, you also need to take DevOps practices into account. Good process orchestration tools allow you to keep using the best practices you want to use anyway, thereby keeping developers in their comfort zone and ensuring they don't have to learn (many) new skills. Important aspects to consider here are:

- **Programming language and environment:** For any reasonably complex automations, you will need to write some code or scripts. The platform should allow your developers to code in the language they are familiar with. This is one of Camunda's superpowers, as it can easily be integrated into different programming stacks (Java, Spring, .NET, NodeJS, etc.).

- **Automated testing:** If the processes you automate are critical, you need automated tests. This is especially important for complex or regulated processes. Test cases will execute a defined set of scenarios and check if their results are as expected. Along the way, they will mock system calls and input data or human decisions. It's best to automate these test cases so that you can run them as part of your CI pipeline. This allows you to verify that any changes you make are not breaking existing functionality (this is called *regression testing*). Overall, this leads to much more stable solutions, which in turn gives your developers the confidence to make changes. If you are interested in more technical detail, you can find more information on tests in Camunda's best practice guide to testing process definitions[15].

- **Configuration management:** Process solutions typically require many configuration parameters. One prime example is the endpoint URLs for systems you integrate, which will be different in test, integration, and production environments. Ideally, your solution only uses parameters that can be set during deployment. This is a well-known concept in software engineering, and the Spring framework, for example, has abstractions to grab properties from various places (property files, configuration servers, environment variables, etc.).

- **Infrastructure provisioning:** Infrastructure as code (IaC)[16] is a common way to manage your various systems, from test to integration to production, via code. The installation process itself is then automated via scripts. This allows you to have clearly defined environments that can easily be reproduced. Changes in the setup of those systems are versioned, so they can be easily understood or rolled back in the event of problems.

- **Continuous integration and deployment:** CI/CD practices and tools enable software development teams to automate the process of integrating code changes made in a shared source code repository (continuous integration) and then automatically deploying those changes to production environments (continuous deployment or continuous delivery). This is typically done by so-called *pipelines* in tools like Jenkins or GitHub.

  CI/CD makes sure software can always be integrated and run. As part of that, it runs test cases with every build to make sure nothing has broken. A CI/CD pipeline can also deploy software, even if the individual making the changes does not know how to or is not allowed to integrate or deploy changes. CI/CD pipelines are essential for process orchestration solutions as well, as you will see when we talk about the process lifecycle in "The Software Development Lifecycle and Model Roundtrips".

Operationalizing AI for Autonomous Orchestration with Guardrails

In the previous section and the section "Enabling Artificial Intelligence", we briefly touched on Artificial Intelligence. AI (which we're using as an umbrella term encompassing generative AI, large language models, and related concepts, for the sake of simplicity) has been around for a while and captured business and public discourse in different waves – but since the launch of ChatGPT in late 2022, which attracted more than 100 million users in only two months, it has taken the world (and the imagination of CEOs) by storm. Alas, two years later we are beginning to see signs of the beginning of a trough of disillusionment, to borrow a term from Gartner's Hype Cycle[17], which describes the adoption curve of new technologies. For example, tech analyst Benedict Evans points out[18] that very few AI use cases make it from pilot to deployment – a phenomenon *The Economist*[19] cheekily labels *pilotitis*.

Technology

And yet, any business person who has ever used ChatGPT undoubtedly has sensed the tremendous potential this technology can provide when applied properly in your enterprise architecture and to your value streams. This has prompted many executives to spring into action, out of fear of missing out and losing competitive advantages. However, AI is certainly an incredibly powerful tool, and like with any such tool, it can both create and destroy value in the blink of an eye. Thus, using it is not just a matter of blindly taking action, but taking the *right* actions (and avoiding the wrong ones). Yet, how can you ensure you take the right actions, when technological developments happen so rapidly and when it's hard to predict how exactly AI will be operationalized in your enterprise?

Research from BCG[20] provides a pointer, highlighting that leaders in AI adoption, among other things, focus on "core business processes and support functions, seeking to deploy AI for productivity, to reshape processes and functions." This indicates the need for a process architecture that allows for adaptability and organizational resilience, which you can achieve through enterprise process orchestration. Such an architecture will allow you to realize value today, for example, by gradually integrating AI tools as endpoints into your processes, and it will ensure you're ready for tomorrow's technology innovations, which you will also be able to plug into your value streams.

Let's sketch out some concrete scenarios of how AI can be operationalized in your value streams in the form of so-called autonomous AI agents and agentic AI. We'll start by defining these terms:

- **AI agent:** An AI system trained to take decisions or carry out actions autonomously (or at least semi-autonomously). Think of it as an endpoint in a process that performs a certain task. An example could be an agent that decides on its own whether to issue a new insurance policy.

- **Agentic AI:** An autonomous system that accomplishes complex tasks on its own, possibly leveraging a set of AI agents.

In the taxonomy used in this book, using an AI agent is simply another form of task automation, because for the overall end-to-end processes it does not matter if a human or AI agent performs a specific task.

Agentic AI typically refers to an agent that controls other AI agents to carry out a more complex task. You could say that this agent orchestrates the task. Doing this in a naive way would simply mean letting it invent its own spaghetti integration – there is no visibility into the process, no governance, and no control. While this approach might be acceptable for simple processes (green in our categorization from "A Useful Categorization of Use Cases"), it is not the way to go for complex end-to-end processes, where you have a need for auditability and adaptability, among other things.

To achieve that, process orchestration allows you to orchestrate whatever agents you have (e.g. for credit scoring or fraud detection) alongside humans and other endpoints, like system integrations. This way, you can still control the end-to-end process while leveraging AI agents wherever they have the most business impact.

Ideally, your process orchestration platform provides the possibility for some level of flexibility in processes, so that agents can decide which tasks to perform. (BPMN, for example, allows for this flexibility by using an ad hoc subprocess, as shown in Figure 3.12.) In this process, an AI agent would decide which tasks needed to be performed for claim investigation, such as an advanced fraud check or a separate policy coverage verification. The agent could also decide to reject the claim, in which case this decision would need to be reviewed by a human. So this model allows an AI agent to orchestrate AI agents, but within clear guardrails, pulling a human into the loop whenever useful (or if the agents hit an exception).

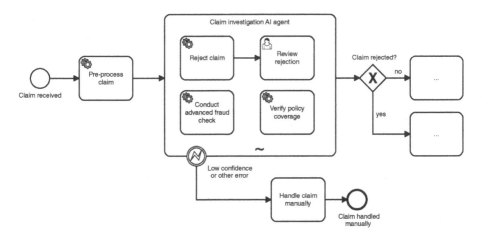

Figure 3.12 Operationalizing agentic AI with BPMN.

Including AI agents as a tool in your task automation toolkit is a pragmatic and highly effective approach. It allows for flexibility during runtime while maintaining control over the end-to-end orchestration logic, enabling you to leverage AI for your processes to generate value without compromising your enterprise architecture. In other words, rather than blindly applying AI to a chaotic spaghetti system and hoping for miracles, you're following a thoughtful, strategic plan to gradually uplevel your processes. This approach not only future-proofs your architecture but also ensures that AI delivers tangible value in your value streams right from the start.

Providing a Process Orchestration Capability to Your Organization

You know by now that the technologies for process orchestration are best made available to your organization by a shared services team or AAT, so that not every project needs to reinvent the wheel and delivery teams don't find themselves drowning in technology that needs to be sorted out. But what does it really take to provide a successful internal platform? Let's take a look at a few key factors.

Enterprise vs. Solution Scope

First, you need to think consciously about the scope of your capabilities. Typically, **the same technical capabilities are used by many development teams** in the organization, as technology is mostly domain-agnostic. The same process orchestration platform can very well be used for order fulfillment, billing, and payments, for example. Other typical examples are databases, document stores, and container orchestrators (like OpenShift). Those technical capabilities are owned by IT and provided as a service to the organization, supported by central CoEs or platform teams. In other words, they have enterprise scope.

Of course, there are exceptions to every rule, so there may be some technical capabilities that are very specifically tied to one domain and as such will only be implemented in a local solution scope. Specific large language models (LLMs) used in the context of AI, such as for fraud detection, are a good example. In this case, the technical capability might directly implement a business capability and not be reused anywhere else (even if your organization has a central enabling team focused on LLMs and AI).

In contrast, **business capabilities are implemented for the business domains**, and they should be **owned by the business departments** (solution scope). Commonly,

160 Enterprise Process Orchestration

there is still a group in IT that owns the application or microservice that implements a business capability. While this is fine, there should be a clear owner on the business side collaborating closely with IT, as IT cannot manage requirements for those capabilities on its own (in contrast to technical capabilities, where this is feasible). Having the right people involved and good collaboration is key for successful digitalization efforts.

Providing a technical capability around process orchestration as a centralized platform will help you in delivering more business capabilities that leverage process orchestration. In Figure 3.13, we depict the different scopes and owners involved in building business capabilities as process solutions, where delivery teams can leverage the technical capability of process orchestration.

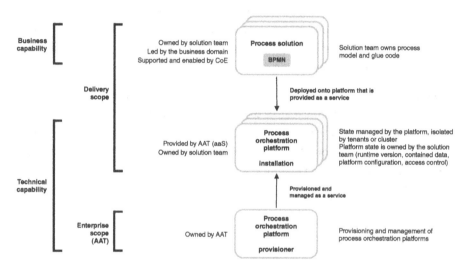

Figure 3.13 Various scopes and owners of technical and business capabilities.

A specific challenge with end-to-end processes is that they **cross domain boundaries**, making establishing clear ownership hard. One process platform leader at a global bank that had been using process orchestration for several years told us that if they could go back and do only one thing differently, they would have assigned clear ownership to every process (on a business and technical implementation level) and established a procedure to update that ownership, even in the case of reorganizations.

Process ownership is almost always a little void that needs to be managed properly. Otherwise, you can find yourself in a situation where you have an important business capability that nobody owns, meaning nobody can make changes or improvements.

If you follow the business architecture sketched out in this book ("Building a Business Architecture to Realize Digitalization and Automation Benefits"), you will not fall into this trap.

Platform Thinking

The process orchestration technologies described in this chapter can be made accessible to delivery teams in the form of an internal platform. In the realm of modern organizational design, platforms are seen as indispensable to reduce cognitive load for development teams and improve time to value (a concept underscored by the previously mentioned *Team Topologies* book[21]). Platforms are the foundational infrastructure required by high-performing teams that produce business value. By providing a common ground for teams to build upon, they promote standardization, reduce friction, and foster a culture of shared responsibility. In short: A platform can be a game changer for automating more with less.

However, a lot of developers we speak with don't have positive associations with the concept of a platform, because of experience with inflexible and proprietary solutions of the past. We will address this in "Why Does This Work Now if SOA Failed a Decade Ago?", but before diving into the challenges of the past, we first want to point out what makes a good platform. A good read on this is Evan Bottcher's article "What I Talk About When I Talk About Platforms,"[22] on Martin Fowler's blog. According to Evan:

> *A digital platform is a foundation of self-service APIs, tools, services, knowledge and support which are arranged as a compelling internal product. Autonomous delivery teams can make use of the platform to deliver product features at a higher pace, with reduced coordination.*

Please keep the following key characteristics of a good platform in mind when you create your own internal offering:

- **Self-service:** A good platform can be used in a self-service way by delivery teams. The goal is to avoid what Evan calls *backlog coupling*, where the delivery team needs to raise tickets with the platform that have to be prioritized properly so as not to hinder the delivery team's progress.

- **Product orientation:** Seeing the platform as a product, with proper product management, is also very important to make sure the platform serves the most important user needs (the users are the internal delivery teams!), but at the same time is not overengineered.

- **Compelling to use:** A platform should provide great support that delivery teams are happy to use, because it solves a problem for them that would be hard to solve otherwise. Evaluating technology for process orchestration and automation, setting it up, and defining your solution architecture is hard work – most delivery teams are happy to just follow the recommended way of doing things, if that path is properly described. This is an approach we've seen at many companies; Spotify describes them as golden paths[23] and Twilio and Netflix as paved paths[24]. Teams in those organizations do not have to make use of the provided platform, but they're responsible for the costs of maintaining their own alternatives.

- **Flexible:** A platform should not enforce an inflexible way of working. Teams might need to configure the platform in a specific way, or extend it; they should be able to do whatever is necessary so that the platform is an actual help, not an obstacle to use.

- **Easy to get started:** In addition to self-service capabilities, you should provide users with additional help to get started with the platform, like tutorials, guides, examples, or templates. This content also needs to be maintained and evolved, which is typically done by the AAT.

- **Rich community:** The platform should have a rich internal community, backed by the international communities around core products used in the platform. This also means that the platform should use out-of-the-box functionality of the core components whenever possible, to make sure users can find help not only via internal resources but also with a simple web search.

- **Secure and compliant:** A core advantage of having your own platform is that you can make sure you meet all important security and compliance requirements. This can help pass regulatory checks.

- **Operated professionally:** For wide acceptance internally, the platform must, of course, work properly.

- **Up-to-date and maintained:** The underlying software components must all be kept up-to-date. It's better to keep the scope of your platform minimal and invest resources in maintenance than to have many features that are half-baked. For example, you should prioritize keeping your Camunda version up-to-date over adding more features around Camunda, as this is typically more mission-critical in the long run.

In his article, Evan describes the responsibilities of the solution (or application) teams and the platform team as follows:

> Application teams build, deploy, monitor, and are on call for the application components and application infrastructure that they provision and deploy on the platform. Platform teams build, deploy, monitor, and are on call for the platform components and underlying platform infrastructure.
>
> The platform team ideally doesn't even know what applications are running on the platform, they are only responsible for the availability of the platform services themselves.

Another good take on this is the article "Run Your Platform Like a Business Within a Business"[25] by Rosalind Radcliffe et al.; it highlights the significance of treating internal platforms as products and developers as customers, emphasizing principles such as development, marketing, sales, delivery, and support to ensure successful adoption and utilization within organizations.

One final important thought we want to call out with regard to building your platform is raised in the article "What Is Platform as a Product?"[26] from the authors of the *Team Topologies* book: When building the platform you should collaborate closely with solution projects in the beginning, but switch to a product-as-a-service model as soon as possible (Figure 3.14).

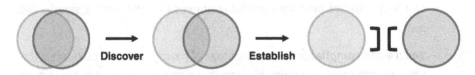

Figure 3.14 Strong collaboration with delivery teams is required for the evolution of the platform, but the platform should then be provided as a service (from "What Is Platform as a Product?").

This is what we also recommend that AATs do: Participate in the early projects until you've learned enough to part ways, then evolve into a central AAT that enables other projects in the organization.

Modern Process Orchestration Platforms Don't Become a Bottleneck

From real-life projects, we know the concerns around centrally run platforms. Many organizations have had bad experiences with proprietary, monolithic tools in the past. One example is the BPM suites that were popular a decade ago: Such tools were operated centrally, but also required very specific knowledge, so that only a central team could work with them. This meant they frequently turned into bottlenecks on two levels: organizationally, as that one team could not do everything it was asked to do, and technically, as the tool was simply not scalable enough to run the load it was supposed to run.

It's important to understand that we have a totally different situation today, for various reasons:

1. Modern platforms are **scalable** enough to run big workloads.

2. A good multitenant design allows tools to **isolate** teams from each other if they have specific requirements (we'll talk more about this in "Isolation Needs and Multitenancy").

3. A good tool has **backward-compatible** APIs, meaning that when the platform itself is updated, this does not affect the delivery teams using the platform. So, for example, the platform team can install important security patches without disrupting the delivery teams, and delivery teams do not need to worry about the health of the platform.

4. Platform teams focus on enablement, making the tool as **self-service** as possible. This means the delivery teams are not slowed down but rather accelerated by the platform teams.

Thanks to these characteristics, a centrally operated process orchestration platform – done right – does not cause any kind of bottleneck.

Why Does This Work Now if SOA Failed a Decade Ago?

Let's address the other typical concern we hear: Wasn't all of this also one of the core promises of the business process management/service-oriented architecture (BPM/SOA) duo many organizations tried and failed to successfully apply 15 years ago? Why should it work now? What has changed?

The big problem back around 2010 was that the whole idea was very vendor-driven and tool-centric. Big vendors sold SOA platforms, Enterprise Service Bus (ESB) products, BPM suites, service registries, and whatnot. Customers were locked into highly proprietary environments that their technologists could not handle (this was touched on, for example, in Bernd's blog post "The 7 Sins of Workflow"[27] from 2017). At the same time, IT was driving this change without involving the business or changing the culture respective to the way they built software. This led to a situation where organizations kept working the way they had been, but using a more complex tool stack that their developers could not handle. The rest is history.

We have a very different situation today, thanks to developments in the following areas:

- **Agility:** As well as theoretical knowledge, practical applications of agile practices around iterative development, minimum viable products (MVPs), and continuous improvement are everywhere now. Important groundwork like the book *Accelerate*[28] proves that agile practices are essential for companies to survive.

- **DevOps:** DevOps evolved from a set of practices aimed at improving collaboration between development and operations teams into a cultural and organizational movement, emphasizing automation, continuous integration, and continuous delivery for faster and more reliable software delivery. Books like *The Phoenix Project*[29] by Gene Kim, Kevin Behr, and George Spafford helped many people around the globe to understand its value.

- **Best-of-breed:** The tide is turning against big monolithic products and vendors. While to some extent we are seeing proprietary software components again with the big hyperscalers (AWS, Azure, GCP, etc.), companies in general no longer accept proprietary and monolithic stacks for core functionality like process orchestration. Instead, they look for the best solutions available for each specific purpose.

- **Products instead of projects:** A mindset shift has begun among internal development teams around providing reusable assets. The idea is that their software should be treated like a product, and in fact, it should be OK to swap internally provided software with off-the-shelf products or SaaS services if possible. Sometimes, the products developed in-house can even be offered externally as services to third parties. This worldview changes how a team manages its software (distribution, documentation, collecting and prioritizing requirements, etc.). Providing products is a key success factor, and it incentivizes teams to create products their users love to use. The alternative is maintaining a reusable service and being annoyed by users constantly coming up with questions or ideas for improvement that could mean additional work. Mik Kersten's book *From Project to Product*[30] is a good read on this, describing the paradigm shift in software development from project-based thinking to a product-centric approach. Kersten argues that aligning software delivery with business goals and customer needs, focusing on continuous delivery, and adopting value stream thinking are essential for organizations to thrive in the digital age.

- **Microservices and domain-driven design:** The architectural style that enables dividing big, monolithic systems into smaller, independent services has greatly matured over the last decade, with an increased understanding of how to design boundaries that help, rather than just adding technical challenges.

- **SaaS and the cloud:** Leveraging SaaS offerings and moving workloads to the cloud is now happening on a broad scale. While many organizations were still pretty skeptical about this a few years ago, today we're seeing customers in all industries moving to the cloud. This approach makes it much easier to take advantage of new capabilities, be they business or technical, as there is no installation to be done or operations team required. You can use services almost instantly, if there's a sound business case for it. Most organizations are also increasing their maturity on settling legal questions around SaaS to enable teams to adopt these offerings more easily (without compromising on compliance and IT security).

All of those developments combined now allow a way of working that enables the architectural vision sketched out in this book.

And to be fair, looking back, not all BPM and SOA initiatives really failed. We have seen customers achieve great results with that approach, largely by applying a lot of the same ideas and techniques we just mentioned. For example, we've seen organizations with best-of-breed development stacks that had developer-friendly tools like Camunda and Apache Camel integrated, with a working CI/CD pipeline and great internal guidance around service design, domain boundaries, and discovery. Such setups tend to yield highly successful business outcomes.

Technology 167

Chargeback Models

An important consideration when providing a platform and enabling services to the organization is how the spend is distributed to the actual business solutions harvesting the business value. Chargeback models address this need by distributing IT costs back to the business units or teams that consume the resources.

The following four models are commonly used:

- **Sponsored:** Internal teams can use the platform and surrounding services for free. This is easy to set up and allows for rapid adoption of process orchestration. However, this model makes it harder to understand the value of the platform for the individual teams, as they are not forced to do their own ROI calculations to justify effort.

- **Fixed costs:** Teams or departments using the process orchestration platform pay a fixed fee based on historical usage or projected needs. Although simple to implement, this model can lack precision, as actual consumption may vary from the fixed allocation (leading to discrepancies in perceived cost fairness).

- **Usage-based:** Teams or departments are billed based on their actual usage of the process orchestration platform. This may be measured in terms of hardware resources and license costs. This model requires that consumption can be tracked, but it may be possible to do this in a low-effort way, such as by collecting usage numbers yearly.

- **Usage and service-based:** With this model, in addition to the usage-based costs, teams or departments are charged on the basis of services consumed (i.e. consulting hours, training courses, accelerators, etc.). While this certainly allows for a more direct allocation of costs, there are potential pitfalls. Tracking such usage can be complicated and expensive, especially for small projects. Your CoEs might also face pressure to increase the internal billable hours, which means that they are more concerned with full utilization of its services than with pragmatically supporting the internal customers.

In general, we advocate for instituting a pragmatic chargeback model to assign costs accurately based on your organization's policy, to foster a culture of understanding value and accountability. This will also create insights into utilization across departments and encourage stronger alignment between IT and business objectives. Accordingly, establishing a sophisticated chargeback model from the get-go shouldn't be your primary concern when establishing your process orchestration initiative (unless your corporate policy or CFO requires it), but you should think about it when scaling your initiative.

Operating a Process Orchestration Platform

Let's switch gears now and assume you want to run a process orchestration platform in your own organization. This section dives into the practical questions you'll have to answer to do this. While we'll use the Camunda platform as an example to avoid too much theoretical palaver, the main points are also true for other tools.

Running the Platform

Figure 3.15 shows a typical Camunda deployment that can cater for advanced scenarios. To run Camunda itself, you'll ideally use the Camunda SaaS offering. In this case, you don't have to deal with installation and operation of the platform as a whole.

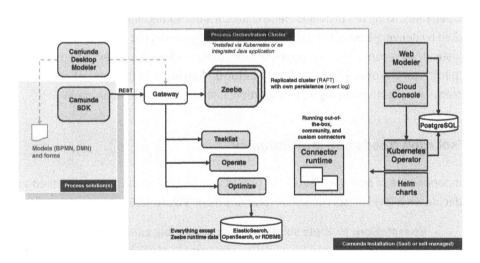

Figure 3.15 A typical Camunda deployment for advanced scenarios.

Unfortunately, however, some organizations still have reservations about using SaaS, even if the business case is compelling. One common concern is around information security and data residency. While understandable, this can be addressed. Camunda, for example, holds ISO 27001, SOC 2, and TISAX level 2 certificates to comfort InfoSec stakeholders. Furthermore, a clever data design can avoid putting sensitive data into the orchestration engine in the first place, as described in "InfoSec".

Another common situation is that development teams are put off by the perceived effort involved in getting approval for a SaaS platform. Those teams may consider it easier to install everything themselves, as this can be organized within IT, in their comfort zone. While this impulse is also understandable, it is typically not a good choice in terms of total cost of ownership (TCO) for the overall organization – and especially if you look at the enterprise scope, where you will end up running many installations, it's shortsighted.

When customers start to really push for SaaS usage in their organization, they're usually positively surprised at how easy it is to get approval in the end. And this is a great deal: Putting in a little effort now will save you a lot of internal maintenance effort on your own installation for years to come. So when you're evaluating the infrastructure for your enterprise initiative, you should definitely give SaaS some consideration, to drive efficiencies and standardization in your operations.

If SaaS is definitely not possible for your situation, you may be able to install a self-managed option. With Camunda, for example, this can be done on Kubernetes (or OpenShift), using the provided Helm charts. It's not something that should be handled by delivery teams, though, as it's not directly connected to business benefits. Instead, we recommend that your AAT sets up the platform – and, even better, operates it – for the delivery teams (see "Platform Thinking"). In this case, the delivery teams are effectively using a SaaS solution, just one that's offered internally.

Isolation Needs and Multitenancy

Independent of how you set up the process orchestration platform, you need to decide what level of isolation your solutions need (Figure 3.16):

- **No isolation:** Multiple solutions work on one big cluster. While this is the simplest setup, it also bears risks – for example, that solutions might define processes with the same identifiers, that operators might get confused by a mix of different processes, or that a noisy neighbor[31] might affect performance.

- **Logical isolation through multitenancy:** To guarantee at least minimal isolation you can set up tenants, so that every solution uses its own tenant. This means they're on the same physical hardware but are isolated logically. This is advisable as it gives each solution its own namespace and makes operators' lives easier. It also saves on hardware costs compared to running dedicated clusters.

- **Physical isolation through separate clusters:** You can also run a separate installation for every solution. By doing so, you guarantee that only that solution uses the cluster's hardware. This is typically useful for use cases that have high load requirements, are sensitive to latency, or have regulatory requirements around isolation.

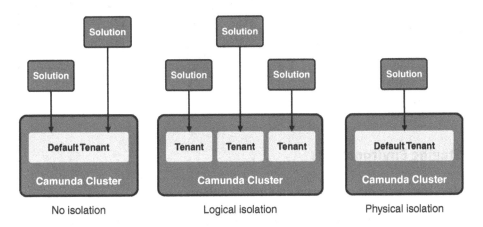

Figure 3.16 Different levels of solution isolation.

Of course, you can mix these styles. Most customers use physically isolated clusters only for selected use cases – typically "dark red" processes (i.e. complex, mission-critical processes, according to our categorization in "A Useful Categorization of Use Cases") – and tenants for all other solutions. For development environments, every developer also gets their own tenant to avoid conflicts or side effects when multiple developers work on different aspects within the same process model.

Figure 3.17 shows a typical example of how customers assign workloads to clusters and tenants in the banking domain. As you can see, departments have separate clusters, which is not necessary but often makes things easier as it requires less coordination. Solutions typically each get their own tenant, even if they are in the same domain. Note that in this setup you cannot use BPMN call activities for communication between solutions.

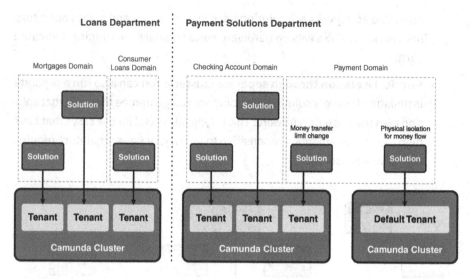

Figure 3.17 A typical setup of clusters/tenants in the banking domain.

Staging Environments

Most customers run three stages for their solutions:

- **Dev:** We strongly recommend using development clusters to avoid development using production systems. While developers can also work with local installations – probably simplified ones – in most cases it's easier to leverage SaaS environments that offload installation and operation responsibilities from the developer. Developers should have their own personal environments, isolated from what other developers are doing, to avoid errors (e.g. due to versioning conflicts with multiple developers working on one cluster). This can be achieved using separate tenants.

- **Int:** On top of functional unit tests performed by developers, most customers want to run integration tests in a close-to-real-life environment. This should be in its own cluster or tenant. This installation does not necessarily require a lot of hardware and using a tenant typically works fine, as this is normally sufficient to run testing workloads. However, the environment needs to be isolated against other test runs to avoid any side effects. Make sure not to run performance tests in such environments.

- **Prod:** The production environment is typically clustered for high availability and resilience.

Of course, there can be additional environments or stages, such as preproduction or test environments. Take functional unit tests: They ideally run in a completely self-contained way, without requiring any external components. With Camunda, for example, you can write JUnit tests in Java and use a testing extension[32] that will run the orchestration engine in-memory for the unit tests. This ensures they will always run in a clean environment and will not need any external elements to work. Similarly, customers running performance tests for performance-critical solutions will need a specific performance test cluster that is sized and configured like a production cluster. Those tests should be run independently of functional or integration testing.

Sizing and Scaling

More than anything else, how you size your environment will depend on the actual tool you're using. For example, Camunda is built for scale, but it is also perfectly fine to run small use cases on it. A good rule of thumb is that if you have less than one process instance per second, you don't really need to think about scale but can just run the smallest cluster setup available. If you are interested in more specific details, check out Camunda's best practice guide to sizing your environment[33]. This gives you an idea of what load a cluster can handle, and what hardware you need to provision if you run it self-managed. It also dives into bigger environments and how to do load tests and benchmarks if scale matters to you. To give a rough example (and prove people wrong who still think orchestration engines are slow), we have customers running more than 10,000 process instances per second on one cluster.

Resilience and High Availability

How resilience is achieved also depends heavily on the tool in use. In the case of Camunda, the core architecture of the platform is engineered so that you can scale horizontally and build resilient setups. By default, Camunda clusters run three nodes and can tolerate the absence of one node. Those nodes can easily be distributed geographically to achieve various levels of resilience. Possible configurations are:

- **Single-zone:** You build a cluster of nodes in one zone. You can stand hardware or software failures of individual nodes.

- **Multizone:** You distribute nodes into multiple zones, increasing availability as you can now stand an outage of a full zone (i.e. data center). Zone outages are very rare.

Technology 173

- **Multiregion:** You distribute nodes into multiple regions (i.e. geographically distributed data centers). You will likely never experience an outage of a full region, as this would only happen because of very exceptional circumstances.

We typically see multiregion requirements because of legal obligations, not so much because of practical matters. Keep in mind that this setup will survive the loss of all data centers in one region. Typically, in those scenarios the goal is to reduce manual cleanup work after an outage, not to eliminate any manual intervention. To be clear, multiregion setups are not a solution for serving customers in different regions faster, as the engine still needs to synchronize between regions, which cancels out any latency that might be saved up front.

More information on resilient setups can be found in Bernd's blog post, "How to Achieve Geo-Redundancy with Zeebe."[34]

Selecting the Right Process Orchestration Technology

There are different types of tools that will generally help you automate processes, but in very different ways, for very different situations. Unfortunately, the lines between different tool categories are blurry, and the category boundaries may differ depending on whom you ask. Let's try to sort this out a little bit.

We'll start by sketching out the typical decisions you need to make when selecting a process automation tool, as visualized in Figure 3.18. The following subsections dive into the details.

Types of Processes: Standard vs. Tailor-Made

One of the first questions to ask yourself is: Do we want to automate standard processes, or do we need tailor-made automation?

Every organization has standard processes, for example, around payroll, tax statements, and absence management. These processes are more or less the same in every company, which is why you can simply buy standard COTS software to automate them. For instance, at Camunda, we use an off-the-shelf tool to manage expenses, automating much of the process around expense management (e.g. receipts collection, approval, reimbursement, etc.).

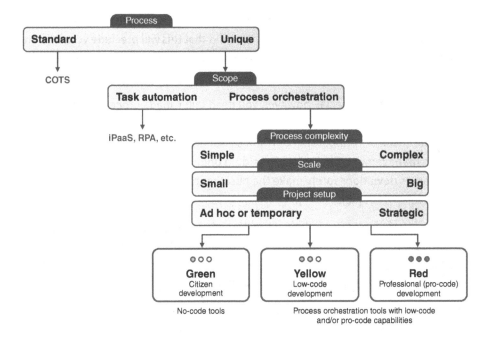

Figure 3.18 Important decisions around tool selection.

In contrast, your core value-driving processes might be unique to your company and require tailor-made solutions. A great example is NASA and its Mars robot[35]. The processes to handle data from the robot and calculate the robot's movements are pretty unique; very few organizations on the planet do this. In this case, the uniqueness is rooted in the fact that NASA has a very **unique business model**. But of course, more down-to-earth processes can also be highly specific to certain organizations. This is frequently the case if you are a first mover in your industry – for example, the first retail bank to fully automate trade requests.

Besides the business model, processes may be unique because they involve a **unique set of IT systems**, typically because of existing **legacy systems** that are in use. Take, for example, the customer onboarding process in a bank. Even if much of the required functionality is available in core banking systems, a unique set of integration requirements (e.g. with your legacy mainframe system) can make the process highly individual and complex. The same is true for claim handling in an insurance company; the process may be very similar but still look quite different from organization to organization, depending on the involved systems and process steps.

If you can automate your end-to-end processes with COTS software, do this. It's probably the cheapest option. Just keep in mind that this will preclude you differentiating your organization via those processes, as your competition may well be using the same tools.

If your processes are special, however, you need tailor-made process orchestration. As a rule of thumb, tailor-made solutions are more often required for core processes, like in the customer onboarding or NASA cases, than for supporting processes like absence management. The latter are seldom unique enough to justify tailor-made solutions, as deviations rarely make the business more successful (exceptions confirm the rule, of course).

Core processes don't *have* to be unique, though. Imagine a small web shop selling sustainable bike helmets made out of coconut fibers (we just made this up). The product is super innovative, but the core order fulfillment process can be standard; an off-the-shelf Shopify account might be all the company needs.

In sum, the answer to the question of whether to use standard software or tailor-made process orchestration is: It depends! If you want to differentiate your organization or have custom requirements, go for tailor-made process orchestration; otherwise, you're probably better off adapting your way of working to how a process is automated in standard software.

Scope: Task Automation and Simple Integrations vs. Processes

The next question to ask yourself is: Do we only need to automate tasks or do local integrations, or do we need to orchestrate end-to-end processes?

We alluded to the difference between process orchestration and task automation earlier, in "Process Automation = Process Orchestration + Task Automation". Plenty of tools can automate specific tasks, and many of them can trigger follow-up tasks as a result of a task's execution. This theoretically allows the automation of complete processes with such tools. But there are serious limitations: The overall process is not visible, and complex processes cannot be addressed because they require complex orchestration logic. Additionally, tools for task automation don't do any kind of state handling to support long-running processes.

There are multiple flavors of task automation and simple integration tools. These include:

- **Application integration tools:** These tools (e.g. Zapier, IFTTT, Tray, Make) can execute actions when some event happens – for example, inserting new data into Airtable when a Trello card is completed. Some of these tools extend beyond the boundary of task automation, also providing basic process automation capabilities.

- **Integration Platform as a Service (iPaaS) tools:** These are typically cloud-based platforms (e.g. MuleSoft, Boomi) that allow integration on a point-to-point basis. They provide prebuilt connectors, data mapping, and transformation capabilities, but don't consider the end-to-end process.

- **Technical task automation frameworks:** These frameworks (e.g. Apache Camel) ease the job of a developer for certain tasks, like communicating with the filesystem, messaging middleware, and other interface technologies. Batch processing also fits into this category, as an (outdated) way to automate tasks with batch jobs that apply them to, say, every row in a certain dataset.

- **RPA tools:** These are so commonly confused with process orchestration tools that they get their own section ("Robotic Process Automation (RPA)").

All of these types of tools can be used in addition to a process orchestration platform to solve integration challenges, but they should not be considered a replacement.

In short, if you're looking at end-to-end processes, you need to look at process orchestration tools.

Process Complexity: Simple vs. Complex

At this point in the decision tree shown in Figure 3.18, you've determined that you want to go for tailor-made process automation. To select the right tool category and specific tool, one important factor to look at is process complexity.

Processes vary hugely in complexity. For example, one of this book's authors runs a personal process around speaking at conferences. A list of conferences is maintained in Airtable, and some additional Zaps (integration flows in Zapier) automate important parts of the call-for-papers process; for example, to remind them on Slack when a call for papers is about to expire, or to ask for the final slide deck to publish online. These processes are relatively simple and deal with a very limited set of applications, all of them with well-known cloud connectors. This makes it a great use for low-code tooling.

Technology

Compare this to an end-to-end business process, like a tariff change for a telco customer that not only needs to take complex pricing rules into account but also interact with many different bespoke IT systems (e.g. to enter the changes into CRM or billing systems, or to provision changes to the telecommunications infrastructure). Or consider the core money flow or trading processes of a bank: They not only need to orchestrate many different systems but also need to run super reliably at scale, 24/7, while fulfilling regulatory requirements. Those processes definitely require a software engineering approach to process orchestration in order to be able to tame the complexity and deliver the quality you need.

Generally speaking, there are different drivers of complexity. These include:

- The **number and nature of systems, applications, or people** involved in the process. For systems and applications, their own complexity and ease of integration is especially important. There's a big difference between connecting to a well-known cloud tool like Salesforce and a legacy mainframe application that's a black box. For people, the complexity of the user interface needs to be taken into account; some processes might not need any UI and some only simple forms, whereas in other cases you might need a fully fledged single-page application to support the users.

- The **number and complexity of activities** involved in the process, and the **control structures** required (e.g. the number of branching points, errors, or exceptions that need to be handled, or the need for advanced constructs like event handling or compensation).

- The **amount and nature of data** handled in the process. This can range from simple text fields to complex documents.

- The **number of developers** required to work on a project.

- The **number of departments** or people involved in discussing how a process is implemented.

- The **number of users** that do operational work as part of the process instances, for example, via human tasks.

- **Compliance or regulatory requirements**. For example, financial processes often need to comply with many legal requirements. Auditors might not only ask about how processes are implemented in general, but also want to look at audit logs to understand what has happened in certain situations.

The more complex the processes are, the more best practices from software engineering you will need to handle them. In contrast, simple processes can also be handled by low-code tooling, where you simply put together a process from standard elements.

Scale: Small vs. Big

Scale is the next aspect to consider. Scale can relate to various things. To avoid confusion, we'll limit it to "load" in this context – so, essentially the number of process instances in a certain time frame. Some consider the number of systems or teams involved as part of "scale," but we explicitly put those factors into the previous discussion of complexity.

For example, one of our customers implements a process that must be able to handle two million payments per hour[36]. This is definitely a big scale and involves considerably different requirements than the management of the abovementioned handful of calls for papers a month. First and foremost, the chosen technology must be able to handle the targeted scale and help you navigate failure scenarios at scale (for example, if a core system faces an outage and many thousands of process instances need to be retriggered once it comes up again).

Volatile loads might lead to further requirements around elasticity, so you need to keep potential changes to the scale in mind. For example, if you provide some service via the internet and run a successful ad, you want your delivery process to be ready to scale to meet the increased demand it generates without interruptions.

Project Setup: Ad Hoc vs. Strategic

As part of the overall Camunda journey, our marketing teams grew quite a bit over the last few years. We hired more people, introduced new functions, and explored a heck of a lot of new ideas about what to do. Many of those ideas required some IT support. During such an exploratory phase, you have no idea what idea will turn out to make the most sense or exactly what the process will ultimately look like. So we did a lot of manual work, but also applied low-code tooling in areas that could be automated. We didn't aim for a stable solution that could run for years; we just needed something quick and dirty to explore or validate an idea. We were fine with the fact that only one individual – the original creator – really understood the temporary solution. And we knew it would need to be shut down in a few months, at most.

But when we understood what really worked, we needed to scale that approach. It became strategically important and required a sustainable and maintainable

Technology 179

solution. This was the moment when we moved toward properly engineered orchestration.

Another good example of ad hoc processes is one-time-only tasks. Maybe you need to run a data cleansing operation just once, then throw it away. Of course, you'll have lower requirements for the stability and maintainability of this process.

At the other end of the spectrum are the organization's core processes. These are highly strategic. Many organizations have entire departments responsible for operating and maintaining single processes. Consider again the example of processing two million payments per hour – that's not something you could ever do on an ad hoc basis.

Part of the decision, then, might also be based on the criticality of the process. If a process is critical for your company to survive, you need to make sure it runs smoothly and is stable. If you can lose real money on process failures, you need operational capabilities that prevent failures from happening or going undetected.

Contrasting Process Orchestration with Adjacent Technologies

The decision tree from Figure 3.18 should help you understand your requirements better. Still, you might be confused by tools or methods that also promise process orchestration and automation in some form. How do they differ from a process orchestration platform? In this section, we'll explore some of the most common adjacent technologies: RPA tools, data flow engines, event-driven architecture, data and event streaming technologies, BPM suites, and microservices orchestrators. Looking at the wider tooling landscape will also help you refine your understanding of what process orchestration really is.

Robotic Process Automation (RPA)

RPA tools (such as UiPath and Automation Anywhere) can automate tasks within legacy systems that don't provide any API. RPA is about screen scraping and simulating mouse or keyboard actions – kind of like the Microsoft Office macro recorder on steroids. It focuses on automating single tasks, not processes, but because the automation of a given task likely requires a series of interactions with the UI, which is typically represented in a graphical flow diagram, it often gets confused with process orchestration. The granularity of an RPA flow is very different from that of a business process, however, as discussed in the blog post "How to Benefit from Robotic Process Automation (RPA)."[37] You might want to quickly flip back to "Process Automation = Process Orchestration + Task Automation" to refresh your memory on task automation vs. process orchestration.

Data Flow Engines and Data Streaming

There are technologies that can automate processes using a set of supposedly loosely coupled components. Event-driven architectures are the most common example, but data flow engines also fall into this category, as do traditional batch processing systems.

Let's look at data flow engines (e.g. Apache Airflow, Spring Cloud Data Flow), data streaming technologies, and extract-transform-load (ETL) tools first. There is one defining difference between these tools and a process orchestration platform: With process orchestration, there is an orchestrator that knows about and controls each instance of a process. You can think of the orchestrator as the conductor that drives the process. It keeps a list of all process instances, together with their current state. It always knows what has to come next in any given process instance. You can ask the orchestrator about the status of any process instance, and it can, for example, escalate the issue if something does not move forward as expected. In a nutshell, the process orchestrator maintains its own state so it knows exactly what is currently going on.

The situation is different with data flow engines or streaming architectures. They're steered by the data flowing through a pipeline. Very often, this follows a pattern where so-called *processors* take work from one place (e.g. a queue), do it, and place the result in another place (e.g. another queue), from which the next processor takes its work. The result is, of course, also a process, but the difference is that the data flow engine does not have its own state. There is no single component you can ask for information on the running instances and their state. Because of this different focus, these tools lack important features for process automation, such as support for control flow constructs like loops.

While in a process orchestrator you typically define the end-to-end process flow, you only define predecessors for processors in a data flow architecture. The resulting challenge with regard to the end-to-end process is that the process logic is pretty hidden. At the same time, the components are not as loosely coupled as it looks at first glance. The book *Practical Process Automation*[38] goes quite deeply into that topic if you are interested.

In summary, we don't see these tools as an alternative to a process orchestration platform, but rather as an addition that can be used for specific use cases. A good example use case for a combination of both technologies is where streams of data are used to generate insights that should lead to certain actions, which are in turn orchestrated. This is described in the blog post "Event Streams Are Nothing Without Action."[39]

Event-Driven Architecture (EDA) and Event Streaming

In event-driven architectures, components react to events, which might be data in a stream. Those components don't know from where this data is coming. Common tooling includes event brokers like Apache Kafka.

A series of event subscriptions might form a logical chain that implements a business process, but this comes with two challenges. First, the process flow does not have its own persistence, making it hard to determine the current state of any instance. Second, the control flow logic isn't visible anywhere, making these architectures hard to understand and maintain. In essence, the problems are comparable to those described in the previous section.

If this is a discussion happening in your organization, we recommend picking up a copy of *Practical Process Automation*, which has a whole chapter on event-driven architecture (also known as choreography) versus process orchestration.

BPM Suites and Low-Code Application Platforms

There is a category of monolithic automation tools that also overlap with process orchestration platforms. Things start to get more nuanced here. The main tools in this category are traditional BPM suites and low-code application platforms (LCAPs). These tools approach process automation from a monolithic perspective, meaning they cannot easily be hooked into your own architecture. They typically come from big vendors in huge packages containing lots of adjacent automation features, making them complex to understand and use (especially because of their black-box nature). They are also often limited in scalability, and as such may not be able to handle core business processes. Integrating endpoints into the process is done in a very proprietary way, meaning that special training is required to use these tools. Finally, they deliberately lock you into their environment instead of facilitating the use of best-of-breed solutions.

Microservice Orchestrators

Microservice orchestrators were invented with microservices in mind and focus fully on those architectures. As such, these tools don't cover the full scope required for end-to-end process orchestration. For example, human task management is not addressed, and legacy software and SaaS services that are not microservices aren't explicitly covered.

On top of this, these tools target solely software developers, which has a few notable consequences. First, the graphical representation of a process model is not considered important, so these tools miss out on the chance to align business and IT. This applies not only to the modeling itself, but also to process intelligence and process improvement. Second, the flow logic is typically kept deliberately simple – but as real-life processes are complex, this leads to a lot of complex workarounds being required, making the flow logic much harder to understand.

Tips on Evaluating Tools

We've found the following differentiators important when evaluating process automation and process orchestration tooling:

- **Support for end-to-end processes:** The tool should be able to orchestrate every human and automated task in an end-to-end business process across components such as systems, APIs, microservices, RPA bots, IoT devices, and AI/ML tools.

- **Support for long-running processes:** The tool should have the technical capabilities necessary to effectively manage business processes that run for hours, days, or even weeks. This is about effective persistence as well as querying possibilities and monitoring abilities.

Technology 183

- **Process-focused analytics and intelligence:** The tool should provide actionable insights based on real-time and historical process data, with features that help you optimize your processes.

- **Developer-friendliness:** The tool shouldn't require software developers to adopt a vendor-specific way of working, but instead should meet developers in their comfort zone. It should provide a good developer experience, including powerful SDKs and getting started guides. Furthermore, the tool should ensure that you are not locked into a low-code layer, where you might hit barriers that you cannot overcome – allowing professional software development makes sure there is no wall you can hit. Finally, developer-friendliness is often also about the small things: for example, having a vibrant community online, providing an open forum, or allowing problems to be solved with Google, Stack Overflow, or AI-powered CoPilot software.

- **Advanced workflow patterns:** Life is seldom a straight line, and the same is true of processes. Therefore, you must be able to accurately express all the things happening in your business processes for proper end-to-end process orchestration. This requires workflow patterns that go beyond basic control flow patterns (like sequences or conditions). If your orchestration tool does not provide those advanced workflow patterns, your developers will need to implement time-consuming workarounds, and you will end up with confusing models. This is explored further in the blog post "Why Process Orchestration Needs Advanced Workflow Patterns."[40]

- **Standards-based collaboration:** The tool should use open standards (namely BPMN and DMN) to facilitate communication and alignment between business stakeholders and IT teams.

- **Flexible architecture:** The tool should allow teams to choose which parts to use and where, integrate seamlessly with other IT tools, and offer on-site, cloud, and hybrid deployment options.

- **Open architecture:** The tool should provide open APIs for integration, allow teams to try it before adopting it, and support community-driven extension and improvement.

- **Low total cost of ownership:** The tool should enable organizations to get started quickly and to make changes easily, with no proprietary or vendor-specific knowledge required.

- **Scalability and resilience:** The tool should be built to align with modern cloud engineering practices to support cloud-first process automation initiatives that can scale horizontally. Supporting a proper level of scaling is important to handle increasing load, whether seasonal or due to overall business success. You need to have a platform that supports whatever your business requires. This will allow you to apply process orchestration to a bigger variety of processes, including core processes running huge loads (like payments or trade processing). To guarantee high availability for your processes, you'll also need to ensure a high level of resilience and high availability, as discussed in "Resilience and High Availability".

It's important to have clarity on what kind of tool you need, as tool categories around process automation, process orchestration, task automation, and integration are blurry. This does not make it easy to select the right tool stack, but hopefully the information in this book will help you make better decisions.

The following are some of the key points to keep in mind:

1. Using standard (COTS) software can be the easiest and cheapest way to automate processes. Note, however, that you won't be able to differentiate yourself by those processes, and you will have to adjust your organization's way of working to the software, not the other way around. For all processes that require a tailor-made process orchestration solution, standard software can be one piece of the puzzle, but it won't be sufficient on its own.

2. Task automation tools (including iPaaS and RPA tools) cannot replace process orchestration, but they can complement a process orchestration platform for specific task automations.

3. Data streaming or event-driven approaches distribute and hide the flow logic, making those bad choices to automate important business processes. There are use cases where those tools are a great choice, though, and use cases where a combination of process orchestration and data or event streaming will work well.

4. BMP suites and LCAPs have some overlap with process orchestration platforms, but they're typically not flexible or developer-friendly and don't have the open architecture required to orchestrate all your processes strategically.

Technology 185

5. Microservice orchestrators are too technical for business processes, lacking features to align business and IT and also typically lacking extended workflow patterns to support all the complexities of core processes.

Ideally, you'll get help when selecting your tool stack. This could mean involving external consultancies or analysts. This decision is vital for the future of your transformation initiative; technology isn't everything, but such transformations can easily get stalled by improper tool choices. The selected tools need to be able to support your strategy.

Run early proof of concept sessions, and let your own employees be part of these. Don't leave the whole decision process in the hands of external stakeholders, as this will not only leave you with limited knowledge of the reasoning behind the choice but can also lead to more shortsighted decisions.

Questions to Assess Your Maturity

For technology, we describe the five maturity levels as follows (see Table P.1):

- **Level 0**: Teams may have implemented disparate automation technologies.
- **Level 1**: Teams are questioning the continued use of legacy systems or monolithic in-house solutions that limit advancement.
- **Level 2**: The focus is on building a single technology stack that covers the entire process lifecycle.
- **Level 3**: Investing in elements that increase solution acceleration, with a focus on enabling multiple teams to build process orchestration solutions at scale.
- **Level 4**: Recognizing that there is no "one-size-fits-all" approach to hyperautomated tech stacks, the organization has instead built one that fits its exact needs; it also has a dedicated process orchestration strategy within the stack.

Questions you should ask yourself to assess your maturity include:

- Do you have a high-level vision of your enterprise architecture around process orchestration, including technical and business capabilities and end-to-end processes?
- Do you have the technical capabilities to establish enterprise process orchestration, and have you selected a tool stack that can implement those capabilities?

186   Enterprise Process Orchestration

- Do you have a clear understanding of why this tool stack was chosen and how it's differentiated from competing categories or tools (in case other parts of the organization challenge your decision)?
- Do you provide the important technical capabilities around process orchestration as a platform within the organization?
- Is this platform operated in a SaaS-like way to ease usage for delivery teams?
- Do you provide enablement around the platform, e.g., through an AAT?
- Do you provide accelerators and reusable components around the platform?
- Do you have best practices on how different domains, teams, and solutions can leverage the platform (like multitenancy and sizing)?
- Do you have enough internal marketing and communications to make people aware of process orchestration and how to approach it?

Takeaways

Here are the key insights from this chapter:

- Process orchestration technology integrates all the endpoints required for end-to-end processes.
- Defined business capabilities serve as building blocks for end-to-end processes. They can also be built as executable processes.
- A good process orchestration platform is composable, allowing integration of best-of-breed components that can be replaced or customized based on evolving business needs, without vendor lock-in.
- A robust process orchestration platform includes an orchestration engine; decision management, task management, and integration capabilities; modeling tools; and analytics.
- Process orchestration platforms provide an environment to operationalize AI agents, enabling automated decision making and task execution within auditable business processes.
- Process orchestration platforms should be offered "as a service" internally, either self-managed by the organization or via SaaS models, to reduce cognitive load for delivery teams and accelerate time to value.

- Process orchestration platforms are differentiated from adjacent tool categories in that they support long-running, end-to-end processes with advanced workflow patterns, integrate diverse endpoints, and provide an open architecture that allows for flexible integration into your environment.

- Process orchestration tools should cater for the level of resiliency, composability, and flexibility your organization needs. They should also support all possible kinds of use cases, blending pro-code, low-code, and AI-based approaches.

Chapter 4: Delivery

Having shaped a great vision, set up a rockstar team, defined a great architecture, and decided on your tool stack leaves you with the most important part of your process orchestration journey still ahead of you: creating concrete orchestration solutions that deliver real value for your organization. So far, everything you've done was kind of a warm-up, with no direct business value contribution delivered just yet. But if you've done all that work well, the solution delivery should run smoothly.

In this chapter, we'll describe the typical steps and iterations involved in developing one concrete solution. Of course, this is also interlinked with architecture work and tool selection, so during your first projects you will typically define and refine your overall architecture and best practices. Only after you've completed those first projects will you be able to scale your solution creation efforts.

Solution Creation Approach

Most often, we see approaches similar to the one sketched out in Figure 4.1. Of course, even though the approach shown in this visual appears to follow a straight line, that is almost never the case in real life; solutions are best created in an agile fashion, continuously delivering business value in small iterations, and not by following rigid waterfall models.

Note that we also advise adopting product thinking in your organization, as discussed in "Product Thinking". This means you want to have stable and long-lasting ownership for every solution, even if the solution is created or improved by dedicated projects. This allows the respective owner to think strategically about the solution.

Let's go through the various steps in the solution creation approach one by one.

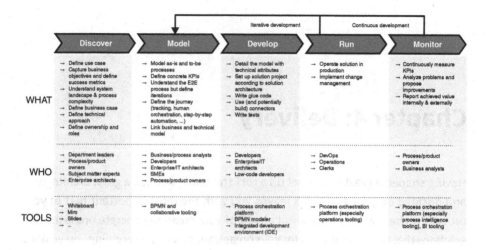

Figure 4.1 The solution creation lifecycle.

Discover

Very often, this step is not really part of a solution project, as typically you have to evaluate process candidates for orchestration and consider the resulting business case first, to come up with concrete next projects.

The aims of the discovery phase are to:

- **Identify a process to orchestrate** and **define the business case** for the automation project.

- **Capture business objectives** and **define success metrics**. It should be clear not only why a process should be automated, but which metrics will define success. These could be, for example, around cycle times, reduced amount of human work, or increased sales through better customer experiences. In our experience, this step is often overlooked, which not only makes it hard to communicate value later but also misses an opportunity to align everyone on a common goal.

- **Define ownership and roles.** Before kicking off your solution, it's crucial to understand how it is connected with the business domains that are holding the use case together (we advocate for clear process ownership) and the roles and enablement that are needed to deliver the initiative.

To dive deeper, we use the following step-by-step guide to build and articulate a strong business case in our customer engagements. You may recognize a few of these from "Building and Prioritizing Business Cases":

1. **Identify pain points.** Start by identifying the current pain points in the organization's processes. These could include inefficiencies, high error rates, long cycle times, or lack of visibility.

2. **Define goals.** Clarify what you aim to achieve with process orchestration. Objectives might include improving efficiency, reducing costs, increasing compliance, or enhancing the ability to adapt to changes. This should include discussing and defining concrete metrics and KPIs, as we will explain further in "Chapter 5: Measurement". Using concrete KPIs helps you hit two targets with one arrow: selling the project internally and defining the right metrics from the start. The latter will also help the automation projects to clearly understand the goal.

3. **Analyze current processes.** Map out the current processes that you intend to orchestrate. Understand the flow of tasks, the involved parties, and the systems used. This will help you pinpoint where orchestration can have the most impact. (Often, this is done when identifying the pain points or validating hypotheses around them.)

4. **Propose desired state.** Define a to-be process model and develop your strategy for how process orchestration will be used. This should include selecting the tool stack and the processes to be orchestrated first, and deciding how the integration with existing systems will be managed.

5. **Estimate costs.** Calculate the total cost of implementing process orchestration. This includes software costs, training, potential downtime during implementation, and ongoing maintenance.

6. **Forecast benefits.** Estimate the benefits of process orchestration in quantifiable terms. This could be in the form of time saved, error reduction, improved customer satisfaction, increased revenue, or other factors.

7. **Conduct a cost–benefit analysis.** Compare the costs and benefits to determine the return on investment. Include a break-even analysis to show when the benefits will start to outweigh the costs.

8. **Address risks by mitigation strategies.** Identify potential risks associated with the implementation of process orchestration and outline strategies to mitigate these risks.

Delivery

9. **Create a phased implementation roadmap.** Develop a phased approach to implementing process orchestration, detailing the timeline, key milestones, and deliverables and differentiating value delivery by phase.

10. **Cultivate stakeholder support.** Present the business case to stakeholders. Highlight the strategic importance and the expected outcomes to gain their support and buy-in.

11. **Review and revise.** Be prepared to review and revise the business case based on feedback from stakeholders and any new information that may arise during discussions. A closed-loop cycle here is critical to develop to an effective business case.

Model

You'll need to model the to-be process to a high standard. The model you create should be clear, understandable, and precise, as it will be the basis for the executable process. Although the primary focus should of course be on the to-be process, as this is where value will come from, it's often helpful to capture the as-is process first, to better understand the changes needed to implement the new process.

While you should aim to get a clear understanding of the end-to-end process, in the early phases of your project you can limit that to a higher level of abstraction and only define the next iteration of your orchestration project in detail. For example, you might start with the happy path and not yet go into all exceptional paths or define all the technical details around the APIs required for the whole process. The end-to-end view is still important for the context, however, and it will help you define the iterations.

When you define your to-be process model for the next development iteration, make sure to start developing as soon as possible to allow for quick feedback cycles. Your first process models might not be suitable directly for execution, but most organizations will get better at this very quickly, especially if they have teams consisting of business people, BPMN experts, and IT folks.

A common topic of discussion is the link between business and technical process models. We've heard a lot of misguided comments in this area, and to shape the discussion we recommend taking a look at the "Camunda house," discussed in detail in *Real-Life BPMN*[1] (see Figure 4.2). The house differentiates a strategic process model,

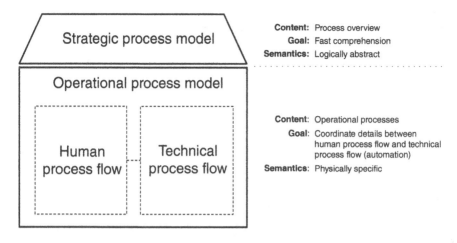

Figure 4.2 The Camunda process house from Real-Life BPMN.

which is a very simplified overview of a process that typically fits on one slide, and the operational model, which is logically correct and directly executable.

The strategic model is a model purely expressing the "why" of a process on a business level, without too many operational details, whereas the operational model contains everything required for a process orchestration engine to do its work and is shared between business and IT. This is the power of BPMN: You do not need two disconnected models for business and IT, but rather can have one joint operational model.

Of course, you might end up with multiple physical copies of that model: For example, one in the collaborative modeling tool, one in the company-internal Wiki, and one in the version control of the IT solution. This is completely fine, and we will describe steps you can take to keep those models in sync later in this chapter.

Develop

Next up is the development of the solution, which means adding all the technical details needed to make a process model executable. For example, this can involve expressions to implement decision points (gateways), glue code to integrate service calls, configuration of connectors (or the implementation of your own connectors), and user interfaces (including task forms). Development should also include writing automated tests, at least for solutions with a certain level of criticality.

Depending on the process at hand, the development phase might involve more pro-code or low-code elements. We will describe the development of solutions at both ends of the spectrum in more detail later in this chapter.

Run

The solution will only generate business value once it's running production. This phase includes setting up the real deployment environment, even if this is hopefully handled as a service by either your SaaS vendor or your internal AAT. Also, before putting your solution into production, it's important to consider change management for the people who will be affected, for example, because they' ll need to switch to using the new task management UI or otherwise change the way they do their work.

The delivery team needs to technically operate the solution and watch for any incidents that might happen. Most customers have a two-layered approach to this. IT runs technical operations, perhaps with someone on call (often 24/7, depending on the criticality of the process). If you have a Platform as a Service in-house, those people are typically connected to your AAT and should resolve failures in the underlying platform themselves. Sometimes solution teams operate their own platforms, in which case they typically resolve those problems. In the meantime, anything that happens in the application and process layer is normally forwarded to the operations part of the delivery team. This might include failures that occur if process instances get stuck because of invalid data or bugs, for example.

As soon as the first iteration is in production, you can immediately begin implementing the next iteration, making improvements or simply implementing the next process phase.

Monitor

Once in production, you should **continuously track value.** Make sure you implement automatic capturing of the KPIs you defined at the start of the project, probably via the process intelligence tool. The process orchestration platform will help you to automatically capture all relevant data and provide real-time dashboards for executives.

Once your process is in production, you should also continuously check for improvement ideas. In our experience, once process owners have visibility on their process's

KPIs they can often quickly and easily identify low-hanging fruit for improvement. If you establish a product mindset around your processes, they will be incentivized to act on those insights, and the visual process model makes it easy to implement such changes.

Being Agile Throughout the Solution Creation Lifecycle

We certainly encourage an agile approach that implements solutions and delivers value incrementally. But we find that one thing is often overlooked: If you want to develop in small iterations, you have to be clear on the goal. Otherwise, you can easily lose sight of your objective, especially if you are wandering into the weeds of implementation.

Take process models as an example. In a first iteration, you might automate just a small portion of the process, or even perform all the steps manually – but you need an idea of how the full process works to even decide on what a useful first iteration might look like. It's similar with architecture, where an up-front understanding of the risks is critical and aspects around security, data protection, authentication and authorization, and so on often need to be properly defined for even the first iteration.

Clearly defining your goals for the end-to-end process will enable you to derive a meaningful first iteration. You can then adapt in an agile manner as you learn.

Setting the Stage for Success: Your Early Projects

We deliberately left out the first projects in Figure 4.1 for simplicity's sake – but of course, your first process orchestration projects are something special. Typically, those first solutions will be developed hand-in-hand with shaping your architecture and selecting your tools. Ideally, a stable team of people will be involved with the first projects, and those folks will then also be involved in building the AAT (or the other way around: Your AAT may actually be doing the implementation work for the first projects to establish the architecture).

Avoid defining too much of a platform without running a concrete project, as this bears the risk of getting into an ivory tower situation that doesn't deliver what people really need.

Delivery 195

The most important additional steps for your first projects are:

- Defining your stack and selecting your tool(s).
- Defining your solution design.
- Piloting your architecture (you'll continue to validate and improve it in later projects).
- Documenting lessons learned.
- Creating enablement material.

As part of the tool selection process, we recommend doing proofs of concept early on, as only those can prove that a tool is working for you – something a spreadsheet with evaluation criteria cannot!

In a PoC, you need to model the process with the goal of the PoC in mind. You likely won't need to model the full process, but can concentrate on specific tasks, such as calling real services in your environment, or executing human tasks if appropriate. You might use existing tools from the vendor (e.g. Camunda Tasklist) as a first step to save effort in developing your own tasklist, unless a tasklist is important for your overall proof. Include some "eye candy," like reporting, to make nontechnical stakeholders happy. The PoC should convey the value of process orchestration to the organization. However, concentrate on just the important aspects to do the proof, and be prepared to throw away the code afterward and start fresh for the pilot. (It's perfectly valid for early PoCs to be "hacky" to keep the focus on the end goals.) See Camunda's best practice guide to doing a proper PoC[2] for more information on this topic.

The early projects often serve as lighthouses and may provide a copy-and-paste template for later projects. Hence, it's important to review those projects after they've gone live. Because of the lighthouse effect, it's worth putting in some extra effort to clean them up. It's better to plan time for this after go-live than to try to make things perfect during early development, as you will have learned a lot by the time the pilot has been running on the live system for a while.

Try to avoid doing too many projects in parallel at the beginning, to allow new learning to influence your future work. If you have parallel pilots, organize knowledge sharing between the teams. Ideally, have the team working on the first pilot implement the next orchestration solution.

Derisking Your Start with Process Tracking

Very often a process that you want to properly orchestrate is already automated in some way, typically through a wild array of point-to-point integrations, hacks in existing legacy systems, or simply chaotic scripts or batch jobs. Unfortunately, you cannot simply get rid of that chaos, as it's generally not easy to understand how the process currently works. Introducing a process orchestrator in this environment, where you have to untangle the spaghetti mess and move integrations to the orchestration layer, might feel like too big an undertaking, with an unacceptable level of risk.

To make it more manageable, this needs to be tackled step by step. The smallest first step, which is completely noninvasive and therefore risk-free, is to introduce the process orchestrator solely to read through what your spaghetti chaos is doing, as visualized in Figure 4.3. Technically, this involves creating a process model as a digital twin for your legacy automation that reacts to events or polls for status information via APIs.

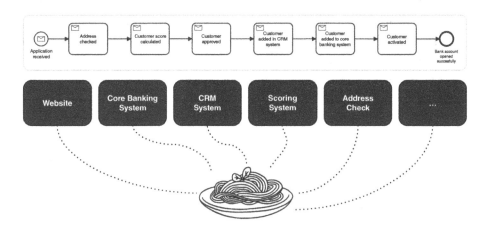

Figure 4.3 To derisk your start, you can introduce a process that only tracks what is happening in your legacy integrations.

This step requires minimal effort and does not interfere with the implementation of the process. At the same time, it provides immediate relevant benefits. By visualizing the process, stakeholders gain a better understanding of how it currently operates. The mapping of events validates whether the process model is merely an idealized concept or reflects reality. In addition, the orchestration platform immediately provides metrics such as idle or throughput times that can offer visibility into potential problem areas or bottlenecks in the process.

Individual instances can also be monitored to detect if the process halts for any reason. For example, if a bank account opening process takes longer than a couple of days to complete, the bank can get notified and take proactive steps to get the process instance back on track, before the customer complains. We've even seen one case where process tracking was used to ensure process cycle times stayed within regulatory time frames, allowing the customer (a bank) to avoid millions of dollars in fines each year.

The biggest value, however, is typically that this provides you with a starting point to work from. You can start implementing the first orchestration steps within the tracking process – for example, integrating an API call to register the customer in a new KYC system. This change does not require reaching into the full bowl of spaghetti, but rather can be implemented within the orchestration tool.

Process tracking thus enables a gradual transformation from spaghetti to orchestrated (micro-)services, guided by process metrics (e.g. "We are losing the most time at step X.") or operational pain points (e.g. "We urgently need to increase the automation rate to achieve the targeted growth."). For example, you might identify address checking as a task that can easily be done via API, reducing the workload on your overworked clerks. As Figure 4.4 shows, you can adjust the process to orchestrate that task.

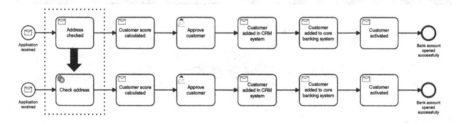

Figure 4.4 The tracking process provides a basis for introducing orchestration (e.g. an automated address check).

This migration typically involves several steps:

1. **Remove the implicit integration logic.** The integration logic that was previously executing this task must be removed. Only then can the task be targeted effectively by the orchestrator.

2. **Provide a suitable interface.** The functionality must be given an appropriate API and made accessible.

3. **Orchestrate the interface.** The API is then orchestrated through the process.

Each incremental improvement can be rolled out productively, with immediate operational benefits in terms of customer experience, process efficiency, or compliance with risk and regulatory requirements. The changes won't all be trivial, but they should be manageable and carry low risk. Over time, you can gradually untangle all the spaghetti and replace it with orchestration, until you reach the desired process model.

Typical Delivery Teams and Roles

At this point, we'd like to revisit the question of what people, roles, and skills you need in your delivery teams. Guess what? It depends! The most important factor is the type of solution you are building. A pro-code approach requires a different setup than a more low-code one, so let's look at those separately.

For **pro-code** solutions, a delivery team requires at least a software developer and a business analyst (for a refresher on how we define these roles, see "Roles"). Very often, you will also see other roles in the team: solution architects, Scrum masters, test engineers, DevOps engineers, methodology experts (e.g. around BPMN), and so forth. The exact team composition that's appropriate will depend on your way of developing software. In other words, you will see normal software development teams, but with added process orchestration experience. This experience can be achieved by training or enablement.

From a process orchestration perspective, the important aspect is that at least software developers and solution architects need to be trained in BPMN and the process orchestration platform. An AAT can either provide full-time team members with the required training or supply part-time team members to help with these tasks as needed. The latter approach is especially useful for very specific skills, for example, around modeling complex scenarios in BPMN or tuning the performance of the process orchestration platform.

For **low-code** solutions, on the other hand, you don't always find software engineers in the delivery teams. This is possible because the complexity of the solutions is lower.

Delivery 199

In this case, the AAT likely provides supporting artifacts like bespoke connectors optimized for internal use in the organization. This removes the need for delivery teams to have engineering expertise themselves. However, expertise around process orchestration and BPMN is still required; again, this can be achieved by training or enablement from the AAT.

Figure 4.5 shows a few possible team compositions.

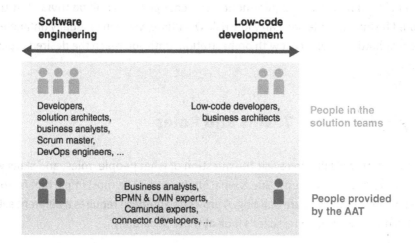

Figure 4.5 Possible compositions of delivery teams.

One very important aspect is that the business must be represented in all delivery projects. This generally happens on two levels: operationally and strategically (as pointed out in "Chapter 1: Vision"). On an operational level, you will need business analysts or subject matter experts that provide concrete input on how to orchestrate the process, dealing with day-to-day requirements. On a strategic level, you need somebody – often from the AAT, but maybe also from the business optimization group – that can connect to business executives, gather their input, understand their priorities, and explain the business value to them. This is a point of failure we often see, as business analysts and business architects do not always speak the language of executives. This role should be filled by someone who really understands the opportunities that technology provides to the business and knows how to capture that and make it transparent to leadership. This is often a central role. In AATs, the task of creating initial awareness within the business is commonly taken on by the AAT leader; solution architects then navigate the business domains along the process development lifecycle, from discovery to modeling, monitoring, and improving.

Solution Design

In this section, we'll get into the weeds of how to design a process solution using process orchestration and process models in BPMN. We'll start by describing the greenfield architecture Camunda has defined for its customers. (Using a concrete tool makes this section much more hands-on; if you use a different tool, you should still be able to draw value from it.)

We differentiate two flavors of the greenfield architecture:

- Greenfield architecture for pro-code use cases (red processes, using the categories from "A Useful Categorization of Use Cases").
- Simplified architecture for low-code use cases (yellow processes).

Of course, as we discussed in the "Introduction", the boundary between red and yellow use cases is blurry. There might, for example, be use cases where 90% of the solution creation is yellow, but a small part of the orchestration process requires custom-implemented code – and for governance reasons, that also means that the overall build and deployment happens via a defined CI/CD pipeline after automated unit tests are run, even if many changes might only affect the BPMN model.

In this case, you could tailor your software development lifecycle so that, for example, a change in the process model made by a business person in your collaborative modeling environment also triggers the deployment pipeline. This is not only possible, but actually a great enabler, as it allows working in a low-code fashion but still can guarantee a high level of quality. In Camunda's case, all the tools in the stack have an API, so you could, for example, pull BPMN models from a milestone in the web modeler and push them to Git automatically on changes or during deployment.

Needless to say, design and architecture depend on hundreds of things, so you'll likely need to make some adjustments to the solution design proposals in this book. Our goal here is simply to provide a sensible default that's a good starting point and has been validated in many situations. This can be quite useful to have when you're getting started with your first project, and you need to make a lot of decisions but still lack firsthand experience!

Many of our customers start with this proposal and adjust it to their organization's needs over time (Camunda leaves a lot of flexibility for this). Those adjusted defaults might then be rolled out through the organization, with the help of the AAT.

Delivery

Greenfield Solution Architecture for Pro-Code Use Cases

Let's explore the solution design and development scenario for red use cases first. Remember, these are your most complex and critical processes, which will be implemented using proven industry best practices around software engineering. This helps ensure that you create high-quality solutions that can be continuously improved over time.

Typically, the process orchestration solution will look something like what you see in Figure 4.6. The exact technologies used will depend on your organization's preferences, so, for example, if you're a Java shop you might want to create a Maven project using Spring Boot and the Camunda Spring SDK[3], and if you're a .NET shop you will likely prefer C# and the Camunda C# client[4] as a NuGet package. (For more technical details, see our best practice guide to deciding about your stack[5].)

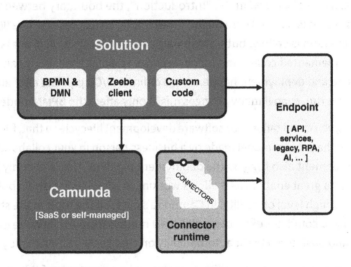

Figure 4.6 The greenfield solution architecture for pro-code use cases.

A solution contains your process or decision models (as BPMN or DMN files), your own code, and the client SDK (as a library) to connect to Camunda. To integrate endpoints, you can either write custom glue code or use existing connectors. The solution should also contain automated unit tests (like JUnit tests in Java) – you can find more information on this in Camunda's best practice guide to testing process definitions[6].

The solution is built via your preferred CI/CD pipeline (e.g. GitHub and GitHub Actions, or Jenkins). This results in a normal deployment artifact (e.g. a Spring Boot JAR) that is deployed into your normal runtime environment (e.g. Kubernetes via Docker images). The BPMN and DMN models will be part of that artifact, and they're deployed to Camunda during startup of the application.

The Software Development Lifecycle and Model Roundtrips

While the solution architecture looks surprisingly similar for most solutions, the way to get the BPMN model in there differs. Most lifecycles start within a collaborative web modeling tool like Camunda Web Modeler[7]. There are two reasons for this:

1. The web modeler brings collaborative features to the table. Especially during early discussions around the business process, using the web modeler makes sure that you can involve all important stakeholders, independent of their role. This facilitates discussions about the process model. Also, the model can be easily hooked into company-internal Wikis. Hence, in many organizations, the web modeler is an important collaboration tool that facilitates the process mindset.

2. The web modeler has a low barrier to entry. You can create your first process model right away, without thinking about version control structures or anything else you need to set up. Typically, you will just create a project folder for your first models; we recommend not worrying about default structures or guidelines for the moment, as this first phase is really just about getting started.

However, solutions will not be solely developed within the web modeler. After this initial stage, the model needs to be put into a development project (e.g. in Git). This offers the following benefits:

- You can write unit tests that run completely locally, accessing the model locally in the developer's filesystem.

- You can set up a CI/CD pipeline that has the process model included, so it can also run unit tests and create a unified artifact containing all relevant elements of the process solution.

- You can tag and release solutions, including the process model and all other code artifacts around it.

- You can use a local Camunda platform for development, enabling a completely offline developer experience.

Delivery   203

Developers typically prefer using a desktop tool (e.g. Camunda Desktop Modeler[8]) to edit the local files. Of course, with this development approach, you will end up with multiple physical copies of your process model: one in the web modeler's repository, and one in the developer's version control system. This requires thinking about keeping those models in sync, which necessitates a roundtrip from one system to the other – the business creates the model, and the developer alters the model in their own environment and syncs it back with the business model. One possibility (the one we see most often in practice) is to use CLI tools[9] to handle the synchronization process, which is triggered manually by the developer. Another possibility is to use the web modeler's API to automatically sync changes back and forth, although this carries some risk of changes being overwritten accidentally.

With that background in mind, let's look at a typical journey, as illustrated in Figure 4.7, concentrating solely on the tools and ignoring which roles are doing what for now.

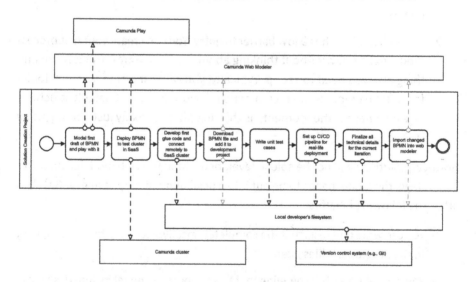

Figure 4.7 An example journey (aka roundtrip) to create an executable BPMN model through the various Camunda tools.

Let's quickly go through this. First, either a developer or a business analyst sketches out the initial version of the BPMN process model to be executed. Using the web modeler lowers the barriers to just start modeling and allows you to involve as many people as possible in this process. The model can be directly deployed to a test cluster in Camunda SaaS, and the Camunda Web Modeler's Play mode can be used to test drive the model in order to improve it.

When service tasks need to integrate systems, either out-of-the-box connectors are used or a development project is created (using tools like Java, Maven, Spring Boot, and Git). In the first step, you might keep using a test cluster in Camunda SaaS and just add API credentials to access it from the developer's machine. In PoC situations, this approach lets you get started quickly, and keeping the model in the web modeler for as long as possible allows you to easily discuss it with all stakeholders.

At some point in time, though, you'll want to move the model into the developer's filesystem, so you can start writing unit tests and create your CI/CD pipeline, or simply because you want to run everything locally on the developer's machine. In Camunda Web Modeler, downloading the model is currently a manual step using the download button (but a feature to automate this step is on the roadmap).

Whenever changes are made to the developer's copy of the model, the model should be copied back to the web modeler to avoid those models diverging. This is done by manually importing the BPMN file into the web modeler (a feature to automate this step is also on the roadmap).

Many projects institutionalize the process for keeping the different versions in sync as part of their development process – for example, when using Scrum this can be done as part of the planning or retrospective sessions. It can also be part of the definition of done (DoD) for development issues.

Simplified Solution Architecture for Low-Code Use Cases

Simpler process solutions – yellow processes, in our categorization – might not require the full-blown software development setup described previously. For such cases, it's often preferable to use a simplified solution architecture that's more accessible to nonsoftware developers. These solutions might not contain dedicated programming code, but just process models, decision models, and forms. Those can be designed using a web-based modeler like Camunda's, so the creator doesn't need any locally installed tools. If a solution requires custom code, for example, to connect to the organization's internal legacy system, the AAT can develop this code and provide it to the solution creator as a reusable connector, to avoid the solution turning into a development project. This is visualized in Figure 4.8.

Delivery

205

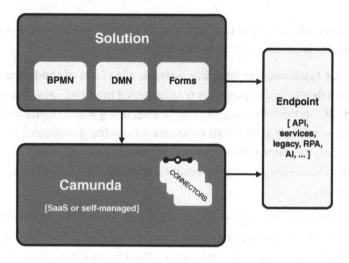

Figure 4.8 A simplified solution architecture for low-code use cases that don't need developer tools.

There are two ways to deploy such a solution:

1. Deploy manually via a button in the web modeler. While this is easy and straightforward, it lacks any kind of quality assurance or controls.
2. Create a milestone and use milestones to trigger a deployment pipeline in your CI tool[10] (e.g. GitHub Actions). This approach provides a good balance between ease of use and quality, but requires your organization to set up those pipelines initially.

At Camunda, we are currently working on improving our low-code experience, so please reach out if you have questions, feedback, or simply want to discuss your vision of the best lifecycle for low-code solutions.

Typical Questions Around the Development Lifecycle

In this section, we'll address some of the questions that commonly arise around the development lifecycle. First, though, one important note. We have learned over the last decade that roles vary widely across enterprises, not only in their responsibilities but also in what they're called. The same responsibilities can be assigned to roles with different names, and roles that have the same name can have completely different responsibilities. And of course, each person fulfilling a role will perform it in their own way. What's more, in smaller projects, one person might take on several (or even all) of the roles we discuss here. That's all OK, but please keep in mind that when giving the following answers we focus on what in our experience is a "typical" scenario.

When do the business analysts stop modeling and developers take over?

The typical approach goes as follows: Business analysts, focusing on the requirements and the communication to stakeholders, typically create the first draft of a model. They should of course have an executable process model in mind, but they might make some mistakes. Ideally, the business analyst collaborates with developers as well as end users to make sure they develop a model that will, later on, be executable. The best situations we have seen are workshops with all those roles together in one room discussing the model. In such a setting, the business analysts might, for example, learn why it is hard to implement a process in the current IT ecosystem, and the developers might learn that legal requirements are what led to such a complicated process. These insights alone have huge value.

Keep in mind that you should not try to sketch a perfect model right away. Most often it is better to focus on an MVP first and make this process model executable going through the whole lifecycle. This helps everybody in the team to understand how things really work, which in turn will ensure the team knows how to create good models when moving forward.

This MVP model is handed over to developers to add all the technical details required to make it executable.

What happens if a business analyst needs to make changes later on?

As described previously, you might work on two physical copies of the model: one in the developer's version control and one in the web modeler. It's important to have clarity on which model is leading, when a business analyst can make changes to the copy in the web modeler, and how changes are merged.

Most often, we see defined points in time where those merges happen. So, the business analyst can make changes in the web modeler and add those changes to a user story to implement (e.g. using the web modeler's diffing features). Those changes are then either merged using an XML merge tool or simply remodeled in the desktop modeler (again, more features for this are on Camunda's roadmap).

Delivery

How do you improve currently deployed processes, and who drives those improvements?

The currently deployed process should have found its way back into the web modeler too, and you can discuss changes there to arrive at a concrete improvement story, which will then be merged into or remodeled in the executable process model. In general, we have found that while remodeling is not very attractive to many people, it's a simple approach that works pretty well, as the actual changes that need to be made to the model are typically small compared to the volume of the discussions that go into them. Diffing features in the modeling tools can help you identify the relevant changes.

Most often, in pro-code scenarios, there are subsequent changes based on process changes anyway; for example, test cases might need to be altered, or data mappings might need to be adjusted. Those changes are driven by the developer, so it makes sense that the same person also does the model changes.

How are models marked as ready for production?

In pro-code scenarios, you use the same mechanisms as for source code, meaning that you tag code in your version control system and run whatever testing and QA procedure you require, and this leads to changes being pushed to production.

While models allow for a shortcut (deploying changed models to production during runtime via an API), we advise against using those shortcuts in most scenarios to make sure you maintain the governance you need for red use cases. Of course, there might be exceptions to this rule; for example, you might allow certain DMN tables to be adjusted by business roles on the fly without QA. You need to make a conscious decision in such cases, keeping in mind the risks of such shortcuts.

How do you prevent unauthorized changes?

Typically, authorization is applied on a version control level, meaning only the developers can make changes to the process models used in production. Access to process models in the web modeler is typically rather liberal, as there is value in many people collaborating. Using the milestone feature, the process owner can make sure to control what's going on and potentially roll back changes.

Does the approach change with the maturity of the organization?

The more mature an organization is, the more standardization typically happens around the solution architecture and project templates. This makes it easier to quickly start a development project, which might reduce the web modeler's role in that respect, but its role for collaboration is still the same.

Who brings the developed models to production? Which parts of this can be done without IT involvement?

In red use cases, models are deployed to production by the production application itself, which is in turn deployed by your CI/CD pipeline. Assuming that this pipeline is automated, you do not need IT to trigger it. So while most often developers will push changes to version control and create the appropriate tags to trigger a deployment, you could also trigger that by new milestones in the web modeler created by business people.

Now we enter a scale of less IT involvement that goes as far as doing deployments from the web modeler manually, without any IT involvement at all.

The approach that is appropriate for you to take depends on your situation, taking into account the roles involved, the maturity of your organization, and also the complexity and nonfunctional requirements of the orchestration solution.

Accelerating Solution Building

In essence, there are two options for accelerating projects:

1. **Use vendor-provided accelerators.** Use components that are shipped with your vendor's product or are available via its ecosystem. The prime examples are out-of-the-box connectors that can be used directly, but solution templates or process blueprints might also speed up your projects.

2. **Build your own accelerators within the organization.** Another very successful way to speed up your projects is to build components yourself that can be reused in various projects. A central function like the AAT can build and own such components, and all federated solutions can make use of them.

Delivery

Let's dive into the example of custom connectors, as they are a great way to make certain bespoke logic reusable across the organization. These connectors need to be maintained as well as operated. Typically, every connector is created and maintained as its own development project, somewhere in your version control system. This is in line with what we do for Camunda's own connectors[11]. Every connector should have a clear owner, which might be the AAT itself, or the team that originally developed the connector.

How the connector is operated is an interesting question. Generally, one or more connectors can be bundled together into a connector runtime, as you can find in Camunda's out-of-the-box connector bundle[12]. The connector bundle is a Java application or Docker image that needs to be run for every Camunda cluster that wants to make use of those connectors.

If you run Camunda self-managed, then you might simply add your custom connector bundle to your Helm charts to be created with every cluster. If you run Camunda SaaS, you run the connector bundle yourself, connecting to Camunda via API credentials.

Some customers run multiple connector bundles to satisfy different nonfunctional requirements. For example, some connectors might need to be colocated with the system they connect to, which also allows hybrid cloud scenarios. This removes the burden of requiring firewall access to the system (instead, the connector polls for work); it also allows credentials to stay out of the process orchestration platform's context, and it means sensitive data might never leave your network at all. You might also want to separate connectors that need to scale massively or that are particularly critical from others.

Of course, as mentioned previously, acceleration is not limited to connectors. Other components that can be reused to speed up projects include:

- Solution templates (e.g. Maven archetypes) and reference architectures.
- Process blueprints.
- Testing frameworks (especially testing mechanisms close to the business, like behavior-driven development [BDD]).
- Modular business capabilities.
- Forms.

Questions to Assess Your Maturity

For delivery, we describe the five maturity levels as follows (see Table P.1):

- **Level 0**: Large gaps between business and IT create silos, leading to slow iterations and limited ability to deliver impactful process solutions.

- **Level 1**: Business starts to recognize the transformational potential of IT, but lack of mature IT methodologies prevents agile delivery in small increments.

- **Level 2**: As business and IT alignment improves and the organization shifts to more agile development, teams begin to deliver continuous improvements in short sprints based on process data.

- **Level 3**: Multiple BizDevOps teams are involved in delivery and establishing best practices that speed up time to value; improved process monitoring allows organizations to track impact on business outcomes.

- **Level 4**: Business teams can self-serve on an increasing number of use cases with minimal IT involvement, enabled by the AAT; processes are purpose-built to drive business value and adjusted through continuous monitoring and improvement to maximize value.

Questions you should ask yourself to assess your maturity include:

- How closely are business and IT teams collaborating to deliver process solutions?

- Do you have a clear understanding of the project lifecycle?

- Do you have a standardized business case creation process that defines tangible success outcomes?

- Have you defined a standardized solution architecture that delivery teams can pull of the shelf?

- Have you defined and are you leveraging modeling conventions that will help teams in the modeling stage?

- Do you have a clear testing approach that is leveraged across the organization?

- Are your delivery teams using iterative development and continuous improvement approaches to deliver value incrementally?

Delivery

211

- Are you systematically tracking the achieved business value of your delivery initiatives?

- How many delivery teams do you have in your organization that are actively working on process orchestration solutions?

- How do you accelerate solution building through reusable components?

- Have you enabled yellow (medium-complexity) use cases to work with as little IT involvement as possible (e.g. by providing connectors)?

Takeaways

Here are the key insights from this chapter:

- During delivery, teams implement specific process orchestration use cases to achieve business value.

- The delivery lifecycle consists of five key phases: discovery, modeling, development, run, and monitor.

- The discovery stage focuses on identifying process orchestration use cases, defining the business case, capturing success metrics, and clarifying ownership and roles to ensure stakeholder alignment.

- The modeling stage involves creating process models via BPMN with a focus on both business and technical details, starting from high-level abstractions and refining as development progresses.

- The development stage turns process models into executable solutions by integrating system services, configuring connectors, adding other technical elements, as well as testing.

- In the run stage, the solution is deployed into production, focusing on operational stability, incident management, and ensuring smooth change management for affected users.

- The monitor stage emphasizes continuous tracking of KPIs defined earlier, ensuring the orchestration solution delivers business value and identifying opportunities for further improvement.

- The phases don't imply a waterfall approach to development, but should be executed iteratively.

212   Enterprise Process Orchestration

- To accelerate time to value, the solution architecture should ideally be predefined by the ATT. They might define a set of architecture possibilities to cater for different levels of complexity. Teams should be allowed to adapt if needed.

- Solution building can be accelerated by leveraging vendor-provided accelerators (like pre-built connectors and templates) or by developing custom reusable components within the organization.

Chapter 5: Measurement

This last chapter focuses on a topic that is (strangely) often neglected in transformation initiatives. It's about measuring the business value that you are achieving through your program. Your process orchestration platform will be a great source for data, but you have to make sense of it and translate it into meaningful business metrics, motivating goals, and effective KPIs. The challenge is to agree on what is worth measuring and how to operationalize it, and to establish a shared understanding about those metrics across the organization. Combine this with a data-driven mindset where measurements will lead to action, and you get the final recipe for your journey toward successful enterprise process orchestration.

Historically, organizations have had a hard time defining metrics to improve their operations through end-to-end digital transformation initiatives. As most processes are implemented in a rather chaotic way, through a mix of islands of automation, spaghetti integrations, and manual work, they cannot properly measure value creation along the value stream, such as improvements in processing speed or operational costs. In such an environment, any process improvement initiative will inevitably end up creating a lot of guesswork without clear feedback on its success. In other words, the missing focus on the end-to-end flow, plus a typical lack of customer-centricity, makes it really hard to measure value (as indicated in Figure 5.1).

With process orchestration you can overcome those problems, as you will not only have an end-to-end view, but also data to track relevant KPIs. This chapter aims to equip you with the tools to do this. We'll look at which value drivers you can leverage through process orchestration, how to define proper KPIs based on those, and ultimately how to operationalize them in your organization and enterprise architecture. But first, let's quickly go over the importance of metrics, especially in IT.

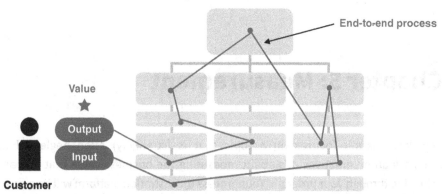

Figure 5.1 When processes touch many organizational units and don't have a clear owner, it's hard to measure and increase their value contribution (taken from this CamundaCon 2024 presentation[1]).

Why Metrics Matter

Somewhat counterintuitively, in many organizations IT is still seen as a cost center whose primary function is to deliver the needed IT capabilities at the lowest cost possible. In such a scenario, the CIO's success will likely be measured by driving down the IT spend per revenue or per employee. Those metrics are easy to capture and easy to benchmark against industry peers. However, this mindset and those metrics fall short in evaluating the strategic contribution IT makes to the organization, in a time when digital competitiveness has become table stakes.

Most likely, every reader of this book will agree that this view is outdated: The role of IT is shifting toward being a strategic enabler for the business. This change, however, requires a mindset shift in the overall company strategy and the business, and it requires IT leaders and team members to adapt and learn to think and communicate in terms of business value. "Speak the language of the business" is an idiom that is often evoked in such scenarios. And rightly so: This is what business leaders understand and listen to.

Process orchestration is a great enabler of bringing together business and IT in the pursuit of business value, as it puts business processes – and therefore operational efficiency, as well as customer experience – front and center. Unfortunately, IT teams are historically bad at quantifying and celebrating their successes and impact on the business. This is somewhat understandable, as it is often hard to measure the precise business value of IT initiatives and disentangle them from other factors influencing the business outcome, such as the overall company strategy and macroeconomic conditions. It is crucial, however, to overcome this, and for IT leaders to have a seat at the tables where strategic decisions are made (i.e. on the board level). To quote an enterprise architect we spoke with recently, "The business does not care about the technology mumbo jumbo your engineers are talking about – but they do care about the impact it is making."

Ideally, you'll connect every IT initiative to leading business indicators. These are metrics that predict the future performance of the organization and are crucial to evaluate whether an initiative will yield a return in the long run. Some common leading business indicators are customer satisfaction, sales pipeline numbers, customer acquisition rates, employee engagement and turnover rates, and operational efficiency metrics. When you are able to show that you will have a positive impact on those numbers, you will have the ear of your CEO.

To illustrate this, let's weave in a real-life story from an insurance company that is strategically deploying process orchestration across the organization. They've orchestrated a few hundred processes, ranging from core processes like claims handling to smaller ones like address changes. Customers can now self-service online, and processing time and quality have improved significantly through the company's transformation effort. The process orchestration initiative looks like a big success.

But unfortunately, the team running this initiative never properly quantified the business value that was enabled by process orchestration. The C-suite weren't even aware why process orchestration was so crucial for their success. When we started to ask various people in IT, they all said process orchestration was critical, but nobody could translate that into concrete, tangible business outcomes business leaders would care about. While advocates secured the budget with the CTO through discussions highlighting the qualitative contributions, there was no visibility on the value beyond these conversations. The process orchestration platform was "just another" expense in the IT budget. The business departments did not have any sense of ownership of the processes, nor did they fully grasp the value of process orchestration. Most of them probably didn't even know if the business solutions they were using were built using BPMN or simply hardcoded in some programming language.

Interestingly, this was in stark contrast to the perception of robotic process automation in the company, which C-level executives raved about, as they saw it as yielding a massive return on investment. A bit of digging showed that RPA projects were

Measurement
217

initiated by business departments, and they always needed to present a sound ROI story to get funded. Showcasing the business value was inherently built into the process of kicking off an RPA project, which led to a positive perception of RPA by leaders.

Of course, it's arguably much easier to calculate the ROI for RPA projects. As bots typically replace human tasks, you can easily calculate x person hours saved multiplied by hourly costs of y equals z dollars saved. In fact, this is so easy that RPA vendors don't even need to provide a ROI calculator.

Measuring value is a harder exercise for process orchestration because typically you do not simply replace human work by orchestrating a process. Instead, you unlock strategic value around improving the customer experience or enabling business agility while driving operational efficiency. But that also means that the value potential goes far beyond what RPA can ever do, which creates a huge potential for IT to underline their importance as a driver of strategic transformation. This is especially true given that the simplicity of RPA can backfire quickly – not only is the initial value it achieves trapped on a local task level, not necessarily improving the overall end-to-end process, but the solution can even create technical debt as RPA bots become prone to errors and hard to maintain. Process orchestration can tame this complexity by orchestrating bots, focusing on the complete end-to-end process and making single bots easily replaceable, for example, by API-driven systems.

When you set out on the journey to express the business value of process orchestration through tangible metrics, you start a communication cycle that will also lead to the business being more closely involved in goal and metrics definition. This will ultimately lead to shared ownership between business and IT, which (as reported by Gartner[2]) is an important building block for improving collaboration between the two. Not only will IT understand its contribution to the business better, but the business itself will gain a better understanding of its value streams and how they can be improved, while taking on more accountability in this change process (e.g. through leveraging process dashboards).

Value Drivers of Enterprise Process Orchestration

To understand how you can track the value of your initiatives, let's look at the three different levels on which enterprise process orchestration can drive value for your organization: the strategic impact of the technology on the business, the value on the operational process level, and improvements on the solution level. Figure 5.2 summarizes some of the main value drivers and possible KPIs at each level.

Figure 5.2 Value drivers of process orchestration on different levels.

The strategic value of process orchestration broadly affects the overall performance of an organization and its success in achieving its business goals. **Strategic** value drivers affect the top and bottom line of the business, such as financial performance, customer satisfaction, market share, and operational efficiency. They should be aligned with the organization's high-level objectives. We sort these value drivers into three main buckets:

- **Customer experience** (measured for example by customer satisfaction, expansion revenue, retention rate, and net new revenue).

- **Operational excellence** (measured by metrics such as productivity ratio, expense reduction, and employee satisfaction).

- **Risk mitigation and compliance** (measured by audit readiness, regulatory compliance, or fines avoided).

You can look at those from three different perspectives: the business, the customer, and the employee. Make sure to properly include all those perspectives – the customer and/or the employee are all too often forgotten. For example, if you define strategic goals for a value stream, you can derive those from the value stream itself, resulting in internally focused metrics around operational efficiency, like cost savings, reduced error rates, or providing services faster. But you can also look at the customer journey, resulting in externally focused metrics around customer experience, like net promoter score, customer retention rates, or cross- or upsell amounts.

Established business process management methodologies typically describe six ways how process improvements can help meet strategic goals: short cycle times, low process costs, high process quality, high product quality, high customer satisfaction, and high employee satisfaction.

Operational process-level value drivers focus on the business performance of individual business processes, mostly on Level 3 (end-to-end processes) and Level 4 (business capabilities) of our business architecture (introduced in "Building a Business Architecture to Realize Digitalization and Automation Benefits"). They indicate how well a particular process is running, thereby enabling continuous improvement. Those KPIs (sometimes also just referred to as "process KPIs") are granular and help process owners, business capability owners, or operational teams to monitor and optimize processes. They show exactly how a business capability or a process is performing, enabling targeted improvements and optimization.

Figure 5.2 gave some concrete examples. In slightly more more general terms, KPIs at this level will focus on:

- Increasing the **automation rate**.
- Reducing **manual work**.
- Increasing **savings** by reducing customer servicing costs.
- **Speeding up** the results for the customer.
- Improving the **compliance rate** of your processes.
- Reducing **error and rework** rates.

The strategic and operational outcomes outlined above can only be achieved when process orchestration solutions are built successfully. Thus, the final set of value drivers focus on the way solutions are implemented and adopted across the organization. At the **enablement** level, you're not directly generating business value per se, but improvements you make here will help you deliver the business value at the other two levels by accelerating teams and giving them reliable tools. Typical areas to focus on are:

- **Development effort** savings or **implementation cost** reduction.

- **Democratization** and **collaboration** (including different roles in solution development, using rare technical resources in an optimal way, making sure to build the right thing by including all necessary stakeholders in a project).

- **Agility** (providing visibility to the business and aligning with business strategies, reducing time to value, enabling continuous improvement with short iterations).

- **Platform performance** (e.g. uptime, throughput, or reuse rate).

- **Adoption** across the organization (e.g. community size, enabled roles, and number of teams using process orchestration).

Keep in mind that different value drivers will be interesting for different people, corresponding with the governance layers of the business architecture described in "Adoption Governance (aka Who Owns the Business Architecture?)". While the strategic value is a top management play, relevant to the executive steering committee, the transformation office, and senior leaders, operational process-level value drivers are important tools for the business process optimization group, business leaders, and process owners looking to operationalize the strategy. Solution-level value drivers, in contrast, are most interesting for IT and the adoption acceleration team, helping them to drive improvements in the way they build solutions and to explain how IT enables the business.

Understanding Metrics

In this section, we'll dive a bit deeper into what makes good metrics and explore the difference between measurements, metrics, and KPIs.

Measurements, Metrics, Goals, KPIs, and SLAs

Let's start with a few quick definitions, to make sure we're all on the same page:

- **Measurements** provide the raw data.

- **Metrics** are created by analyzing and interpreting measurements.

- **Goals** set the strategic direction and desired outcomes for metrics.

- **KPIs** track the progress of metrics toward the goals.

For example, for a loan application process, you will track the cycle time of each process instance. This is your **measurement**. On its own, this will only give you a table full of data. To make sense of it you need to create **metrics**, like the average time from application submission to loan disbursement, or to better help you judge if your processing speed is on track, that is, the median application submission to loan disbursement time (often there will be a small number of outliers that are processed very slowly – of course, you'll also want to analyze why that is the case, but that's a different story).

Now you need to define the **goal** for that metric: for example, you want to disburse within three business days. This goal is typically informed by the status quo, but also by your strategy, as you might need to decide if you want to be fast at the expense of thoroughness (a great example of a company that took this approach was PayPal, which prioritized simplicity and speed over risk mitigation – the opposite of what banks were doing back then), or if it's better to take a bit more time to reduce the risk of making a wrong decision. Truth be told, most of the time nowadays automation gives you both – faster and more reliable results – but this is not always the case.

Once you know the goal, you can set up a **KPI** to measure the progress of your metric toward that goal. Technically, this might simply mean properly visualizing the metric, as shown in Figure 5.3.

The final concept to mention here is service level agreements. SLAs are also based on metrics, but whereas you can think of KPIs as a sort of North Star helping an organization to move in the right direction, SLAs provide a minimum baseline over which the metrics need to perform. You might have both internal and external SLAs:

- **Internal SLAs** are used to define nonfunctional requirements of your business capabilities. For example, the underwriting capability might agree to underwrite within a maximum of five business days, which is an SLA the loan application capability is counting on to meet its own goals.

- **External SLAs** are often rooted in compliance, or contracts. For example, the loan disbursement may be operated for a reseller that white-labels the loan contract. In this case, the bank might need to commit to an SLA that 99% of all contracts are dispersed within seven business days.

Figure 5.3 Example dashboard showing how to compare a metric to your goal, making it a KPI.

The big difference from a KPI is the element of commitment, as often there are fines or other penalties involved if an SLA is not met.

Figure 5.4 summarizes these concepts.

What Makes a Good KPI?

It's important to establish clear and measurable KPIs that align with top-line business objectives. The KPIs need to be derived from your business strategy and overall business goals. They act as guideposts, tracking progress and driving the project toward overarching success, and help to communicate value clearly. You can draw inspiration from the framework that we laid out in "Value Drivers of Enterprise Process Orchestration".

The same metric might lead to different KPIs depending on if you want to be the fastest on the market, the cheapest, or perhaps simply grow as quickly as possible. It's important to consider the following factors when selecting the most relevant KPIs for an organization:

- **Alignment with business goals:** KPIs must align with the overarching business objectives to ensure that process orchestration efforts contribute to the company's success.

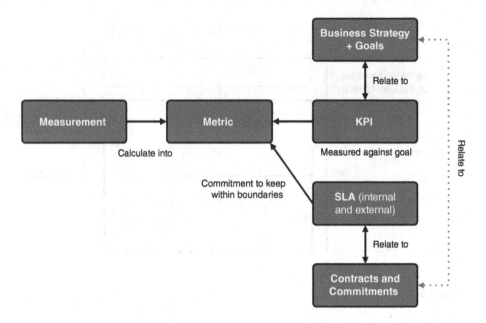

Figure 5.4 Connections between measurements, metrics, goals, KPIs, and SLAs.

- **Relevance to the process:** In the context of process orchestration, each process may require unique KPIs tailored to its specific requirements and characteristics.

- **Measurability:** Effective KPIs must be measurable, with clear data points to track progress accurately and assess performance. Process orchestration platforms should inherently measure the processes they execute and be able to derive metrics and track KPIs, which simplifies this factor.

- **Actionability:** KPIs should provide actionable insights that enable organizations to take meaningful steps toward process improvement. Having a metric available in your process orchestration platform does not automatically qualify it as a KPI.

If you want to keep it short, you can simply say your KPIs need to be **SMART** (specific, measurable, achievable, relevant, and time-bound).

It's also important to limit the number of KPIs. There is a reason they are called *key performance indicators* – if you define too many of them, the signal-to-noise ratio will be too low and people will lose sight of the most important information. A related point is that you should keep your stakeholders in mind when defining KPIs. While a typical process owner might want to dive deeper into all sorts of metrics, C-level executives will likely only want to look at two to three KPIs per process.

Example Metrics and KPIs

Let's look at some possible metrics and derived KPIs you might want to track, sorted according to the value drivers we introduced earlier. We will use the bank account opening process of a fictional bank, which we'll call Flow Bank, to give concrete examples.

Strategic KPIs / Customer experience:

- **Customer satisfaction:** Assesses customer feedback and satisfaction levels related to processes. Improved satisfaction scores can indicate the positive impact of streamlined and well-orchestrated processes.

  Flow Bank fights for new customers, but also needs to retain existing ones. Net promoter score (NPS) is the typical metric for customer satisfaction, but they also want to track the number of new customers.

Strategic KPIs / Operational efficiency:

- **Expense reduction:** Quantifies the reduction in costs due to improved process efficiency and resource utilization. These include labor costs, operational costs, and overheads.

  Process orchestration has enabled Flow Bank to reassign a team of 10 full-time employees (FTEs) to other tasks than handling bank account openings, resulting in savings of around $500,000 per year.

- **Employee satisfaction:** Gauges employee happiness – a sometimes forgotten but important factor in today's world, with the talent shortages companies face. You can measure the employee engagement score, for example, which will rise if you set up a meaningful process orchestration practice that can take tedious coordination tasks or double-work off employees' plates and let them concentrate on the work they like doing.

  Flow Bank's frontline clerks no longer take calls from frustrated users asking for their onboarding status. Instead, they concentrate on proactively handling failures whenever the orchestration process runs into a problem, making their daily work more fulfilling.

Strategic KPIs / Risk and compliance:

- **Service level agreement (SLA) compliance:** Measures the adherence to predefined SLAs. High compliance rates indicate that processes are meeting or exceeding service expectations.

  Flow Bank uses process orchestration for trade settlements, which need to be done within one business day (T+1) to avoid fines. Previously, the bank had "thrown people at the problem" and needed a huge team of more than 25 externals to speed up trade settlement manually. The orchestration solution saves the company roughly $1.2 million per year and avoids fines from regulators.

Operational process-level KPIs / Process efficiency:

- **Process cycle or completion time:** Measures the average time taken to complete a process from end to end. Shorter times positively link to a variety of strategic KPIs: For example, customer experience, as customers don't like to wait, and regulatory compliance, as processes are able to keep within regulated SLAs.

  Flow Bank brought down the time required to open a bank account from five days to two business hours by using an orchestrated process.

- **Automation rate:** Tracks the percentage of processes or activities that are automated. Higher automation rates correlate with more efficient and consistent process execution. This can mean less human work for each process instance, which results in cost savings, as well as the possibility to scale the process to handle more new customers.

  Flow Bank fully orchestrated the bank account opening process and reduced manual involvement in resolving (lesser) problems. The automation rate increased from less than 10 to 95%.

- **Throughput:** Tracks the number of processes completed within a given time frame. Higher throughput allows the process solution to scale.

  Flow Bank was able to create a new low-cost offering that attracts a large number of customers, handled by a stable number of employees.

Process efficiency KPIs typically directly influence strategic KPIs (especially related to operational efficiency and customer experience).

Operational process-level KPIs / Quality and compliance:

- **Error rate:** Tracks the frequency of errors or exceptions in processes. Lower error rates suggest more reliable and effective process orchestration. This influences not only customer experience, but also compliance.

  Orchestrating the bank account opening process increased the quality of the process and made it consistent for nearly every customer. Flow Bank was able to reduce the percentage of bank account opening cancellations due to technical problems by 3.5x, resulting in thousands of net new customers per year.

- **Compliance rate:** Assesses the level of risk associated with process execution. Lower risk levels imply that orchestration has made processes more predictable and controlled.

  The orchestrated bank account opening process allows Flow Bank to assess customer scores consistently, avoiding potential biases of individual employees. It also ensures no important risk controls or Know Your Customer (KYC) checks are missed. This is estimated to avoid 100 customer contracts a year ending up in trouble, saving considerable human labor and legal costs (an estimated savings of $200,000–$750,000 per year). In addition, it ensures FlowBank does not receive negative press due to allegations of discrimination against certain customer groups.

Solution level KPIs / Solution-building efficiency:

- **Time to market:** Measures the time it takes to launch new products or services.

  Flow Bank was able to accelerate development and reduce onboarding time for projects by 50%, based on analysis of similar project implementations.

- **Business agility:** Provides an indication of how easy it is to make changes to the business. Having a handle on end-to-end processes is a key enabler of agility.

  Within their orchestrated processes, Flow Bank can discuss the use of AI and easily start using the technology for tasks where it is applicable. They can roll these changes out risk-free by using AB testing or humans as backups.

- **Development cost:** Quantifies the savings made by reducing the technical complexity while increasing business/IT collaboration. Executable models eliminate translation errors during the implementation phase, lessening the effort and time required to build automation solutions.

At Flow Bank, the ratio of FTEs required for developing traditional solutions versus process orchestration solutions was 6:1.

Most of the abovementioned metrics should of course be monitored over time, to facilitate a continuous improvement process.

Operationalizing Your Metric-Driven Approach

Now that we have the basic definitions, let's look at how to operationalize such an approach.

Metrics Are Not an Afterthought

We want to highlight one important aspect first: Metrics on business value should not be an afterthought for your program! They should actually drive the discussion about process orchestration use cases. Metrics will help you to strategically plan your automation efforts and prioritize areas for automation. Be sure to think about metrics and KPIs up front.

Unfortunately, in reality this advice isn't always followed, especially when IT is introducing process orchestration in a bottom-up fashion to solve certain technical challenges. While there is nothing wrong with such a bottom-up approach per se (as discussed in "Amplifying Organic Bottom-Up Initiatives"), the people behind those initiatives often start to think about measuring the achieved value too late – that is, after the initial projects have successfully gone live, when they recognize that they need to improve their communication to get heard internally. This is commonly an aha moment, as nobody seems to be interested in their great achievements. At this point it is often harder to track the right metrics. Also, benchmark data showing how the process was performing before the new solution was implemented is often not available anymore – for example, you can only attribute a 50%-error rate reduction to your automation solution if you start to measure error rates before implementing it.

To reemphasize this point, it's important to understand process-level and strategic KPIs even in bottom-up scenarios. We often hear from our customer development teams that they want to mature the process orchestration capabilities in the organization as they understand and recognize the value of this approach at the technology

228   Enterprise Process Orchestration

level. But because they fall short in expressing the business value, this negatively impacts their own experience and morale – you only get the resources required for broader adoption (which would require quite a transformation and enablement effort) if you are able to show the impact on the business.

By treating metrics as first-class citizens, you can make sure that you have them top of mind when building your new automation solutions, and that you implement the solutions in a way that allows you to measure the business outcomes.

Mapping Metrics and KPIs to Value Drivers

So, let's dive deeper into how you can treat metrics as first-class citizens. Metrics and KPIs need to be mapped and traced through the various levels of value drivers.

This works in top-down as well as bottom-up initiatives. To give a bottom-up example, an automation project might have orchestrated the loan disbursement process. This shortened the cycle time to loan disbursement (an operational process-level KPI). This in turn increased customer satisfaction, measured by NPS (a strategic KPI) – and the project was only possible because the use of process orchestration technology reduced time to value and lowered the overall development effort (solution-level KPIs).

A top-down story might start in your annual company planning process. Your senior leadership defines a North Star vision connected to measurable strategic KPIs: For example, your organization wants to enable fully digital electronic loan applications (meaning a maximum 1%-customer interaction rate), at a competitive price (meaning that customer acquisition costs are below $15), with a decision in under 24 hours.

Now, your SVP of consumer loans gathers their leadership team and derives operational KPIs for the loan application process: cycle time < 24 hours, automation rate > 99%, resource utilization for clerks < 10 FTEs, raised service requests < 150/month.

Sitting down with IT, they scope the project with a budget and settle on the development approach: agile, with continuous deployment.

One important observation here is that strategic business KPIs are hard to control directly. They are often influenced by external market forces. A recent example is that the demand for loans was heavily influenced by global interest rate developments that are beyond the control of a single bank. However, organizations can effectively drive their operational process-level KPIs, which in turn also influence these higher-level strategic KPIs. For example, by improving operational efficiency and the effectiveness of the loan application process through an automation solution, they are able to reduce their own surcharge on the premium, creating a ripple effect that positively impacts strategic business outcomes.

Also, providing self-service with blazing-fast loan decisions (the operational process-level KPI of cycle time) will lead to more customers coming to you, affecting customer or revenue growth (strategic KPIs). You can compare this to lean principles, which emphasize continuous improvement and waste reduction, demonstrating that enhancing the way an organization operates can lead to significant gains in performance metrics.

The challenge is that metrics on different levels are often only indirectly connected, especially looking at how project-level KPIs influence strategic KPIs. But communicating this link is actually the trick you need to learn to make the important people in the organization aware of the transformative power of process orchestration.

We like to use concrete stories to illustrate this. For example, suppose you decide to start offering loans via a new channel (e.g. a new app), and therefore create not only the user interface, but also a solution orchestrating the back office process behind it. The app might be hugely successful in driving new revenue and increasing customer satisfaction, affecting strategic KPIs. Is all of this because your process-level KPIs, like automation rate or cycle time, improved? Of course not – it's also because you leveraged new user interface technologies, probably ran a big advertising campaign, and probably also adjusted your product to the channel. So, it's a mix.

Still, you need to link some of that development to the streamlined process due to the automation solution. It doesn't matter too much if that's 82% or 49%; the important thing is to tell a consistent story of how those KPIs unlock the business impact.

The next step in this exercise is to clearly articulate the value contribution of process orchestration to achieving the operational process-level KPIs. This is now less about linking specific KPIs directly, and more about telling a story that shows how using process orchestration technology allowed you to build your automation solution faster, better align it with the real business requirements, operate it more reliably, and continuously improve the underlying business process. In other words, process automation not only makes the automation solution possible in the first place, but also makes it better.

This relationship is visualized in Figure 5.5. It's quite similar to the layering of KPIs, but visualizes the same information from a higher level that allows you to explain the contribution of process orchestration to business outcomes.

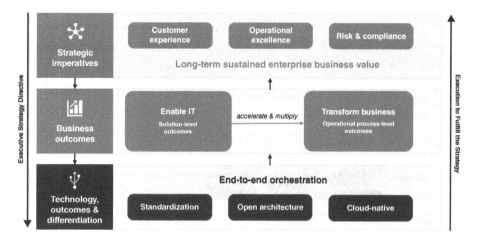

Figure 5.5 Value relationship across different dimensions.

Mapping Value Flow Through Business Architecture Layers

In "Building a Business Architecture to Realize Digitalization and Automation Benefits", we defined a business architecture that contains customer journeys, value streams, and business capabilities that can be mapped to executable processes. This is a great basis to implement strategic KPIs.

You start by defining the strategic goals of your value stream (Level 2 of the architecture). When you have those KPIs, you need to connect them to a business capability (or, more likely, several business capabilities) implementing the value stream. For example, your organization might want to speed up the time from customers looking for a loan to the loan disbursement. This might be separated into two KPIs: one for the marketing folks to process people in the funnel faster, for example, through limited-time offers for prospective customers visiting your home page, and another looking at the end-to-end application submission to loan disbursement process as part of the loan application business capability.

The latter capability will require other capabilities to work, so its KPI needs to be distributed further. For example, in order to meet a three-day loan disbursement KPI, you need to look at where time is spent. You might identify that underwriting is typically taking too long to make this goal realistic, so you need to discuss improvements with the team responsible for that business capability.

This is also where KPIs meet SLAs, as internally you might want to work with SLAs for every business capability, as part of their definition. This avoids the need to look into a business capability when discussing processing speed at a higher level. In our example, the owner of the loan application capability should negotiate an improved SLA with underwriting in order to meet their own targets. SLAs are an important tool to distribute KPIs across various business capabilities. This is visualized in Figure 5.6.

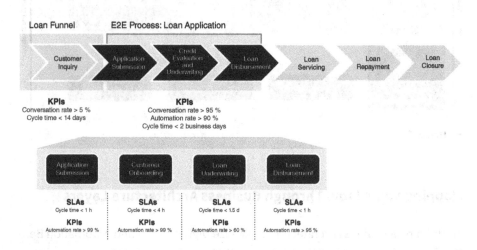

Figure 5.6 Tracking KPIs and SLAs across the different business capabilities of an end-to-end process.

When using executable processes to implement a business capability, you can easily make sure the required metrics are available to measure KPIs. It's important to have those target KPIs top of mind when designing processes, as the process design will influence how easily metrics can be calculated by the platform. For example, you might want to use separate end events for failure scenarios, so you can calculate error rates without any additional logic (the next section will look into this in more detail). Figure 5.7 shows how SLAs and KPIs can be measured for the onboarding process. The visualized KPIs and required metrics should be directly available through your process orchestration platform, as they relate to generic process concepts.

In this example, you would probably also want to break down the cycle time further into specific tasks. For example, the identity verification task might take the longest, and you'll want to define an SLA with the group owning this capability. The process model and the defined SLAs will help you understand that in order to provide a faster onboarding service, you will need a faster identity verification process.

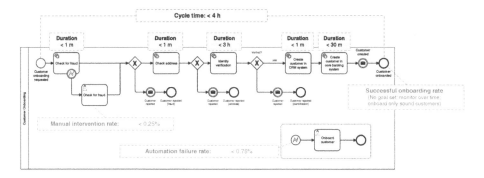

Figure 5.7 Measuring KPIs and SLAs for an onboarding process.

While you will only define a small number of relevant KPIs on the end-to-end process level, the data available in your process orchestration platform will allow you to drill down into those. For example, looking at the cycle time (how long does it take to disburse loans after the submission of an application?), you can use the data the process orchestration platform delivers to dive into questions like: Are there any differences based on specific data, like the loan amount? Which step in the process takes the longest, and can the SLA for that business capability be negotiated to speed up the processing? Or, looking at the approval rate (how many loans are approved?), you can dig deeper into the data to answer questions like: What's the main reason applications are denied? Can we do anything about it? This will ultimately help to improve the company's top and bottom line and give the business an important stake in your transformation journey.

Modeling for Measurement

Let's get a bit more operational now and equip you with some tips and tricks for creating executable BPMN process models that make measuring your KPIs and SLAs easy. This is a great example of where business stakeholders, process modelers, and developers need to collaborate to create a great solution. The aim of this section is not to list every possible pattern, but to give you an idea of how the modeling will influence your ability to measure important metrics. Done right, your process orchestration platform can collect the right data so that you can create dashboards with almost no effort. You should make sure not to miss out on this opportunity.

As an example, let's use the Identity Verification business capability. An executable process model for implementing this capability is shown in Figure 5.8.

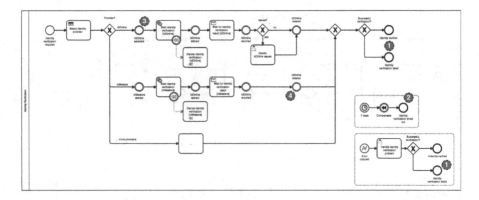

Figure 5.8 Executable process model implementing the Identity Verification business capability.

In this process model:

1. There are different end states, depending on whether verification succeeded or failed. The same end states are also used if the process escalates verification to a human due to technical errors. This makes it very easy to calculate success rates.

2. There is a separate end state for timeouts, making it easy to calculate timeout rates and allowing you to drill into timed-out process instances and look for root causes in the scenarios where processes most often time out.

3. Intermediate events can mark milestones in a process, such as that identity verification has started or succeeded. This indicates a meaningful business state to operators and allows you to get a more fine-grained understanding of cycle times (e.g. When did a particular event happen? In which state was the most time spent?). It also helps to keep the customer journey top of mind, as milestones most often relate to events that matter to the customer.

4. The same milestones are included for every process branch to make them comparable, even if in the case of "IdMasters" the milestones happen one after another without any tasks in between.

Note that you always add information about important key performance indicators implicitly; for example, by the start and end events. Additionally, you often add more business milestones by modeling intermediate events. These event elements might not have any execution semantics other than leaving a trace in the history of the workflow engine; the milestone is met as soon as the process has passed the event, so its status can either be passed or not passed. Furthermore, you can add business phases by modeling (embedded) subprocesses.

In addition to modeling for reporting, you can also add specific data to the process model for reporting purposes. In the previous example, it might make sense to add some anonymized customer data to enable digging into causal relationships. For instance, if process instances for customers from a specific age group are more likely than others to time out, this can give you an indication of where you might be able to improve your process. A potential hypothesis could be that elderly people might have more problems doing identity verification on their smartphones.

Setting Up Continuous Measurements and Communication

When you have defined your metrics and KPIs, you have to set up a communication plan around those. Some KPIs might be communicated very selectively, while others warrant a monthly or weekly update. The presentation will differ depending on the stakeholders you want to address, as will the channels. Typical target people include:

- **Executive leadership:** Include very condensed information (e.g. as traffic lights) in existing regular reports, often made weekly. Set up quarterly meetings to discuss the most important KPIs from all important end-to-end processes with them directly, possibly even presenting them to the board of directors. Focus on strategic KPIs, as they link to business outcomes, or some selected operational process-level KPIs that directly influence the strategic KPIs. This discussion should be easy for a CEO to follow, while making sure everybody stays aligned. It is worth investing some manual effort into determining how best to present the selected KPIs.

- **Middle management:** Create a dashboard with a mix of strategic and operational KPIs that allow a detailed analysis of the process's performance and challenges and enable assessment of potential improvement plans. Ideally, this dashboard is fed with real-time data and can be accessed on a self-service basis. However, make sure to set up regular meetings – say, once a month – to make sure all important stakeholders are leveraging and understand the data presented. This can also take you a long way toward creating a process-first mindset.

- **Process owners and team leads:** Include detailed operational KPIs and specific end-to-end process metrics. The team will be interested in incidents and

Measurement 235

love to drill down further into the details of various metrics whenever something catches their eye. Real-time dashboards are key for this, probably with an additional weekly reporting cadence to make sure nobody forgets about the dashboard. A weekly meeting to analyze the data, perform root cause analysis of issues, and discuss short-term action plans will also be helpful. Some teams even include the dashboard in daily standup meetings or keep it on permanent display on a hardware monitor in the team room, as shown in Figure 5.9. This can be a great way of encouraging more process-centric and data-driven thinking at the same time.

- **Engineers and software developers:** Engineers often have a different way of looking at metrics. Providing general process KPIs, with the possibility to drill deep into them, combined with general monitoring metrics around system load might make them much happier and trigger better feedback than pestering them with net promoter scores.

Figure 5.9 Still a good tool: a hardware dashboard visible to everyone in the office.

As always, exceptions validate the rule, and not every individual is the same. We have seen developers focusing on the company's bottom line with dedication, as well as CEOs that love to dive deep into operational measurements to get to the bottom of some discussion.

To make this more tangible, we want to highlight a practical example. In customer scenarios we regularly run value engineering workshops, where we work with our customers to come up with relevant KPIs to track the business impact of their initiatives. When doing this for an omnichannel account onboarding process with an international bank, we ended up with the following list of important metrics, all of which could be compared by channel:

- Journey throughput (number of onboardings per day).
- Average time spent for journey completion (with an SLA set to 15 minutes), but allowing drilling into the various high-level phases of the process.
- Close rate (percentage), with a distribution of the typical drop-off points.
- Percentage of journeys without exceptions.
- Percentage of journeys canceled.
- Percentage of journeys abandoned.
- Percentage of journeys with escalations.
- Customer satisfaction (surveyed specifically for onboardings).

This is a lot of data, and it's all interesting to look at on the operational level or during improvement projects. The company ended up creating a dashboard for the operations team that made all of this data available. This was very helpful in enabling business and technical team leads to efficiently operate the process, understand problems, and think about improvements.

However, it was too much information to distribute to others in the organization. We agreed to distill a more strategic view of this data into a second dashboard, which was mainly for the SVP of consumer loans and focused on the aggregated median of the key operational process metrics (journey throughput, SLA compliance, close rate, and error rate).

We also agreed to focus on only three main KPIs to report to a wider audience, including C-level executives:

- **Close rate:** The close rate is important to judge the effectiveness of the onboarding process.
- **Duration median:** The duration is an indicator of operational efficiency and should directly influence customer satisfaction. Using the median is important to soften the effect of outliers.

- **Online application ratio:** The organization had a specific focus on increasing the usage of its digital channels, so the online ratio was especially important.

In order to make the desired information accessible, you should build real-time dashboards like the example shown in Figure 5.10 (which is admittedly not from a real-life scenario).

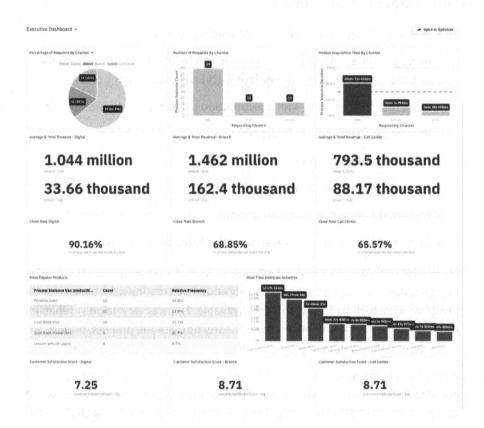

Figure 5.10 Example executive dashboard showing operational project-level KPIs.

In addition to dashboards, you'll probably want to provide qualitative reports. For example, whenever you complete an automation project, you should consider crafting an internal case study that highlights the achievement and lists all the relevant measurable metrics, with some impressive graphics and numbers. You can then share this with the organization at internal forums or events (as well as at external events, if you like). In our experience, investing some effort in putting together some sort of report or presentation and making sure it is communicated internally is definitely worthwhile.

But while we emphasize the importance of all this communication, it is still true that often less is more. Don't flood people with information and overload them with metrics, as that will probably lead to most people simply ignoring them. Instead, decide what KPIs are really important and what is a good cadence for communicating them – and then feel free to pester people a little bit to make sure they have received and understood that information.

Can't We Just Delegate This to Our Existing Data Warehouse Folks?

Before wrapping up, let's quickly discuss one common question: Isn't measurement about reporting, and isn't that what our business intelligence or data warehouse teams are responsible for? In other words, can't I just delegate creating the right dashboards and reports to them?

The short answer is: No, you can't. First of all, tracking the value of your use cases is not an afterthought that you can delegate to another team. You really have to understand what the important goals are and how you can measure those within the team creating automation solutions.

Second, traditional BI tools lack the process context the process orchestration platform has. They don't look at the business through the lens of end-to-end processes, and it's actually very hard to get a process view in those tools. Typically, it's easier to keep the process context in the process orchestration platform (and its own process intelligence tools), and use the BI tools additionally for other correlations (e.g. with accounting data to calculate costs per process).

Furthermore, the loading processes required to get data from the process orchestration platform into the BI tools can easily become dependent on process specifics (e.g. because you want to calculate durations around milestones). But setting up an ETL process that is dependent on details of the business process torpedoes your business agility, as you can no longer adjust your process without also adjusting that ETL process, which is probably owned by another team.

You might still want to add data from the process orchestration platform into your BI solution. This is of course possible, but not always straightforward. Most of the time, the problem is less technical, but because of silos within the IT organization and the lack of process understanding in the BI teams. Our recommendation is to reduce the amount of data passed to those tools to a minimum, refraining from adding too much process-specific data to maintain business agility. The BI tools can then service high-level reports, but the process orchestration platform should remain the source for any more detailed information on process performance and KPIs.

Questions to Assess Your Maturity

For Measurement, we describe the five maturity levels as follows (see page xxv):

- **Level 0:** Processes are not well enough defined to measure anything.
- **Level 1:** Teams are focused solely on completing projects; success is defined as "project is in production." Process metrics are gathered manually, or only technical metrics from an engine are used.
- **Level 2:** Meaningful KPIs are defined and used for individual projects and/or processes. KPIs are mostly operational and not linked to strategic business value.
- **Level 3:** Clear success metrics and KPIs have been established for most processes, with a clear narrative to link those to business goals.
- **Level 4:** The contribution of process orchestration to business outcomes can be clearly shown using continuously measured strategic and operational KPIs. Those KPIs are also driving investment decisions.

Questions you should ask yourself to assess your maturity include:

- What are the value drivers you are pursuing with process orchestration?
- Do the delivery teams (or your program) have a clear picture of which metrics to track in their initiatives?
- How deeply are IT and business teams collaborating in the early stages of a project to define and track metrics for use cases?
- Which metrics are you and your teams actively tracking (strategic, operational, solution-level)?
- Are you modeling your BPMN processes to effectively track and measure their business impact?

240   Enterprise Process Orchestration

- How do you report the achieved value inside of your organization? Are you using process intelligence dashboards? Do you have regular meetings with your key stakeholders to track and report the important metrics? Do you communicate the achieved value inside your organization, through case studies or events?

Takeaways

Here are the key insights from this chapter:

- Measuring the business value of process orchestration initiatives is essential for tracking and communicating success, yet it is often overlooked.

- Business outcomes need to be widely communicated to ensure alignment and understanding across IT and business leadership.

- IT's role is shifting from a cost center to a strategic enabler, requiring alignment with business goals and communication through business metrics.

- Challenges regarding lack of data to define metrics and KPIs can be overcome by process orchestration, which provides an end-to-end view and data for relevant KPIs.

- Linking IT initiatives to leading business indicators is key for demonstrating value as well as building and sustaining stakeholder buy-in. If you can't show the direct relation to strategic value drivers, you can use operational KPIs as a proxy to tell a story about the impact.

- Keep the strategic value drivers in mind, such as customer experience, operational excellence, and risk mitigation.

- Effective KPIs should be aligned with business goals, measurable, actionable, and relevant to the specific process being analyzed.

- Solution-level KPIs, such as time to value, can indicate the impact that your ATT is having on your organization in terms of driving adoption and accelerating delivery teams.

Closing Thoughts

Congratulations, you made it through the book! We hope we've been able to provide you with a clear understanding of how process orchestration can empower you and your organization. More importantly, we hope you feel ready to embark on your own successful journey, as have the countless people who inspired this book. And, of course, we hope you enjoyed reading the book as much as we enjoyed writing it!

As this book has shown, process orchestration is a crucial success factor for digital transformation, IT modernization, and strategic automation initiatives. It also serves as a foundation for unlocking the value of AI. As you've seen, process orchestration is far more than a technical solution – it's a new way of envisioning how work flows across an organization, integrating people, processes, and systems. At its best, it unifies diverse functions, breaks down silos, and enables swift adaptation to changing market demands, regulatory pressures, and customer expectations.

Enterprise process orchestration is a strategic endeavor that requires a vision, clear leadership, and structured efforts to develop both technological capabilities and an organizational culture that supports them. It demands effort, perseverance, a transformational mindset, and commitment from top management. And you always need to put a strong focus on continuously delivering business value through use cases that are grounded in specific business problems.

But first and foremost, it requires committed and enthusiastic people like yourself, who are willing to change their organizations. We are always impressed by what impact passionate individuals can have in the enterprise and how they can change the trajectory of even large organizations through their persistence and commitment.

As you move forward, we hope these final guiding principles will help you navigate your transformation journey:

Vision – Think big, but start small: Create a vision of how process orchestration can transform your organization and what your target operating model will look like, but in the near term focus on achievable, quick wins to build momentum. Afterward, you can gradually increase the maturity of your practice to work toward your vision. The most important thing is to get started. Don't wait for your plan to be perfect – take the first steps now, and learn and iterate on the way.

People – Empower and accelerate teams with an AAT: An adoption acceleration team (your process orchestration CoE, which can, of course, be named something different) speeds up solution building by providing best practices, technology, and enablement of autonomous delivery teams. It ensures consistency and creates a community to share knowledge and create visibility for your program. Putting together a dedicated group of skilled people to drive process orchestration strategically will create a strong foundation from which to scale.

Technology – Provide process orchestration and automation capabilities: Enable your organization by providing a composable orchestration and automation platform, augmented with accelerators. This will help reduce the cognitive load of your delivery teams, allowing them to increase quality and improve time to value at the same time. You can use SaaS platforms or operate the technology yourself, most likely in your AAT. Just make sure your platform follows best practices and allows as much as self service as possible to avoid bottlenecks.

Delivery – Stay focused on value creation: Keep sight of the overarching goals of your process orchestration initiative – enhancing customer experiences, increasing operational efficiency, and sustaining the agility to innovate in a dynamic business environment. While it's essential to anchor any initiative strategically with top management, make sure to deliver tangible, hands-on value from day one and to onboard as many teams as possible.

Measurement – Learn, adapt, and communicate: Assess your process orchestration maturity and prioritize continuous improvement toward your target vision. Use metrics for every orchestrated process to measure the value of orchestration, and derive insights from the data you collect – not only for the use cases you've put into production, but also for the capabilities that you are building to create those use cases. Communicate the achieved value across your organization to build and sustain the buy-in that will help your program snowball.

Remember, technology is only as powerful as the people and strategy that guide it. With these principles in mind, you're equipped to embark on – or evolve – your process orchestration journey.

So, get going and orchestrate the heck out of your business! Become the catalyst for lasting change that your organization will celebrate as essential to its future success. Please don't hesitate to provide us with feedback, ask questions, join forums or conferences, and connect with peers to share your ideas and experiences.

And above all, enjoy the journey!

List of Abbreviations

AAT: Adoption acceleration team. A centralized team of experts (often sitting under the CIO) that drives strategic, scaled adoption of process orchestration across the enterprise.

AI: Artificial intelligence. For the sake of simplicity, in this book we use this as an umbrella term encompassing generative AI, large language models, and related concepts.

BPMN: Business Process Model and Notation. An ISO-standardized modeling language that can express workflows visually, but is also executable. It supports complex workflow patterns and is understandable by both business users and technical teams.

CEO: Chief executive officer. The top executive responsible for the overall direction and success of the organization.

CFO: Chief financial officer. The executive overseeing financial planning, reporting, and the organization's fiscal health.

CIO: Chief information officer. The executive managing the company's IT strategy and ensuring technology supports business goals. The CIO ensures that technology aligns with business goals, improves operational efficiency, and fosters innovation.

CoE: Center of excellence. In general, a central team that enables and supports the rest of the organization with a specific methodology or technology. In the context of enterprise process orchestration, the AAT and POG are the most relevant CoEs.

COO: Chief operating officer. The executive responsible for managing day-to-day operations and process optimization. The COO ensures seamless execution of the business's operational plans.

COTS: Commercial off-the-shelf. Pre-built software products that are purchased and used with minimal customization.

CRM: Customer relationship management. Systems and tools designed to manage the customer relationship.

DDD: Domain-driven design. A software design approach that emphasizes collaboration between technical and business teams to create models based on the core domain of the business.

DMN: Decision Model and Notation. A standard for modeling and executing decisions, often within business processes. Complements BPMN for complex decision making.

ERP: Enterprise resource planning. Integrated software systems used to manage core business areas, such as accounting, supply chains, or human resources.

KYC: Know Your Customer. A regulatory process where businesses verify the identity, financial profile, and risk level of their customers. KYC is essential for compliance and preventing fraud in sectors like finance and insurance.

NPS: Net promoter score. A metric used to measure customer loyalty and satisfaction by asking how likely they are to recommend a product or service to others.

POG: Process optimization group. A centralized team of experts (often sitting under the COO) that drives continuous improvement and maintenance of business processes to ensure alignment with organizational goals.

ROI: Return on investment. A metric used to evaluate the profitability of an investment, vital for decision-making.

RPA: Robotic process automation. Technology for task automation that allows mimicking human interactions with software systems to automate tasks via the user interface.

SDLC: Software development lifecycle. The process used for developing software applications, encompassing stages such as planning, design, coding, testing, deployment, and maintenance.

SLA: Service level agreement. A contract between a service provider and a customer that defines the level of service expected, including performance metrics and responsibilities. SLAs ensure clear expectations and accountability for service delivery.

TCO: Total cost of ownership. A comprehensive assessment of all costs associated with acquiring, deploying, operating, and maintaining a product or system over its lifecycle. TCO helps organizations evaluate the long-term value of investments.

TEI: Total Economic Impact. A framework developed by Forrester Research to assess the financial impact of a technology investment. TEI includes cost, benefits, flexibility, and risk to calculate ROI and value creation.

References

Preface

[1] Camunda (n.d.). Enterprise process orchestration: A hands-on guide to strategy, people, and technology. https://camunda.com/ccon-video/enterprise-process-orchestration-a-hands-on-guide-to-strategy-people-andtechnology (accessed 16 December 2024).

[2] Camunda (2023). Atlassian + Camunda = Hyperautomation. https://camunda.com/blog/2023/01/atlassian-camunda-hyperautomation (accessed 16 December 2024).

[3] Forrester (n.d.). Techniker Krankenkasse Excels with Customer Experience Through Process. https://www.forrester.com/report/techniker-krankenkasse-excels-with-customer-experience-through process/RES180454 (accessed 16 December 2024).

[4] Camunda (n.d.). State of Process Orchestration. https://camunda.com/state-of-process-orchestration (accessed 16 December 2024).

[5] Evans, B. (2024). The AI Summer. https://www.ben-evans.com/benedictevans/2024/7/9/the-ai-summer (accessed 16 December 2024).

[6] Boston Consulting Group (2024). Where's the Value in AI? https://www.bcg.com/publications/2024/wheres-value-in-ai (accessed 16 December 2024).

[7] Fenergo (2023). KYC Trends 2023 Report. https://resources.fenergo.com/reports/kyc-trends-2023-report#main-content (accessed 16 December 2024).

[8] Bureau of Labor Statistics, U.S. Department of Labor (2023). Labor force and macroeconomic projections. https://www.bls.gov/opub/mlr/2023/article/labor-force-and-macroeconomic-projections.htm#:~:text=BLS%20projects%20that%20the%20annual,from%20164.3%20million%20in%202022 (accessed 16 December 2024).

[9] The Economist (2022). There are not enough Germans to do the jobs Germany needs. https://www.economist.com/europe/2022/10/06/there-are-not-enough-germans-to-do-the-jobs-germanyneeds (accessed 16 December 2024).

[10] BNP Paribas (n.d.). T+1 Settlement Ready. https://securities.cib.bnpparibas/t1-settlement-ready (accessed 16 December 2024).

[11] Camunda (n.d.). State of Process Orchestration. https://camunda.com/state-of-process-orchestration (accessed 16 December 2024).

[12] Gartner (2024). Quick Answer: Beyond RPA, BPA and Low Code – The Future Is BOAT. https://www.gartner.com/en/documents/5577427 (accessed 16 December 2024).

[13]Camunda (n.d.). Process Orchestration Maturity. https://camunda.com/process-orchestration/maturity (accessed 16 December 2024).

Introduction

[1]Freund, J., & Ruecker, B. (2019). Real-Life BPMN: Includes an Introduction to DMN. Independently Published.

[2]Camunda (2024). Forrester Total Economic Impact^{TM} Study 2024. https://page.camunda.com/wp-forrester-tei-study-2024 (accessed 16 December 2024).

[3]Camunda (n.d.). Workflow Patterns Concept Overview. https://docs.camunda.io/docs/components/concepts/workflow-patterns (accessed 16 December 2024).

[4]Ruecker, B. (2022). Why Process Orchestration Needs Advanced Workflow Patterns. https://camunda.com/blog/2022/07/why-process-orchestration-needs-advanced-workflow-patterns (accessed 16 December 2024).

[5]ResearchGate (n.d.). IBM System Science Institute: Relative Cost of Fixing Defects. https://www.researchgate.net/figure/IBM-System-Science-Institute-Relative-Cost-of-Fixing-Defects_fig1_2559 (accessed 16 December 2024).

[6]Camunda (n.d.). T-Mobile Austria: A Case Study. https://camunda.com/case-study/t-mobile-austria (accessed 16 December 2024).

[7]Camunda (n.d.). Connectors in Camunda Modeler. https://camunda.com/platform/modeler/connectors (accessed 16 December 2024).

[8]Camunda (n.d.). Camunda Tasklist: Simplified task management for complex business processes. https://camunda.com/platform/tasklist (accessed 16 December 2024).

[9]Camunda (2022). Why Goldman Sachs Built a Brand New Platform on Camunda Platform 8. https://camunda.com/blog/2022/03/why-goldman-sachs-built-a-brand-new-platform (accessed 16 December 2024).

[10]Camunda (2018). The 'Platformization' of Workflow at Goldman Sachs: A Camunda Day NYC Recap. https://camunda.com/blog/2018/07/camunda-days-nyc-goldman-sachs-workflow-platform (accessed 16 December 2024).

[11]BIAN (n.d.). BIAN Banking Industry Architecture Reference Model version 12.0. https://bian.org/servicelandscape-12-0-0 (accessed 16 December 2024).

[12]ACORD (n.d.). ACORD Reference Architecture. https://www.acord.org/standards-architecture/reference-architecture (accessed 16 December 2024).

[13]tmforum (n.d.). Model of the Open Digital Architecture (MODA). https://www.tmforum.org/oda/moda (accessed 16 December 2024).

[14]Wikipedia (n.d.). ITIL. https://en.wikipedia.org/wiki/ITIL (accessed 16 December 2024).

Chapter 1

[1] Lamarre E., & Smaje, K., Zemmel R. (2023). Rewired: The McKinsey Guide to Outcompeting in the Age of Digital and AI. Wiley. https://www.mckinsey.com/featured-insights/mckinsey-on-books/rewired (accessed 16 December 2024).

[2] Hohpe, G. (2020). The Software Architect Elevator: Redefining the Architect's Role in the Digital Enterprise. O'Reilly Media. https://architectelevator.com/book (accessed 16 December 2024).

[3] BIAN (n.d.). BIAN Banking Industry Architecture Reference Model version 12.0. https://bian.org/servicelandscape-12-0-0 (accessed 16 December 2024).

[4] ACORD (n.d.). ACORD Reference Architecture. https://www.acord.org/standards-architecture/reference-architecture (accessed 16 December 2024).

[5] tmforum (n.d.). Model of the Open Digital Architecture (MODA). https://www.tmforum.org/oda/moda/ (accessed 16 December 2024).

[6] Freund, J., & Ruecker, B. (2019). Real-Life BPMN: Includes an Introduction to DMN. Independently Published.

[7] Camunda (2024). A Hands-on Approach to Measuring Strategic Value With Top-down Process Orchestration (Camunda & Ibo). https://camunda.com/ccon-video/a-hands-on-approach-to-measuring-strategic-value-with-top-down-process-orchestration (accessed 16 December 2024).

[8] Goldratt, E. M., and Cox, J. (1984). The Goal: A Process of Ongoing Improvement. Great Barrington, MA: North River Press. https://en.wikipedia.org/wiki/The_Goal_(novel) (accessed 16 December 2024).

[9] Schank, M. (2023). Digital Transformation Success: Achieving Alignment and Delivering Results with the Process Inventory Framework. New York: Apress.

[10] Wikipedia (n.d.). PDCA. https://en.wikipedia.org/wiki/PDCA (accessed 16 December 2024).

[11] Wikipedia (n.d.). Crossing the chasm. https://en.wikipedia.org/wiki/Crossing_the_Chasm (accessed 16 December 2024).

[12] Bain & Company (2020). Intelligent Automation: Getting Employees to Embrace the Bots. https://www.bain.com/insights/intelligent-automation-getting-employees-embrace-bots/ (accessed 16 December 2024).

Chapter 2

[1] Forsgren, N., Humble, J., & Kim, G. (2018). Accelerate: Building and Scaling High Performing Technology Organizations. Portland, OR: IT Revolution Press. https://itrevolution.com/product/accelerate (accessed 16 December 2024).

[2] Techbeacon (n.d.). 7 takeaways to "Accelerate" your DevOps. https://techbeacon.com/app-dev-testing/7-takeaways-accelerate-your-devops (accessed 16 December 2024).

[3] DORA (n.d.). Accelerate State of DevOps Report 2024. https://dora.dev/ (accessed 16 December 2024).

[4]Kestern, M. (2018). Project to Product: How to Survive and Thrive in the Age of Digital Disruption with the Flow Framework. IT Revolution Press. https://flowframework.org/ffc-project-to-product-book (accessed 16 December 2024).

[5]McKinley, D. (2015). Choose Boring Technology. https://mcfunley.com/choose-boring-technology (accessed 16 December 2024).

[6]Toyota (2021). What is Toyota Lean Management? https://www.toyotaforklift.com/resource-library/blog/toyota-solutions/what-is-toyota-lean-management (accessed 16 December 2024).

[7]Skelton, M. & Pais, M. (2019). Team Topologies: Organizing Business and Technology Teams for Fast Flow. IT Revolution. https://teamtopologies.com/book (accessed 16 December 2024).

[8]Team Topologies (n.d.). Key Concepts. https://teamtopologies.com/key-concepts (accessed 16 December 2024).

[9]Team Topologies: Organizing Business and Technology Teams for Fast Flow. IT Revolution. https://teamtopologies.com/book (accessed 16 December 2024).

[10]Spotify (2020). How We Use Golden Paths to Solve Fragmentation in Our Software Ecosystem. https://engineering.atspotify.com/2020/08/how-we-use-golden-paths-to-solve-fragmentation-in-our-software-ecosystem (accessed 16 December 2024).

[11]Backstage (n.d.). An open source framework for building developer portals. https://backstage.io (accessed 16 December 2024).

[12]McKinsey & Company (2021). Unleashing developers' full talents: An interview with Twilio's CEO. https://www.mckinsey.com/industries/technology-media-and-telecommunications/our-insights/unleashing-developers-full-talents-an-interview-with-twilios-ceo (accessed 16 December 2024).

[13]Camunda (n.d.). State of Process Orchestration. https://camunda.com/state-of-process-orchestration/ (accessed 16 December 2024).

[14]Schank, Michael. (2023). Digital Transformation Success: Achieving Alignment and Delivering Results with the Process Inventory Framework. New York: Apress.

[15]Camunda (2022). Ramping up Camunda Usage at NBC: Successes and Failures. https://page.camunda.com/camundacon-2022-national-bank-of-canada (accessed 16 December 2024).

[16]Camunda (n.d.). Process Orchestration Maturity. https://camunda.com/process-orchestration/maturity/ (accessed 16 December 2024).

[17]Ruecker, B. (2021). Practical Process Automation: Orchestration and Integration in Microservices and Cloud-Native Architectures. Sebastopol, CA: O'Reilly Media. https://processautomationbook.com (accessed 16 December 2024).

[18]Camunda (2023). Scaling Automation: Lessons Learned From Provinzial's Center of Excellence. https://page.camunda.com/camundacon-2023-provinzial (accessed 16 December 2024).

[19]Evan B. (n.d.). What I Talk About When I Talk About Platforms. https://martinfowler.com/articles/talk-about-platforms.html (accessed 16 December 2024).

[20]Prohl, K. & Kleinaltenkamp, M. (2020). Managing value in use in business markets, Elsevier. https://doi.org/10.1016/j.indmarman.2020.03.017 (accessed 16 December 2024).

[21] Camunda (2022). How do you create and grow a Center of Excellence? https://camunda.com/blog/2022/12/how-to-create-grow-center-of-excellence/ (accessed 16 December 2024).

[22] Cloud Native Foundation (n.d.). Cloud Native Landscape. https://landscape.cncf.io/ (accessed 16 December 2024).

[23] McKinsey & Company (2022). Your questions about automation, answered. https://www.mckinsey.com/capabilities/operations/our-insights/your-questions-about-automation-answered (accessed 16 December 2024).

[24] Camunda (2022). How do you create and grow a Center of Excellence? https://camunda.com/blog/2022/12/how-to-create-grow-center-of-excellence/ (accessed 16 December 2024).

[25] HubSpot (2023). Lunch and Learns: How to Host One That Your Team Will Want to Attend. https://blog.hubspot.com/service/lunch-and-learn (accessed 16 December 2024).

[26] Camunda (n.d.). The Process Orchestration Conference Experience. https://www.camundacon.com/ (accessed 16 December 2024).

[27] Camunda (n.d.). Camunda events. https://camunda.com/events/ (accessed 16 December 2024).

[28] Camunda (n.d.). Welcome to the Camunda Community. https://community.camunda.com (accessed 16 December 2024).

[29] Camunda (n.d.). Browse our case studies. https://camunda.com/case-studies (accessed 16 December 2024).

[30] Camunda (n.d.). Welcome to Camunda Academy. https://academy.camunda.com (accessed 16 December 2024).

[31] Camunda (n.d.). Camunda 8 Docs – Best Practices Overview. https://docs.camunda.io/docs/components/best-practices/best-practices-overview (accessed 16 December 2024).

[32] Camunda (2022). What's in Your Hyperautomation Tech Stack? https://camunda.com/blog/2022/02/whats-in-your-hyperautomation-tech-stack (accessed 16 December 2024).

[33] Ruecker, B. (2021). Process Automation In Harmony With RPA. https://blog.bernd-ruecker.com/process-automation-in-harmony-with-rpa-720effdb0513 (accessed 16 December 2024).

[34] Spotify (2020). How We Use Golden Paths to Solve Fragmentation in Our Software Ecosystem. https://engineering.atspotify.com/2020/08/how-we-use-golden-paths-to-solve-fragmentation-in-our-software-ecosystem (accessed 16 December 2024).

[35] Camunda (2023). Scaling Automation: Lessons Learned From Provinzial's Center of Excellence. https://page.camunda.com/camundacon-2023-provinzial (accessed 16 December 2024).

[36] Camunda (2024). CamundaCon NYC On-Demand Recordings. https://page.camunda.com/camundacon-nyc-2024-on-demand (accessed 16 December 2024).

[37] Camunda(2023). Automating Citizen Services in the City of Munich. https://page.camunda.com/camundacon-2023-city-of-munich (accessed 16 December 2024).

[38] Camunda (2022). Hyperautomation: How Camunda Is Put to Good Use. https://page.camunda.com/camundacon-2022-desjardins (accessed 16 December 2024).

References

[39] Camunda (2022). Why Goldman Sachs Built a Brand New Platform on Camunda Platform 8. https://camunda.com/blog/2022/03/why-goldman-sachs-built-a-brand-new-platform (accessed 16 December 2024).

[40] Camunda (2022). Enabling Technically Challenging Business Use Cases Using Camunda Platform 8 at Scale. https://page.camunda.com/ccs2022-client-use-cases-by-goldman-sachs (accessed 16 December 2024).

[41] Camunda (2022). Ramping up Camunda Usage at NBC: Successes and Failures. https://page.camunda.com/camundacon-2022-national-bank-of-canada (accessed 16 December 2024).

[42] Camunda (2023). 6 Years of Camunda at NatWest: Impacts, Changes, Learnings and the Future. https://page.camunda.com/camundacon-2023-natwest (accessed 16 December 2024).

[43] Camunda (2021). Wie gelingt digitale Transformation wirklich? https://page.camunda.com/de/process-automation-forum-live-dt (accessed 16 December 2024).

[44] Camunda (2023). Scaling Automation: Lessons Learned From Provinzial's Center of Excellence. https://page.camunda.com/camundacon-2023-provinzial (accessed 16 December 2024).

[45] Camunda (2024). Designing your CoE Toolbox. https://docs.google.com/presentation/d/1fyVtpYAcGqdrLT5xeKCEeuLp3TsCLJzeVFl351xEulc/edit#slide=id.g29dceac4d0b_0_0 (accessed 16 December 2024).

Chapter 3

[1] Harvard Business Review (2016). Know Your Customers' "Jobs to Be Done". https://hbr.org/2016/09/know-your-customers-jobs-to-be-done (accessed 16 December 2024).

[2] Gartner (2024). Quick Answer: Beyond RPA, BPA and Low Code – The Future Is BOAT. https://www.gartner.com/en/documents/5577427 (accessed 16 December 2024).

[3] Forrester (2021). Automation Is The New Fabric For Digital Business. https://www.forrester.com/report/Automation-Is-The-New-Fabric-For-Digital-Business/RES164798 (accessed 16 December 2024).

[4] Camunda 8 Docs (n.d.). Tasklist Introduction. https://docs.camunda.io/docs/components/tasklist/introduction-to-tasklist (accessed 16 December 2024).

[5] Camunda 8 Docs (n.d.). What are Camunda Forms? https://docs.camunda.io/docs/components/modeler/forms/camunda-forms-reference (accessed 16 December 2024).

[6] BPMN.io (n.d.). Visually edit and embed JSON-based forms. https://bpmn.io/toolkit/form-js (accessed 16 December 2024).

[7] Camunda (n.d.). Camunda Operate: Intuitive dashboard for real-time process observability and troubleshooting. https://camunda.com/platform/operate (accessed 16 December 2024).

[8] Camunda (n.d.). Camunda Modeler: Orchestrate business processes and build decision models. https://camunda.com/platform/modeler (accessed 16 December 2024).

[9] Camunda (n.d.). Welcome to Camunda Marketplace. https://marketplace.camunda.com (accessed 16 December 2024).

[10] Cooper, D. & Stol, K. (2018). Adopting InnerSource. O'Reilly Media. https://www.oreilly.com/library/view/adopting-innersource/9781492041863/ch01.html (accessed 16 December 2024).

[11] Camunda 8 Docs (n.d.). Handling data in processes. https://docs.camunda.io/docs/components/best-practices/development/handling-data-in-processes/ (accessed 16 December 2024).

[12] Ruecker, B. (2021). Process Automation In Harmony With RPA. https://blog.bernd-ruecker.com/process-automation-in-harmony-with-rpa-720effdb0513 (accessed 16 December 2024).

[13] Camunda (n.d.). Camunda Optimize: Holistic process intelligence and analytics. https://camunda.com/platform/optimize (accessed 16 December 2024).

[14] Camunda 8 Docs (n.d.). Reporting about processes. https://docs.camunda.io/docs/components/best-practices/operations/reporting-about-processes/#connectingcustom-business-intelligence-systems-bi-data-warehouses-dwh-or-monitoring-solutions (accessed 16 December 2024).

[15] Camunda 8 Docs (n.d.). Testing process definitions. https://docs.camunda.io/docs/next/components/best-practices/development/testing-process-definitions/ (accessed 16 December 2024).

[16] Wikipedia (n.d.). Infrastructure as code. https://en.wikipedia.org/wiki/Infrastructure_as_code (accessed 16 December 2024).

[17] Gartner (n.d.). Gartner Hype Cycle. https://www.gartner.com/en/research/methodologies/gartner-hype-cycle (accessed 16 December 2024).

[18] Evans, B. (2024). The AI Summer. https://www.ben-evans.com/benedictevans/2024/7/9/the-ai-summer (accessed 16 December 2024).

[19] The Economist (2024). Why your company is struggling to scale up generative AI. https://www.economist.com/business/2024/11/04/why-your-company-is-struggling-to-scale-up-generative-ai (accessed 16 December 2024).

[20] BCG (2024). Where's the Value in AI? https://www.bcg.com/publications/2024/wheres-value-in-ai (accessed 16 December 2024).

[21] Skelton, M. & Pais M. (2019). Team Topologies: Organizing Business and Technology Teams for Fast Flow. IT Revolution. https://teamtopologies.com/book (accessed 16 December 2024).

[22] Evan B. (n.d.). What I Talk About When I Talk About Platforms. https://martinfowler.com/articles/talk-about-platforms.html (accessed 16 December 2024).

[23] Spotify (2020). How We Use Golden Paths to Solve Fragmentation in Our Software Ecosystem. https://engineering.atspotify.com/2020/08/how-we-use-golden-paths-to-solve-fragmentation-in-our-software-ecosystem (accessed 16 December 2024).

[24] McKinsey & Company (2021). Unleashing developers' full talents: An interview with Twilio's CEO. https://www.mckinsey.com/industries/technology-media-and-telecommunications/our-insights/unleashing-developers-full-talents-an-interview-with-twilios-ceo (accessed 16 December 2024).

[25] IT Revolution (2022). Run Your Platform Like a Business within a Business. https://itrevolution.com/articles/run-your-platform-like-a-business-within-a-business (accessed 16 December 2024).

[26] Team Toplogies (n.d.). What is Platform as a Product? Clues from Team Topologies. https://teamtopologies.com/videos-slides/what-is-platform-as-a-product-clues-from-team-topologies (accessed 16 December 2024).

[27] Ruecker, B. (2017). The 7 sins of workflow. https://blog.bernd-ruecker.com/the-7-sins-of-workflow-b3641736bf5c (accessed 16 December 2024).

[28] Forsgren, N., Humble, J., & Kim, G. (2018). Accelerate: Building and Scaling High Performing Technology Organizations. Portland, OR: IT Revolution Press.

[29] Kim, G., Behr, K., & Spafford, G. (2013). The Phoenix Project: A Novel About IT, DevOps, and Helping Your Business Win. Portland, OR: IT Revolution Press.

[30] Kersten, M. (2018). Project to Product: How to Survive and Thrive in the Age of Digital Disruption with the Flow Framework. Portland, OR: IT Revolution Press.

[31] Azure Learn (n.d.). Noisy Neighbor antipattern. https://learn.microsoft.com/en-us/azure/architecture/antipatterns/noisy-neighbor/noisy-neighbor (accessed 16 December 2024).

[32] Camunda 8 Docs (n.d.). Testing process definitions. https://docs.camunda.io/docs/components/best-practices/development/testing-process-definitions (accessed 16 December 2024).

[33] Camunda 8 Docs (n.d.): Sizing your environment. https://docs.camunda.io/docs/components/best-practices/architecture/sizing-your-environment/#sizing-yourruntime-environment (accessed 16 December 2024).

[34] Ruecker, B. (2022). How to Achieve Geo-redundancy with Zeebe. https://camunda.com/blog/2022/06/how-to-achieve-geo-redundancy-with-zeebe (accessed 16 December 2024).

[35] Camunda (n.d.). NASA Jet Propulsion Laboratory: Using Camunda for JPL Common Workflow Service (CWS). https://camunda.com/customer/nasa (accessed 16 December 2024).

[36] Camunda (2020). Enabling Core Banking Use Cases with Camunda Cloud. https://page.camunda.com/cclive-2021-goldman-sachs (accessed 16 December 2024).

[37] Ruecker, B. (2018). How to benefit from robotic process automation (RPA). https://blog.berndruecker.com/how-to-benefit-from-robotic-process-automation-rpa-9edc04430afa (accessed 16 December 2024).

[38] Ruecker, B. (2021). Practical Process Automation: Orchestration and Integration in Microservices and Cloud-Native Architectures. Sebastopol, CA: O'Reilly Media. https://processautomationbook.com (accessed 16 December 2024).

[39] Ruecker, B. (2021). Event Streams Are Nothing Without Action. https://www.confluent.io/de-de/blog/data-streams-are-nothing-without-actionable-insights-leading-to-actions (accessed 16 December 2024).

[40] Ruecker, B. (2022). Why process orchestration needs advanced workflow patterns. https://camunda.com/blog/2022/07/why-process-orchestration-needs-advanced-workflow-patterns (accessed 16 December 2024).

Chapter 4

[1] Freund, J., & Ruecker, B. (2019). Real-Life BPMN: Includes an Introduction to DMN. Independently Published.

[2] Camunda 8 Docs (n.d.). Doing a proper POC. https://docs.camunda.io/docs/components/best-practices/management/doing-a-proper-poc/ (accessed 16 December 2024).

[3]Camunda 8 Docs (n.d.). Getting Started with Spring Zeebe. https://docs.camunda.io/docs/apis-tools/spring-zeebe-sdk/getting-started (accessed 16 December 2024).

[4]Camunda 8 Docs (n.d.). Getting Started with C#. https://docs.camunda.io/docs/apis-tools/community-clients/c-sharp (accessed 16 December 2024).

[5]Camunda 8 Docs (n.d.). Deciding about your stack. https://docs.camunda.io/docs/components/best-practices/architecture/deciding-about-your-stack/ (accessed 16 December 2024).

[6]Camunda 8 Docs (n.d.). Testing process definitions. https://docs.camunda.io/docs/components/best-practices/development/testing-process-definitions (accessed 16 December 2024).

[7]Camunda 8 Docs (n.d.). About Modeler. https://docs.camunda.io/docs/next/components/modeler/about-modeler (accessed 16 December 2024).

[8]Camunda (n.d.). Download Camunda Modeler. https://camunda.com/download/modeler/ (accessed 16 December 2024).

[9]Camunda Community Hub (n.d.). Web Modeler GitHub Sync Example. https://github.com/camunda-community-hub/web-modeler-github-sync-example (accessed 16 December 2024).

[10]Camunda 8 Docs (n.d.). Integrate Web Modeler into CI/CD. https://docs.camunda.io/docs/guides/devops-lifecycle/integrate-web-modeler-in-ci-cd (accessed 16 December 2024).

[11]Camunda GitHub (n.d.). Camunda out-of-the-box connectors. https://github.com/camunda/connectors/tree/main/connectors (accessed 16 December 2024).

[12]Camunda GitHub (n.d.). Camunda Connectors Default Bundle. https://github.com/camunda/connectors/tree/main/bundle/default-bundle (accessed 16 December 2024).

Chapter 5

[1]Camunda (2024). A Hands-on Approach to Measuring Strategic Value With Top-down Process Orchestration (Camunda & Ibo). https://camunda.com/ccon-video/a-hands-on-approach-to-measuring-strategic-value-with-top-down-process-orchestration/ (accessed 16 December 2024).

[2]Gartner (2018). The True Business Value of IT. https://www.gartner.com/en/podcasts/thinkcast/the-true-business-value-of-it (accessed 16 December 2024).

Index

accelerators 119–20, 148–9, 209–10

adjacent technology comparisons 180–3

adoption acceleration teams (AAT) 61–3, 66, 84–135, 148–9, 160–4, 170

adoption frameworks xxi–xxiv, 60–77, 221, 229

agile/agility approaches 12–14
> business architecture 38, 69, 72–5
> delivery aspects 195
> measurement/metrics 221, 227–9, 239–40
> people aspects 81, 84, 110–12, 125
> technology 166

alignment aspects 32–8, 56–8, 62–3, 67–9, 73–7, 223

anti-money laundering (AML) 24

anti-patterns 123–5

APIs 67–8, 139–43, 147, 150–4, 162, 165, 183–4

artificial intelligence (AI) xiv–xv, 108
> enablement 14, 29
> technology 142–3, 151–2, 157–60, 183–4

audit data 11–12, 15

automation xvi–xix, 1–29
> delivery 190–8, 201–5, 209
> measurement/metrics 217–33, 238–9
> people and software aspects 79–85, 88–100, 103–7, 110–33
> technology 137–9, 142–59, 162–3, 166, 169, 174–87
> vision aspects 31–54, 58–9, 67, 71

banks 2–3, 9, 21–5, 175, 197–8
> business architecture 33, 36–40, 43–9, 54

best-of-breed approach 166–7, 183, 187

bottom-up initiatives 69–72, 229

business analysts xxvi
> delivery 199–200, 204, 207

people aspects 101–2, 109–10, 133
> vision 58–9, 86

business architecture xxvi, 14, 38–76, 137–57, 162, 220–1, 231–3

business capabilities 40–5, 60–2, 65–70, 138–41, 146, 160–2

business cases 65–9, 110–13

business domain process orchestration 33–4, 38–9, 58, 63, 66, 78, 160–2

business intelligence (BI) 145, 153, 239–40

business leaders xxvi, 32–4, 58, 62–3, 75–7, 216–17, 221

business orchestration and automation technologies (BOAT) xix, 142–4

business processes 2–5, 12–28, 41–2, 50–1, 54–62, 66

Business Process Model and Notation (BPMN) 5–6, 12–13, 30
> business architecture 39–40, 44, 48–50
> delivery aspects 190–3, 199–206
> measurements/metrics 233, 240
> technology 147, 159–61, 169–71, 182–5

business process optimization groups 61–2, 66, 89–93, 99, 118, 127

business requirements 84, 103–5, 185

Camunda xxvii, 5–8, 13–14, 20–3
> delivery 192–3, 196, 201–7, 210
> people 88, 96–7, 102–3, 107–11, 115–19, 123–33
> technology 146–53, 156, 169–74, 179
> vision 31, 56, 70

Center of excellence (CoE) xiii, xxii, xxvi, 244
> people 87–93, 96–101, 107–15, 125
> technology 142, 160, 168
> vision 60–7, 71–5

centralization levels/centralized teams 86–97, 108–9, 114–16, 121–2, 127–31, 134–5

change implementation 59–71

chargeback models 168–9

CHATGPT xiv, 108, 157–8

chief financial officers (CFO) 35, 60, 169

chief information officers (CIO) 12, 31–2, 35, 60–1, 81, 91–3, 99, 216

chief operating officers (COO) 35, 60–1, 89, 92–3

chief technical officers (CTO) 35, 61, 217

claim processes 9–10, 17–18, 25

cloud 28–9, 167

commercial off-the-shelf (COTS) solutions 138–9, 174–6, 185

communications 7, 23, 26–9, 32–78, 115–16, 230–1, 235–9

community of practice (CoP) 95–6, 107–8, 113, 123, 130

complexity aspects 5–6, 15–16, 112, 177–80

compliance 11–12, 24–5, 28–30
    adoption acceleration teams 121
    measurement/metrics 219–22, 226–7, 231, 237
    vision aspects 37, 67

composable platform technology 144–5

connector accelerators 148, 210

continuous integration/continuous delivery (CI/CD) 14, 17–18
    delivery 201–6, 209
    people and software aspects 81, 84, 102, 117–20
    technology 144–6, 149, 156–7, 166–7

continuous measurements 235–9

core process orchestration capability 145–7

corporate strategy 32, 77

credit 37, 42–3, 47–8, 51

cross-functional teams 62, 64–5

C-suite executives xxv–xxvi, 31–6, 59–61, 89–93, 99, 216–17, 237–8

culture aspects 122–3

customer relationship management (CRM) 9, 14, 17–18, 27, 147, 178, 197–8

customers xiii–xxiv, 3–30, 243–4
    business architecture 33–67, 71, 76–8
    delivery aspects 190–1, 194, 197–201, 210
    measurement aspects 215–20, 225–38, 241
    people and software aspects 81–3, 88–9, 92–4, 107–10, 113–18, 123–7, 132
    technology aspects 137–43, 147, 150–1, 164–79

data-driven mentality 54, 58

data flow engines 181–2

data streaming 181–2, 185

data warehouses 239–40

decentralization 87–8, 95–6, 121–2

decision automation 13, 142

decision engines 146

decision-making 53–4

Decision Model and Notation (DMN) 13, 109, 116, 146, 202–3, 206, 208

delivery xxi–xxv, 189–213, 244
    adoption acceleration teams 86–99, 103–5, 108–15, 118–35
    business architecture 62–5, 68, 75

Deming cycle 63–4

demographic change xvii, 31

de-risking strategies 3, 57, 81, 153, 197–9

developer-friendly tooling 12, 13–14, 167, 184

developers xxvi, 13–15
    delivery 185, 199–200, 203–9
    measurement 236
    people 111–12, 127–9
    software 103–4, 236–7
    technology 144–8, 154–7, 162–8, 171–3, 177–8, 183–5
    vision 59, 70–1, 84–6, 103–5, 109–12

DevOps 79, 81, 84, 109, 156–7, 166

digitalization/digital processes 16–18, 38–52, 66

discovery delivery solution phase 190–2

domain-driven design (DDD) 57, 87, 137, 167

early maturity stages 98, 195–6

endpoint aspects 5, 150

end-to-end processes 4
    business architecture 40–4, 48–62, 65–8, 76–8
    technology 137–8, 141, 145, 158–61, 176–8, 182–7

260   Enterprise Process Orchestration

enterprise architects/architecture xxvi, 30
measurement 215–17
people 90–1, 100–1
technology 137–60, 186
vision 38, 41, 61, 72–5
enterprise capability 160–2
enterprise resource planning (ERP) 9, 14, 17–18, 40, 140, 153, 248
enterprise-wide process orchestration 33–8, 41, 59–66, 69, 72–8
enterprise work streams 60, 62–5
evaluating tools 183–6
event buses 150
event-driven architectures (EDA) 182, 185
executable processes 6–7, 12, 41, 48–51, 82, 106–7, 233–5
executive sponsorship 68

federated delivery 72–5, 86–98, 114, 122, 125, 128–35
focused software components 80–5
fully centralized delivery 96–9
fully decentralized delivery 95–6

goals
business architecture 44, 53, 57–61, 65–9, 73–7
delivery solution creation 191
measurement/metrics 215, 218–24, 231–3, 239–41
graphic modeling 147
greenfield choice of delivery 92, 110, 128–9, 133, 201–3
green use cases/processes 20–3
guardrails 157–60

human task management 142, 146–7, 154, 183
hyperautomation stacks 118–19

identity verification 6, 48–50, 55–6, 232–5
industry-specific reference models 40–1
InfoSec 154–6
insurance 9–10, 14, 18, 23, 25–6, 217
integration 3–6, 11–19, 21, 27–30
business architecture 40, 65–7, 70
delivery aspects 198, 201–6, 209

people and software aspects 81, 84, 96, 102, 104, 106–9, 117–20, 122, 126
technology 138–51, 154–9, 166–9, 172–8, 183–7
inventory 27
investment management 24, 53–4, 66, 68, 78
isolation needs 170–2
ISO standards 6, 12, 155, 169–70
see also Business Process Model and Notation
IT xviii, xix, xxii–xxvi, 243
business architecture 31–6, 40–1, 45, 52, 59, 65, 68–70, 74, 77
delivery aspects 192–4, 207–12
measurement 215–18, 221, 227–31, 239, 240–1
people aspects 79–84, 90–2, 95, 98–104, 109, 112–13, 125, 133–5
technology 143–4, 160–1, 166–70, 175, 178–9, 183–6

key performance indicators (KPIs)
business architecture 44–6, 54, 58–9, 67, 75
delivery aspects 191, 194–5, 212
measurement/metrics 215, 219–41
people 120
Know Your Customer (KYC) xvi, xvii, 14, 24–5, 138, 198, 227

language aspects 12–14, 156–7, 160
large language models (LLM) 14, 157, 160
launching adoption frameworks 73–5
law enforcement 27
legacy technology 29, 70, 175
lighthouse projects 98, 196
line of business (LoB) leaders 36–7, 63, 89, 94, 100, 103
loans 23–4, 37–54, 65–7, 229–30
local automation xviii–xix, 2–4
local task process orchestration 33, 53–8, 64, 67–9
low-code application platforms (LCAPs) 182–3, 185
low-code solutions 20–3

Index   261

low-code solutions (*Cont.*)
    delivery aspects 194, 199–201, 205–6
    people 91, 104, 107, 117, 120, 129
    technology 139–43, 148, 151, 175–9,
        182–5
    vision 75, 85–6

machine learning (ML) 14, 54, 142–3, 183
mapping measurements/metrics 229–33
market pressure xvii, 82
maturity assessments xxi–xxiv, 68, 75–7, 134,
    186–7, 211–12, 240–1
maturity phases 114, 209
measurements/metrics xxi–xxv, 215–41, 244
    vision aspects 34, 37–8, 44–6, 50, 54,
        58–61, 67, 77
media industries 28, 42
microservices
    business architecture 57, 62, 70
    people and software aspects 80, 87, 122
    technology 137–42, 161, 167, 180, 183–6
minimum viable products (MVP) model 207
mining tools 153
models
    adoption acceleration teams 126–34
    delivery aspects 192–3, 203–5
    measurements/metrics 233–5
monitoring delivery 194–5
monolithic platforms 144–5
multitenancy technology 170–2
mutual vision 32, 112

net promoter score (NPS) 24, 225, 229
network management 25, 26
non-functional requirements 18–23, 209–10,
    222

onboarding process 6, 16–21, 24–5
    business architecture 37, 49–52
    measurements 225–7, 232–3, 237
    people and software aspects 82–3
    technology 175–6
operational efficiency 10–11, 27, 30, 46, 81, 89,
    216–40
operational stakeholders 35–9
operations engineers 105

orchestration components 145–57
orchestration engines 6–7, 12–16, 70, 193
    technology 146–7, 151, 155, 170, 173
order fulfillment 16, 18, 26, 41, 160, 176
order management 27
organizational structures 41, 47, 53–60, 65
owner/ownership relationships
    business architecture 37, 46, 53–68, 76
    delivery solution creation 190
    measurements/metrics 235–6
    people and software aspects 82–3, 89–93,
        96, 105–6, 122, 130, 135
    technology 184

pain points 66–7, 70, 74, 191
PDCA cycles 63–4
people xxi–xxv, 79–135, 235–7, 244
platform technology 140–2, 147, 162–4, 169–74,
    183
policy administration 25–6
process automation 1–4, 7–11, 16–22, 30
    people and software aspects 80–5,
        88–100, 103–7, 110–33
    vision aspects 31, 37
process complexity 5–6, 177–80
process definition 6, 15–16, 156, 202
process efficiency 219, 225–7
process hierarchies 50–2
process intelligence 152–3
process mindsets 58–9, 112, 235
process optimization groups (POG) 61–2, 66,
    89–93, 99, 118, 127
process orchestration 1–16, 22–30
    benefits of 7–16
process ownership 37, 83
process selection technology 174–80
process tracking 197–9
pro-code solutions use cases 19–23
    delivery aspects 194, 199–203, 208–9
    people aspects 79, 86, 91, 117, 120
    technology 139, 175, 188
productivity 7–8, 14
    people aspects 79, 84–5, 103, 111–12,
        119, 148, 158
product-oriented delivery (POD) 60, 62

product owners 37, 105–6
product thinking 82, 84, 109–10, 135, 166–7
public sector 26–7
pull/push approaches 66–7, 70, 74

quality aspects 112, 227

rainmakers 101–2
red mission-critical processes 19–23
    delivery aspects 194, 199–203, 208–9
    people aspects 79, 86, 91, 117, 120
    technology 139, 175, 188
reference models 40–1
registry connectors 149
regulatory pressure xvii, 243
resilience aspects 173–4, 185
resource aspects 45, 52–3, 58, 71
retail industry 27
risk mitigation 11–12, 191, 219, 222, 241
roadmaps 32, 35, 59–76, 192
robotic process automation (RPA) xviii, xx, 2–3
    measurement/metrics 217–18
    technology 137–9, 142–6, 151–2, 175–7, 180–1
runtimes 12, 152–3, 159–61, 169, 194, 202–3, 208–10

SaaS services 80–1, 119, 127, 202, 205–6
    technology 139–41, 166–72, 183, 187
scale
    adoption acceleration teams 113–14
    adoption frameworks 75
    operating at 4–5
    process automation 88, 90, 94–7, 110–14, 119, 126, 131
    technology 173, 179, 185
self-service options 9, 217, 230, 235, 244
    adoption acceleration teams 109
    business architecture 53, 71
    technology 162–5
senior vice president (SVP) leaders 36–7, 44, 46, 55, 229
service level agreements (SLA) 3, 46, 153, 222–6, 231–3, 237
service-oriented architecture (SOA) 165–8
setup aspects 179–80

skill development 79, 90, 100–7, 127–35
SLA 46, 153, 222–6, 231–3, 237
software 5, 12–14, 17–22
    developers/engineering 103–4, 236–7
    lifecycles 203–9
    people aspects 79–88, 98, 102–6, 109, 119–21, 124–7, 133
    technology 137–9, 144–51, 156–7, 163, 166–7, 173–9, 183–5
solution architects 102–3
solution capability 160–2
solution delivery 120–1, 189–95, 201–9
Spotify 87–8, 163
staging environments 172–3
stakeholders 32–8, 58–62, 66, 69–77, 112–13, 192
standard processes 17–18, 174–6
state machines 70
steering committees 60–3, 69, 221
strategy techniques 32–44, 48–55, 58–74, 76–8
streaming platforms 150

T+1 regulations xvii, 24, 226
tailor-made processes 16–18, 20–2, 174–6
target operating models 126–34
tariff changes 26, 178
task aspects
    adoption acceleration teams 114–23
    people and software aspects 82, 86–91, 102–8, 114–23, 128
    vision aspects 33–4, 47–58, 64, 67–9, 73–7
task automation 1–4, 17, 29
    technology 142–54, 158–9, 169, 175–7, 180–1, 184–5
teams
    business architecture 35, 38–9, 42, 47–8, 53–77
    delivery aspects 199–200
    measurements/metrics 235–6
    people aspects 79–98, 103–15, 119–35
technical capabilities 140–2, 147, 160–5
technical debt avoidance 15–16
technical use cases 28–9
technology xxi–xxv, 137–88, 244
template accelerators 148

Index   263

time to value 12–14, 31, 59
tool aspects 22–3, 118–20
top-down strategies 54, 66, 71–2, 78, 229
tracking strategies 197–9
transformation office 61–3, 66, 69, 221
transformation roadmaps 32, 35, 59–76
transparency 9–10, 27, 53

underwriting 42–54, 222, 231–2
use cases/processes 19–23
    delivery aspects 194, 199–209
    people aspects 79, 86, 89–92, 97–9, 104, 107, 113, 116–18, 120, 127–34
    technology 139–44, 148, 151–2, 157–9, 171, 174–9, 182–5, 188
    vision aspects 32, 35–6, 59, 62–77, 85–6
user interface technology 150–1

value
    communication 32, 34–72, 74–8
    delivery 124–5

measurement/metrics 215–25, 228–31, 239–41
pyramids 111
streams 28, 39–54, 57, 61, 66–9
traps xviii–xix
vendor rationalization 22–3
vision xxi–xxiii, xxiv, 31–78, 157, 243–4

wave patterns 72–4
web modelers 201, 203–9
workflow engines *see* orchestration engines
workflow pattern technology 184
work streams 60–1, 62–5, 75

yellow use cases/processes 19–23
    delivery aspects 194, 199–201, 205–6
    people aspects 86, 91, 104, 107, 117, 120, 129
    technology 139–43, 148, 151, 175–9, 182–5
    vision 75, 85–6